To John Matthias,

Here it is, such as it is,
with thanks to you for your
benevolent influence. Having
you to read this made writing
it possible.
Gratefully,
Gail

The Phoenix Paradox:

A *Study of Renewal Through Change*
in
the Collected Poems *and* Last Poems
of D. H. *Lawrence*

GAIL PORTER MANDELL

Introduction by Sandra M. Gilbert

SOUTHERN ILLINOIS UNIVERSITY PRESS
Carbondale and Edwardsville

Library of Congress Cataloging in Publication Data

Mandell, Gail Porter, 1940–
  The phoenix paradox.

  Bibliography: p.
  Includes index.
  1. Lawrence, D. H. (David Herbert), 1885–1930—
Poetic works.   2. Lawrence, D. H. (David Herbert), 1885–
1930—Criticism, Textual.   I. Title.
PR6023.A93Z676   1984   821'.912   83-10563
ISBN 0-8093-1121-6

For
my husband,
Daniel Neil Mandell, Jr.

Permission to quote from materials listed below is gratefully acknowledged.

Selected published and unpublished poems and passages from the prose of D. H. Lawrence, by permission of the estate of D. H. Lawrence, the estate of Mrs. Frieda Lawrence Ravagli, and Laurence Pollinger, Ltd.

"Dreams: Old," "Dreams: Nascent," "Troth with the Dead," and "The Street-Lamps" from the private collection of L. D. Clarke.

"Wealth" and "Fidelity" from a typescript of *Pansies* in the private collection of George Lazarus.

Drafts of "Dreams: Old," "Dreams: Nascent," "Two Wives," and "The Street-Lamps" from the Henry W. and Albert A. Berg Collection, New York Public Library, Astor, Lenox, and Tilden Foundation.

"The Songless," "Sorrow," "The Wild Common," "Dreams: Old," "Dreams: Nascent," "Virgin Youth," "Discipline," and "Last Words to Miriam" from manuscript LaL2, by permission of the D. H. Lawrence Collection, Manuscripts Department, University of Nottingham Library.

Pages 527 passim from *Sensibility to Romanticism: Essays Presented to Frederick A. Pottle,* edited by Frederick W. Hilles and Harold Bloom (New York: Oxford University Press, 1965).

Page 188. Reprinted by permission of the University of South Carolina Press from *Another Ego: The Changing View of Self and Society in the Work of D. H. Lawrence,* by Baruch Hochman (copyright © 1970 by the University of South Carolina Press).

"Dreams: Old" and "Dreams: Nascent" from a holograph manuscript of four poems; "The Blind"; drafts of "Wealth," and "Fidelity" from a notebook containing *Pansies;* "Two ways of living and dying," "So let me live," "Gladness of Death," "The Ship of Death" (2 versions), "Bavarian Gentians" (4 versions), and "Phoenix" from the notebooks containing *Last Poems* and "More Pansies" from the Humanities Research Center, The University of Texas at Austin.

Contents

Preface

D. H. Lawrence belongs to a group of writers that includes Montaigne, Goethe, Wordsworth, and Whitman—a revisionary company so obsessed by a character (often themselves, thinly disguised if disguised at all) or by an idea that they wrote and rewrote the same material until they died. As he himself and his ideas changed, Lawrence rewrote many of his poems, not once but several times, often taking advantage of the opportunity to revise that various publications of a poem gave him. His final revision of the published poetry occurred in 1928, two years before his death, when he put together *Collected Poems*. At that time, Lawrence worked for several months revising the early verse, rewriting entire poems and rearranging all the poetry to give it narrative coherence. Lawrence confessed in his preface to the collection that he had ordered the poems not only to conform to his experience but also to reveal his "inner history," or essential autobiography.

Because the autobiographical content of much of Lawrence's writing has long been recognized, such an admission does not surprise us. Lawrence is as candid about his true subject as is Montaigne when he writes that he himself is the matter of his book. What fascinates us in both authors is not so much their self-revelation, per se, as their conscious struggle to grasp the protean self. Lawrence is after the elemental identity, the "carbon" of the personality, of his fictional characters and, ultimately, of himself. As he explains in an unpublished foreword to *Collected Poems*, he has found and revealed the essential self through the poetry. This self manifests not only the fully personal but also the transcendent in human life; consequently, Lawrence invents a mythic name, the "demon," for what he perceives to be the "carbonate" self—that which in another age he might have called the soul. As the demon's biography, *Collected Poems* recounts the emergence of the "new" from the "old" self. The speaker of the poems becomes increasingly conscious of his connection with all that is, and is not, the self, even as the poet himself did in the course of his development.

The close connection between Lawrence's emerging idea of himself and his evolving verse underscores the intimate connection in his writing between life and art, both of which bear out his motto, "Art for my sake!" From the poetry spun from his experience, Lawrence finally created a conscious myth of the self in *Collected Poems* and *Last Poems*. Reading Lawrence's work in the order in which he wrote it, one perceives implicit ideas coming to consciousness; Lawrence systematized these ideas and often used them to reform the verse. He once pointed out that all of his "doctrine," or "pollyanalytics," as he called his philosophical and psychological musings, originated in his art, which served as the midwife to conscious understanding. He persistently attempted to formuate his creative insights in nonfiction prose. Consequently, the reader of Lawrence's work shares the author's deepening awareness of the basic patterns of his art and the psychic structure at its source. This awareness culminates in *Collected Poems*. It is the key to comprehending Lawrence's idea of himself and his art.

In my study of Lawrence's verse, I emphasize the controlling consciousness of the mature poet at work. The evidence of the surviving manuscripts supports the view that Lawrence was from the first a deliberate craftsman. The myth of the spontaneous poet was one that Lawrence himself invented to buy time for his experiments in verse. Granted: Lawrence only secondarily rewrote for form; his first purpose in revising the poetry was to clarify his ideas and imagery. He sought above all to communicate that "complete state of mind" that he described in his introduction to the definitive edition of *Pansies*. Whenever he wrote about his poetry, Lawrence encouraged his reader to regard it as an entity. My book is intended to aid the reader of Lawrence's poetry in doing just that—understanding the "state of mind," often conveyed through myth, that informs and connects the verse.

His poetry was Lawrence's way of coping with change on an experiential as well as theoretical level. At crucial times in his life—at his mother's death, for example, and in anticipation of his own—he returned to poetry, often after years away from it, finding through it, perhaps, a consoling order. He also heard in his poetry the voice of the demon—the self that, phoenix-like, shows its indestructibility through change. In the images of his own poetry, Lawrence's verse was for him a ship that allowed him to ride the destructive flood of death, or a gentian that guided him through interior darkness. In his art, the poems are his first and last words. Are we surprised that the spirit that shaped them reveals itself profoundly through them?

For permission to quote from the work of D. H. Lawrence, I wish to thank Laurence Pollinger, Ltd., and the estate of Frieda Lawrence Ravagli. George Lazarus and L. D. Clarke have generously allowed me to quote from their private collections of Lawrence's verse; I thank them. I also thank the University of Nottingham Library for permission to quote from its Lawrence collection; members of its staff deserve special mention for their eagerness to be of service when I visited their collection. The Humanities Research Center of the University of Texas at Austin has frequently allowed me to use microfilms of several of Lawrence's manuscripts in their collection: I am indebted to their staff for its helpful cooperation, and to the Center for permission to quote from manuscript material. In addition, I thank the New York Public Library for permission to quote from manuscripts in the Berg Collection, and also the University of South Carolina Press and the Oxford University Press for permission to quote from books published by them.

In completing this study, I have depended on the work of many scholars, but in particular, I wish to acknowledge my indebtedness to the variorum of Lawrence's poetry through 1919 produced by Carole Ferrier. Without her work, I could not have begun my own. I am also grateful to Sandra Gilbert for her suggestions about expanding my study to include Lawrence's *Last Poems*. She has been for me the responsive, intelligent reader that every writer desires.

With a keen sense of all I owe them for their encouragement and support, I affectionately thank William A. Hickey and Bruno P. Schlesinger of Saint Mary's College. They fostered this project from its beginning. For his invaluable criticisms of this book in its early stages, I would like to thank John Matthias of the University of Notre Dame. The superb staff of librarians at

Saint Mary's College is also due thanks, in particular Lola Mae Philippsen and Robert Hohl, both of whom helped me countless times to obtain necessary materials.

Thanks go to others, too: Linda Guyton, who cheerfully and efficiently typed a most demanding manuscript; Connie Maher, who offered indispensable help early in the project; Susan McGury, who was always willing to talk about Lawrence and refresh my flagging spirits; and my family, who offered their unconditional support as I pursued a project that diminished my time with them (especially my husband, Dan, my mother, Genevieve Henneman, my father, Howard Porter, and my mother-in-law, Elizabeth Mandell).

Finally, I owe a special word of appreciation to Joyce Atwood, Senior Editor at Southern Illinois University Press. Fortune blessed me by entrusting my manuscript to her care. With exceptional competence and intelligence, she has seen this project through to completion.

Introduction

Sandra M. Gilbert

From T. S. Eliot, who claimed in 1933 that D. H. Lawrence was incapable of "what we would ordinarily call thinking," to R. P. Blackmur, who declared in 1952 that "Lawrence developed as little art as possible, and left us the ruins of great intentions," to Donald Davie, who argued in 1972 that "Lawrence . . . tolerate[d] poetic skill as little as poetic technique," critics have seen the author of majestic poems like "Bavarian Gentians" and "The Ship of Death" as an impulsive anti-craftsman, a recorder of spontaneous responses who made no attempt to shape or refine the style in which he transcribed experience, even a witless victim of his own passions. Now Gail Mandell's book effectively explodes these images that have shadowed the reputation of one of our century's major poets, revealing them for the myths they are. At his best, she shows, Lawrence was not only majestic but also magisterial, and specifically magisterial in his command of an uncannily invisible craft, a skill he would himself have called a "naïveté . . . sufficiently sophisticated to wring the neck of sophistication." Indeed, as Mandell's careful studies of Lawrence's revisions suggest, and as her appended publications of Lawrentian manuscript sequences even more dramatically document, the prophet of "blood-consciousness" was always, also, an acolyte of "nerve-brain consciousness" who devoted the keenest intelligence to his poetic art so as (in the words of his "Man Who Has Come Through") to "blur no whisper, spoil no expression."

How and why have so many readers failed to understand these truths about Lawrence? To begin with, the novelist-poet's own rhetoric may well have led to misunderstandings of his aesthetic. Certainly what would seem to have been his valorization of the "dark gods" of "blood-consciousness" over against the "frictional white seething" of "nerve-brain consciousness" appears to imply a preference for not knowing (and therefore not revising) as opposed to knowing (and revising). In what sense, after all, can even the richest and most intuitive blind-ness—a condition this artist often used as a metaphor for crea-tivity—be compatible with the meticulous vision that is essen-tial to revision? In addition, Lawrence's images of inspiration also seem at first to preclude any conscious shaping by the imagination. Despite the longing of the man who has come through to "be a good fountain, a good well-head" in order to "blur no whisper, spoil no expression," he does, we must con-cede, define himself as an instrument of wise passiveness, a fountain involuntarily spouting language rather than a father intentionally begetting texts. In fact, he goes so far as to insist that the source of his energy is wholly distinct from himself: his genius, he tells us, is "Not I, not I, but the wind that blows through me."

It is no wonder, then, considering the charisma of such conceits, that some critics anxious about control (as well as some readers anxious to lose control) might associate this poet with the eccentricities of sheer expressiveness and with a kind of anti-intellectual ecstasy that refuses attention to the materiality of verse—to words, to stanzas, to rhythms and line-breaks— that is, to all the minutiae of what Blackmur called "rational form." Given Lawrence's background, moreover, it might have been simple for even the most sympathetic critics to take the writer's own rhetoric at what seemed to be its face value. A coal miner's son, lacking both the social graces of the literary middle class and the intellectual capital bestowed by "Oxbridge," the impassioned author of "Snap-dragon" and "Love on the Farm" could be easily romanticized as (or reduced to) a kind of twenti-eth-century ploughboy poet, an uncultivated genius who could not tell strophe from antistrophe, thesis from antithesis, and whose allusions would never be properly Greek.

Yet if we read Lawrence's own aesthetic statements care-fully we can see that he was never the literary wild man such thinkers as Eliot, Blackmur, and Davie have implicitly called him. For one thing, he did continually articulate a concept of poetic skill that, though it may have seemed antithetical to the severe assumptions of high modernists, was nothing like as alien

as they thought. Declaring that "it needs the finest instinct ima-
ginable, much finer than the skill of the craftsman, to get an
emotion out in its own course, without altering it," he defined
an aesthetic which required precisely the linguistic exactitude to
which contemporaries like Yeats, Hulme, Pound, and Eliot were
committed. Or perhaps the exactitude he needed was paradoxi-
cally more intense, for as we can see in reviewing the texts Gail
Mandell has examined here, Lawrence's revisions were never
merely stylistic alterations; they were always, in the truest sense,
re-*visions,* so that he was always necessarily his own *miglior
fábbro.* More important, however, as Mandell insightfully
argues, Lawrence was not only the *miglior fábbro* of his own
frequently revised poems, he was also the maker of his own
poetic self, a point that explains why his rhetoric may some-
times be misleading even while it reveals exactly how artful his
aesthetic was.

The *Collected Poems* of 1928, Mandell explains, were "the
demon's biography," and in that volume, as elsewhere, Law-
rence himself devised "the myth of the spontaneous poet" in
order "to buy time for his experiments in verse." Thus, just as
the *Plumed Serpent* "hymns disembodied from the novel lack
their full meaning" so do "the *Collected Poems* detached from
the orienting context of Lawrence's biography." It is important
to remember, though, that that "orienting complex" was for
Lawrence at least as fictive as any of the texts it fostered, per-
haps as fictive in its way as the fantastic plot of *The Plumed
Serpent.* Even more than Yeats's supreme fiction was Yeats,
Lawrence's supreme fiction was Lawrence. Whether man or
mask, after all, Yeats frequently devoted himself to a cosmic
vision by which he hoped to transcend what Lawrence crucially
called "the burden of self-accomplishment." For Lawrence,
however, cosmos and microcosmos, spiritual achievement and
self-achievement could not be disentangled. As Mandell ob-
serves, like Whitman he belonged in that "revisionary com-
pany" which had continually to reconstruct the character of the
self in order to re-envision the characters of the world. What
Wordsworth saw as the "types and symbols of Eternity" were
therefore present to him as a calligraphy within the soul which
constantly required translation and transcription in new poems
and new versions of old poems.

To be more specific, then, just as it was Lawrence himself who brilliantly invented the warring figures of "the young man" and "the demon" (by whose battles critics from Blackmur to Bloom to the present writer have been intermittently enthralled), so it was Lawrence who re-created himself as a "man who is loved" and a "man who has come through," Lawrence who fictionalized himself as a speaker who had "missed [his] chance with one of the lords / of life," Lawrence who renamed himself "Red Wolf," Lawrence who masked himself as "Quetzalcoatl, of the Two Ways," and Lawrence who transformed himself into a Phoenix "willing to be made nothing" personally, even to be "burnt alive," in order to renew his youth and self in art. For, as Mandell rightly notes, Lawrence is and always was "after the elemental identity, the 'carbon' of the personality, of his fictional characters and, ultimately, of himself."

Once we understand these points, it becomes easier to understand the blurring of fiction and manifesto as well as the eliding of urge and demiurge in some of Lawrence's late poems about creation. As much as any of his essays and prefaces, verses like "Demiurge," "The Work of Creation," "Red Geranium and Godly Mignonette," and "The Body of God" reiterate the familiar Lawrentian rhetoric of spontaneity even while they indirectly reveal Lawrence's strategies of re-vision. The first stanza of "The Work of Creation," for instance, characteristically repudiates intentionality:

> The mystery of creation is the divine urge of creation,
> but it is a great strange urge, it is not a Mind.
> Even an artist knows that his work was never in his mind,
> he could never have *thought* it before it happened.
> A strange ache possessed him, and he entered the struggle,
> and out of the struggle with his material, in the spell of the urge
> his work took place, it came to pass, it stood up and saluted his mind.

At the same time, however, the poem's conclusion defines the reciprocal relation or urge and demiurge, the dependence of creation on the *miglior fabbro* who is sworn to "blur no whisper, spoil no expression." For as the divine "urge takes shape in flesh . . . God looks himself on it in wonder, for the first time," musing "Lo! there is a creature, formed! How strange! / Let me think about it! Let me form an idea!" Clearly, as he finds and fictionalizes himself in flesh, Lawrence's divinity, like the poet himself, will persistently struggle toward revisions as he forms and reforms his ideas.

As Mandell reminds us, Lawrence insisted in one of his most famous essays on his own poetics that "in poetry of the present, nothing is finished," a statement that has often been interpreted to mean that *vers libre* of the kind Lawrence wanted to write was deliberately unfinished in the sense of unpolished, organic, asymmetrical. Yet even while such a reading may accurately capture Lawrence's consciously romantic aesthetic, the statement, as Mandell also observes, can be supplementarily interpreted in another way: for Lawrence, no poem is ever "finished" because every poem is always subject to re-vision, to a continual (demi)urge toward refinishing whose end is an ever more accurate refinement of the supreme fiction of the self. One of modernism's best-known claims about the poetic process is to be found in Yeats's "Adam's Curse":

'A line will take us hours maybe;
Yet if it does not seem a moment's thought,
Our stitching and unstitching has been naught.
Better go down upon your marrow-bones
And scrub a kitchen pavement, or break stones
Like an old pauper, in all kinds of weather;
For to articulate sweet sounds together
Is to work harder than all these.'

Plainly, even if his rhetoric of spontaneity may have been misleading, Lawrence would not have shared such a view of what has lately been called "the scene of writing." Rather, his philosophical allegiance would have been to Keats's romantic dictum: "If Poetry comes not as naturally as the Leaves to a tree it had better not come at all." Yet if we put Keats's simile together with Mandell's interpretation of the lack of "finish" in Lawrence's "poetry of the present," we can perhaps best understand the thought behind Lawrence's revisionary passion. Every tree, after all, revises itself every spring as it grows toward its own uniqueness. For Lawrence, therefore, there was in practice no discrepancy between romantic form and rational revision, between inspiration and what Yeats called "stitching and unstitching." Indeed, because of Gail Mandell's revealing study, we can now understand how truly this poet was the demiurge of his own life and art, looking back at the leaves of his own inexorable imagination and, like the wondering God in his "Work of Creation," murmuring "How strange! / Let me think about it! Let me form an idea!"

Abbreviations, Symbols,
and Editorial Method

Am	*Amores*
CP	*Collected Poems*
(illeg.)	Illegible
LP	*Love Poems*
MS	Manuscript
NP	*New Poems*
TS	Typescript
⸜ ⸝	Interlinear deleted or emended material
[ ]	Multilinear deleted or emended material
{ }	First letter(s) or word emended to second
Δ	Inserted material
*	Footnote
⟨ ⟩	Author's note

As far as possible, I have transcribed each manuscript version of a poem as Lawrence wrote it and each printed version as it appeared in its first edition. Where a number of versions of a poem resemble each other closely, as in the case of the versions of "Dreams Old and Nascent" that appear in manuscripts 5 and 9 and in the *English Review,* I have reproduced the published version of the poem and indicated manuscript variations, where they occur, in angle brackets at the end of the verse line. In a few cases, as with "Discipline," where nine versions of the poem remain, many almost identical, I have included all published versions of the poems, but only those manuscript versions that display substantive changes. Almost always, however, I have chosen to reproduce each distinct version of a poem as it appears in manuscript or in print, arranging all variants of a single poem in chronological order. Thus, the reader has a sense of each version of a poem as an entity; its evolution becomes apparent as one compares emendations within and between the versions of a poem.

In my transcriptions of manuscript poems, I intend for the reader to read upwards through successive emendations to Lawrence's final text. In the few cases where his writing is illegible, I have so indicated by the abbreviation *illeg.* Where Lawrence has occasionally misspelled a word or written one clearly wrong for its context, I have so indicated by using *sic.* However, I have transcribed mistakes in punctuation without comment. Where Lawrence has used ampersands, I have changed them silently to "and." While I make no attempt to note every peculiarity of Lawrence's holographs, I consistently note what strike me as significant features of his handwritten drafts, for example stanzas squeezed into margins.

Except for references to *Last Poems,* in which I follow Richard Aldington's designations because he distinguishes between the manuscript notebooks, I have adopted the numbering system that Carole Ferrier uses to list Lawrence's verse manuscripts in her unpublished doctoral dissertation, "The Earlier Poetry of D. H. Lawrence: A Variorum Text" (see app. A). My descriptions of these manuscripts are also based on information supplied by Ferrier in her dissertation. Where Ferrier assigns a new number to a particular verse manuscript in her article "D. H. Lawrence's Pre-1920 Poetry: A Descriptive Bibliography of Manuscripts, Typescripts, and Proofs," *The D. H. Lawrence Review* 6 (1973): 333–59, I have indicated it in angled brackets. The other listings in the appendix refer to the bibliographies of Warren Roberts and E. W. Tedlock.

I had direct access to manuscript 1 and four poems that form part of manuscript 14, but I used photocopies or microfilms of manuscripts A, B, 31, and 79, and of the typescript of *Collected Poems.* In the case of poems published in books and periodicals, I used first editions and photocopies, respectively. In other instances, most notably the manuscripts in various private collections, I depended upon Ferrier's variorum.

The scope of my study of Lawrence's verse determined which poems and, in a few instances, which versions of poems, I included in the Appendixes. I chose poems that I judge to be the best representatives of Lawrence's typical method of revision, and that illustrate conclusions based on an analysis of all of his extant revisions. I have not tried to present a survey of Lawrence's revisions of the poetry or of the notebooks that contain most of them, nor have I necessarily chosen to transcribe the existing versions of his best poetry—or of his best known. In short, I have been as thorough as space and the purpose of my book allowed, but like all Lawrence scholars, I await the Cambridge edition of Lawrence's poems as the definitive variorum of his poetry.

The Phoenix Paradox

1. Lawrence's Design for *Collected Poems*

D. H. LAWRENCE arranged *Collected Poems* (1928)[1] to tell a story. The genre of the story is biography, he tells his readers in the note to the two-volume edition,[2] although poems of other kinds, namely the imaginative or fictional and the dialect poems, are not excluded. Nevertheless, not all the poems that he wrote are included in the collection; only those poems that have the "demon" in them—the "real poems," he adds by way of clarification—find a place. Some, he says, he had to rewrite in order to free the demon.

Chronology, specifically the chronology of their composition, determines the arrangement of the poems because, asserts Lawrence, the order of time reflects the order of experience. The story told represents "an emotional and inner life" which, he implies, moves through three cycles: the first, the "death-experience," presented in volume 1 and the first few poems of volume 2; the second, the start of the "new cycle," opening with "Bei Hennef" and closing with "Frost Flowers" (for the most part poems first collected in *Look! We Have Come Through!* [1917]); and the conclusion of the new cycle, consisting of the whole of *Birds, Beasts and Flowers* (1923) and the *Tortoise* poems (1921), which had been printed separately in America. According to Lawrence, the total time period represented in *Collected Poems* is twenty-two years, which by inference includes the years 1906 through 1928.[3]

The foreword[4] to *Collected Poems,* dated the same day as the note, which superseded it, contains in more extended form a similar explanation of the story and structure of the two volumes. It treats in greater, more personal detail the autobiographical background of the poems, especially the early ones, written before 1912. It is, as well, considerably more explicit about the role of the demon in *Collected Poems.* Of course, one can only guess at Lawrence's reasons for publishing the note

rather than the foreword. Because the note in no way contro-
verts the content or the tone of the foreword (it is simply less
detailed), the choice may have been prompted by Lawrence's
fear that he had been too explicit in the foreword about his plan
for *Collected Poems*. A passage from the travel book *Etruscan
Places,* which he was composing at approximately the same
time that he was working on the two versions of the foreword,
illuminates Lawrence's apprehension about telling too much:

> The people are not initiated into the cosmic ideas, nor into the
> awakened throb of more vivid consciousness. Try as you may,
> you can never make the mass of men throb with full awakedness.
> They *cannot* be more than a little aware. So you must give them
> symbols, ritual and gesture, which will fill their bodies with life
> up to their own full measure. Any more is fatal. And so the actual
> knowledge must be guarded from them, lest knowing the formu-
> lae, without undergoing at all the experience that corresponds,
> they may become insolent and impious, thinking they have the
> all, when they have only an empty monkey-chatter. The esoteric
> knowledge will always be esoteric, since knowledge is an experi-
> ence, not a formula.[5]

Added as an apparent afterthought (the original date and place
of composition having been scored out in the holograph manu-
script to make room for it), the final paragraph of the foreword
makes clear the true subject of *Collected Poems:* the demon.
This paragraph begins with an apology for the personal tone of
the entire foreword. Its tone is justified, says Lawrence, because
it reflects the personal approach of the poems themselves. Being
personal, they "hang together in a life." Furthermore, the per-
sonal foreword is meant to "give the demon his body of mere
man, as far as is possible."

In other words, it would seem that we, the readers, are to
read the story of *Collected Poems* not as autobiography, as
some have done,[6] but as the biography of Lawrence's demon.
He is the "timeless" Lawrence, we are told, distinct from the
"ordinary meal-time" Lawrence who "has yesterdays." He
unites the twenty-year-old "young man" with the forty-two-
year-old poet who sits at Scandicci on 12 May 1928, writing his
foreword to *Collected Poems*. He is the "same me" who wrote
the best of the early poems (examples of which Lawrence cites
as "The Wild Common" and "Renascence") and *Birds, Beasts*

and Flowers. It is he, the demon, who oversaw the revision of many of the early poems, not only in the autumn and winter of 1927/28, when Lawrence was in the process of collecting the poems, but also presumably throughout the many earlier periods of revision that preceded and often followed the publication of the verse in periodicals and books. Lawrence indicates that he met and continues to meet his demon in his poetry, and that on this ground we too shall meet him and face, if we stand fast, that new knowledge of self that is still "a sin and a vice," i.e., forbidden by conventional morality and by custom.

The language and tone of both the note and the foreword introduce the mythic structure that underlies *Collected Poems.* Lawrence is obviously mythmaking when he introduces the demon (also called the "ghost"[7]) to explain the unconscious creative urge and give a name to the unknown, unique self that refuses conventional determination. The figure can be looked upon as a complex objective correlative meant to signify a reality that defies precise definition. This fully individual self is, as the foreword says and the note suggests, at once the creator and the central figure of *Collected Poems.* The historical D. H. Lawrence provides the body through which the demon manifests himself in order to give a shape to the "emotional and inner life" of which *Collected Poems* is the biography.

What Lawrence means by the demon and the ghost has been variously interpreted. Some see the demon as a personification of the poetic process; others find it to be the equivalent of inchoate emotions.[8] Based on references to the demon and the ghost in other writings of D. H. Lawrence, I agree with Aldous Huxley's suggestion in his introduction to the *Letters of D. H. Lawrence* that Lawrence's idea of the demon stems from the pre-Christian Greek concept of "daimon."[9] Most likely, the concept first came to him by way of the Romantic poets, who rediscovered it and extensively used it in their poetry (e.g., Byron in *Manfred* and Shelley in *Alastor*).[10] In any event, Lawrence certainly encountered a systematic description of the daimon in John Burnet's *Early Greek Philosophers,* which he read most probably sometime in 1916 and by which he was greatly influenced, according to his friend Richard Aldington.[11] The traditional moral ambiguity of the "daimon," its role as mediator between gods and men, and its intimate connection with saving knowledge invite Lawrence to adapt the symbol to his own mythopoeic ends.

Baruch Hochman, in his book *Another Ego,* which considers Lawrence's changing artistic view of the self and society, sees the leadership novels, particularly *Kangaroo* and *The Plumed Serpent,* asserting that

> the quiddity of the self stems from the natural entities that Lawrence calls "dark" and "demonic" and that hold selves centered in their own, extra-social integrity. The "dark gods," who preserve individual identity, are integrally related to the societal instinct. Together, and, in a manner of speaking, dialectically, they counteract the effect of socialization—or of participation mystique—which draws the individual into the community by shattering his individual integrity, yet which nonetheless fails to satisfy his dark, "somatic," societal needs.[12]

As Hochman implies, the demon becomes for Lawrence a "true self," but one that assumes the role of an "anti-self" when viewed from the perspective of conventional social, moral, and artistic norms. The demon exists as a mystery within man, and also outside him, in nature, by which Lawrence means the physical world. The demon unites man and nature in a dark, because unconscious, relationship.[13] Duality is implicit in this view, in the separation of spirit and matter, the struggle between conscious and unconscious existence, and the tension between creation and destruction.

"Demon" is a word used infrequently and then, for the most part, late in Lawrence's writings, although the concept of the demonic occurs throughout the work. Much more often, especially in some of the letters, essays, and novels written in the period betwen 1914–15 (the respective dates of the composition of the *Study of Thomas Hardy* and "The Crown," the first lengthy explorations of this idea) and 1925 (when *Reflections on the Death of a Porcupine,* in which the concept finds its fullest expression, was published), Lawrence refers to the concept later called the demon as the "Holy Ghost," a designation clearly borrowed from Christian nomenclature. In the foreword, Lawrence's shortening of the name to "ghost," capital letter deleted, emphasizes that by 1928 he had relegated Christianity to one among many mythological expressions of the divine. In *Apocalypse,* written in 1929, all reference to the ghost has disappeared, although the concept remains a central one to the book.[14]

Lawrence's concept of the Holy Ghost, even when he first uses the term, does not coincide with its Christian signification. He explains in *Reflections* that the name was created by Jesus to describe what he saw only vaguely: the "third thing," the timeless spark that springs out of the balance of "me" and "thee" (i.e., subject and object) in any act of creation.[15] Lawrence, however, refuses to identify the Holy Ghost with love, as Christ did; he maintains that it is both love and hate (or, more properly, individuality, which is the true opposite of love in his view); that it is opposition and attraction both. In a letter written in 1915, Lawrence makes an early attempt to articulate what he means by the Holy Ghost. Still tied to the Christian paradigm, he tries to explain as a temporary lapse Christ's misrepresentation of the Holy Ghost as love alone. "In His purest moments," concludes Lawrence, "Christ knew that the Holy Spirit was both love and hate—not one only."[16]

By 1925, the year in which he wrote all but one of the essays published in *Reflections*, Lawrence has worked out the concept of the Holy Ghost in some detail. It resembles, he says, the spark that the ancient Greeks called "equilibrium" (a term he eschews as being too mechanical), which arises from the perfect balance of opposite forces, the tension between "two creatures, two things that are equilibriated, or in living relationship" (*Reflections* 433). Equilibrium, Lawrence maintains, implies dualism. "Everything that exists, even a stone, has two sides to its nature. It fiercely maintains its own individuality, its own solidity. And it reaches forth from itself in the subtlest flow of desire" (*Reflections* 456).

Like the pre-Christian "daimon," the Holy Ghost is the "glue" of the dualistic universe. Lawrence makes this function explicit in the title essay from *Reflections:* "All existence is dual, and surging towards a consummation into being. . . . The Holy Ghost is that which holds the light and dark, the day and the night, the wet and the sunny, united in one little clue."[17]

In a similar way, the Holy Ghost unites the individual person, who is implicitly dualistic from conception, as Lawrence makes clear in *Fantasia of the Unconscious* (1922): "The intrinsic truth of every individual is the new unit of unique individuality which emanates from the fusion of the parent nuclei. This is the incalculable and intangible Holy Ghost each time—each individual has his own Holy Ghost."[18] Developing this idea later in the same book, Lawrence writes of the Holy Ghost in a way that recalls Socrates' description of his "daimon" in *Apology*:

> It is the individual in his pure singleness, in his totality of consciousness, in his oneness of being: the Holy Ghost which is with us after our Pentecost, and which we may not deny. When I say to myself, "I am wrong," knowing with sudden insight that I *am* wrong, then this is the whole self speaking, the Holy Ghost. It is no piece of mental inference. It is not just the soul sending forth a flash. It is my whole being speaking in one voice, soul and mind and psyche transfigured into oneness. This voice of my being I may *never* deny.[19]

Just as the Holy Ghost springs from the union of the diverse elements of the self, so it can glance from the person's recognition of the other as other, the "not-me." As Lawrence puts it in *Reflections:* "In so far as I am I, a being who is proud and in place, I have a connection with my circumambient universe, and I know my place. When the white cock crows, I do not hear myself, or some anthropromorphic conceit, I hear the not-me, the voice of the Holy Ghost" (481).

It follows for Lawrence that the Holy Ghost in man is that timeless element, that link with the divine called the "soul": "But what is the soul of a man, except *that* in him which is himself alone, suspended in immediate relationship with the sum of things?" (*Reflections* 434) Indeed, asserts Lawrence in *Studies in Classic American Literature* (1923): "The multiplicity of gods within us make up the Holy Ghost."[20] The "God-flame" restlessly seeks new incarnations, ever new "blossomings" in "the establishing of a pure, *new* relationship with all the cosmos" (*Reflections* 471).

True to its nature, the Holy Ghost, or demon, assumes many shapes in *Collected Poems,* some human, some divine. Most obvious among them is that of the historical D. H. Lawrence, developing in time from an "old" self to a "new" self. He begins as the young man of volume 1, who struggles for equilibrium in relationship with others and with the world, but fails to achieve it. In volume 2, he becomes the adult male of *Look! We Have Come Through!,* who attempts to establish a living relationship with a woman, and partially succeeds; and emerges as the mature human being of *Birds, Beasts and Flowers,* who searches to establish relationship with the nonhuman world, and in large measure succeeds. This temporal development of the self, the most obvious ordering of *Collected Poems,* Lawrence signals in his titles for volumes 1 and 2 of the edition: "Rhyming Poems" and "Unrhyming Poems," respectively. In an unpublished letter to Amy Lowell dated 5 April 1919, Lawrence writes the following, which clarifies his choice of titles: "I agree with you that the poetry of the future, and the poetry that *now* has the germs of futurity in it, is rhymeless, naked, spontaneous rhythm. But one has an old self as well as a new."[21] These sentiments echo those expressed one year earlier by Lawrence in his introduction to the American edition of *New Poems,* which he says should have preceded *Look! We Have Come Through!,* that being the book to which it belonged.[22] Both the letter and the introduction make clear that the titles must be understood metaphorically; otherwise, they appear to be misnomers, since Volume 1 contains a number of unrhyming poems and volume 2 includes a sizable number of poems that rhyme.

Apparently, the new self, which begins to reveal itself in volume 2 of *Collected Poems,* does not depend as heavily on the particulars of time, place, and circumstance as does the old self. Of the poems first collected in *Birds, Beasts and Flowers,* Lawrence writes in the foreword, "They are what they are," implying that they perfectly reveal themselves, and leaving us to conclude that they manifest the demonic self, who "makes his own form willy-nilly, and is unchangeable." But this demonic self is the "same me" who wrote the best of the poems in volume 1, stresses Lawrence, emphasizing thereby that the structure of *Collected Poems* goes beyond chronology, either of experience or of composition.

Without doubt, Lawrence does order the poems more or less chronologically—although not always so; he also arranges them to reveal the self that refuses to recognize limitations of time or place or circumstance. This self-demon-ghost provides continuity in the midst of ephemera; it transcends particular existence even while embedded in it. He effects this ordering by choosing a deliberately nonchronological approach, the mythological. This

mythopoeic method, akin to the "mythical method" that T. S.
Eliot described after reading James Joyce's *Ulysses*,[23] introduces
the ahistorical Lawrence as the central figure of the biography:
Lawrence as avatar. The demonic Lawrence can be one god or
many. He assumes the shapes of Attis, Dionysos, Osiris, Or-
pheus, and Christ and the roles of son, brother, and lover as the
situation warrants. Against him, the eternally dying and resur-
rected male, stands the female: the mother, sister, and beloved.
As the archetypal situation demands, she becomes the earth
goddess in any of her forms: Demeter, Persephone, Cybele, Se-
mele, or Isis; she may appear as Eurydice or the virgin wife and
mother, Mary; or she may assume any of the three incarnations
of the moon: Selene, Artemis, or Hecate. Why so many faces?
Lawrence gives his answer in *Apocalypse:* "The older a myth,
the deeper it goes in the human consciousness, the more varied
will be the forms it takes in the upper consciousness."[24] Law-
rence is rarely explicit about the mythic identities of those who
appear in the poems; similarly, he conceals the actual identities
of "Miriam," the "Betrothed," and "Helen." The significance
of the people and situations represented in *Collected Poems* lies
in their participation in a cyclic structure of death and resurrec-
tion that underlies both volumes. Lawrence hints at this struc-
ture: he refers in the note to the "death-experience" explored in
Volume 1 and to the rebirth motif treated in the "new cycle" of
volume 2. He does not develop it as he does the chronological
structure, quite possibly, as I have suggested, to avoid misunder-
standing by the uninitiated.

The individual experience of the historical Lawrence is ex-
tended, primarily through metaphor and symbol, to the mythic
experience that reveals its full import. Thus, for example, the
spiritually exhausted world of the young scholar and teacher,
vitiated by callousness, willful perversion, and violence, be-
comes an underworld that must be explored, integrated, and
transcended. Ordinary settings like a classroom, a bedroom, or
a garden become the scenes of cosmic realizations. Temporal
and mythic realities intertwine in each poem to form the web
that unites the collection and makes it of a piece with *Last
Poems* (1932).

That Lawrence had some such plan in mind when he ar-
ranged the poems and that the plan dictated a number of his

revisions becomes clear when one compares the order of the contents of *Collected Poems* with the shape of the earlier volumes that it incorporates and examines in manuscript form the nature of the revisions Lawrence made for this collection. Furthermore, a detailed study of the progressive revision of the poems from their earliest extant forms, often in the college notebooks that Lawrence has called "the foundation of the poetic me," demonstrates his growing consciousness of the psychic shape that lay implicit in his work, waiting to be refined and fully revealed.

From such study, patterns of revision emerge that uncover the craftsman industriously at work, trying for the distinctive word, the succinct phrase, the limpid image, and the appropriate rhyme and meter. They also reveal a developing artist, fighting toward artistic identity by consciously overturning conventional forms and ideas in his work to establish unique themes and modes of expression. The evolution—or unfolding, as Lawrence would prefer to name it—of his poetic technique and style parallels a corresponding development in his personal vision of himself and the world.

Collected Poems provides the key to this unfolding, recording as it does a twenty-year search for knowledge through experience that approaches the epic. The two volumes also exist as an emblem of the self. Lawrence's eagerness to publish his collected poems in America because they were "in such a scattered mess"[25] betrays his sense of their participation in the mystery of his identity.[26] This particular study, a type of poetic archaeology, seems particularly appropriate to Lawrence, the lover of Etruscan places, and to *Collected Poems,* the strata of successive selves. Uncovering layer upon layer of whatever remains of the previous forms of the poems will add yet another dimension to our understanding of Lawrence's creative development.

2. The Incorporation of *Love Poems,* *Amores, New Poems,* and *Bay* into "Rhyming Poems"

Although Lawrence paid seemingly little attention to the order established in their separate collections when arranging the volume 1 "Rhyming Poems," an examination of some of the manuscript collections of Lawrence's verse, especially the two extant Nottingham University College notebooks (see app. A), reveals that Lawrence consistently grouped thematically related poems together as he made fair copies of them, thereby indicating his recognition of their intrinsic connection as well as his desire that they be read consecutively. As the poems were published, he often kept such clusters intact; indeed, in *Collected Poems,* he restored to their original clusters several poems that had been separated when first published. Frequently among these groups are poems that Lawrence united in early manuscript form under a general heading, such as "The Songless" poems in manuscript 1.[1] Also often grouped together are the poems he reduced in manuscript to two or more independent lyrics as he revised them, as in the case of an early poem called "Silence," which in manuscript 5 includes the stanzas that later become "Silence" (*Am* 34, *CP* 75) and "Listening" (*Am* 35, *CP* 76),[2] poems that remain proximate in both *Amores* and *Collected Poems.* On the other hand, Lawrence occasionally disperses in *Collected Poems* other clusters that he maintained throughout various revisions and printings, most obviously "Dreams Old and Nascent: Old" (*Am* 10, *CP* 22) and "Dreams Old and Nascent: Nascent" (*Am* 11, *CP* 144), which as "A Still Afternoon in School" had formed a unit in five manuscript versions, in *The English Review* for November 1909, and in *Amores.*

Is there a coherent method in Lawrence's incorporation of *Love Poems, Amores, New Poems,* and *Bay* into "Rhyming Poems"? I propose to show in the following pages that Lawrence in fact reorders the poems according to a controlling idea expressed in the foreword and note to *Collected Poems:* the story of the interior experience of the poet, his "psychobiography," as one critic has called it.[3] The structure that develops this idea consists of three planes: the chronologic, the thematic, and the mythic. Put simply, Lawrence respects earlier sequences when they serve his new design and rejects them when they do not. Furthermore, I suggest that Lawrence takes full advantage of certain chronologic, thematic, and mythic groupings present in the manuscripts and the published volumes, particularly *Amores,* as he shapes the story of the demon and his relation to Lawrence's old self in "Rhyming Poems." By doing so, Lawrence tacitly acknowledges that this story, or myth, is implicit in the earlier material. Consequently, his primary concern in "Rhyming Poems" would seem to be to structure the individual poems to reveal their inherent psychic shape, as he had already done in *Look! We Have Come Through!* and *Birds, Beasts and Flowers,* the volumes that compose "Unrhyming Poems." Lawrence's task in arranging volume 1 of *Collected Poems* can be summed up as making explicit the mythic form of his early experience, whose fullest implications he has only retrospectively realized.

As its title suggests, *Love Poems* contains many of the poems that Lawrence wrote about his early love affairs, especially those with Jessie Chambers and Helen Corke (the "Miriam" and "Helen," respectively, of the verse). Many of the fictional and dialect poems belong to this volume, also, as do a few of the poems about schoolmastering. The most plausible explanation of the volume's diversity is that Walter de la Mare, who selected and arranged the material for *Love Poems,* used personal taste as his primary editorial criterion. In essence, he seems to have chosen from Lawrence's notebooks those poems he considered artistically best and ordered them in a way he thought aesthetically pleasing.[4] Consequently, although Lawrence places most of the poems from *Love Poems* early in "Rhyming Poems," indicating thereby that they represent some of his earliest poetic ventures, he frequently inserts among them poems on similar subjects or themes from *Amores, New Poems,* and even *Bay* (see app. B).

Three poems about Miriam, "Aware" (*LP* 12, *CP* 35), "A

Pang of Reminiscence" (*LP* 13, *CP* 36), and "A White Blossom" (*LP* 14, *CP* 37), form the longest sequence transferred intact from *Love Poems* to *Collected Poems*.[5] In addition, two pairs of poems from this volume remain contiguous in *Collected Poems:* a couple of Helen poems, "Return" (*LP* 16, *CP* 51) and "The Appeal" (*LP* 17, *CP* 52),[6] and two poems that were originally part of a seven-poem sequence called "Transformations" in manuscript 5, "Morning Work" (*LP* 21, *CP* 43) and "Transformations" (*LP* 22, *CP* 44). Not apparent until one consults manuscript 5 is that Lawrence reunited "Corot" (*LP* 20, *CP* 38) and "Michael Angelo" (*LP* 25, *CP* 39) in *Collected Poems,* placing them near most of the other poems from the "Transformations" sequence, of which they had also been a part.[7] Conversely, Lawrence separates the only clear sequence in *Love Poems,* the "Schoolmaster" group, which includes "A Snowy Day in School" (*LP* 30, *CP* 48), "The Best of School" (*LP* 31, *CP* 21), and "Afternoon in School" (*LP* 32, *CP* 46: "Last Lesson of the Afternoon").[8] Lawrence apparently made this decision because "The Best of School" is thematically closer to "Dreams Old and Nascent: Old" (*Am* 10, *CP* 22) than to the other school poems, with which it shares only a common subject.

Both *New Poems* and *Bay* follow a pattern of transposition to "Rhyming Poems" similar to that of *Love Poems*. Every now and then, two or more poems from these volumes will remain in their original order relative to each other, or shift position only slightly, but most often Lawrence rearranges them freely in *Collected Poems*. Several of the poems from *New Poems,* however, do find themselves reunited in the collection as Lawrence reestablishes early manuscript sequences. These are "A Letter from Town: On a Grey Evening (*CP:* Morning) in March" (*NP* 9, *CP* 26) and "Letter from Town: The Almond-Tree" (*NP* 6, *CP* 27), coupled originally in manuscript 1; "Hyde Park at Night, Before the War: Clerks" (*NP* 11, *CP* 40) and "Piccadilly Circus at Night: Street-Walkers" (*NP* 18, *CP* 41), grouped as "The Songless" in manuscript 1 and as "Songs of Work People at Night" in manuscript 19; and "Embankment at Night, Before the War: Charity" (*NP* 22, *CP* 114) and "Embankment at Night, Before the War: Outcasts" (*NP* 26, *CP* 115), part of "London Nights" in manuscript 26.

Neither *Love Poems* nor *New Poems* has a strong unifying

motif; the arrangement of the poems in these volumes reveals no significant connection among them. *Bay* does possess a certain thematic unity because all of its poems relate to a common topic, the war; yet the actual sequencing of the poems in the volume seems quite as arbitrary as that in the other two books. Nevertheless, if one excludes *Love Poems,* which he did not personally assemble, one finds that Lawrence betrays an early tendency towards thematic arrangement of his verse (surely the novelist in him coming out), even though he does not fully achieve it in any of the books collected in "Rhyming Poems." For example, Lawrence's intention to name *New Poems* either *Chorus of Women* or *Coming Awake*[9] indicates that he conceived of the volume as having at least potential thematic unity. In the end, however, the publisher Martin Secker expeditiously decided on the title *New Poems,* even though all except a handful have their origins in the college notebooks that date from as early as 1906. After the publication of *Amores,* at the time at which he was putting together *Bay, Look! We Have Come Through!,* and quite possibly *New Poems,* Lawrence had relatively few unused poems left in the notebooks; as he admits to his agent at the time, J. B. Pinker, these books represent the final reaping from the old notebooks.[10] Consequently, any convincing thematic arrangement of *New Poems* would have been difficult without extensive alteration of old material (which is, indeed, what happened in *Bay*) or entirely new composition. Lawrence apparently feels compelled to rearrange most of the poems from *Love Poems, New Poems,* and *Bay* as he integrates them into *Collected Poems* because they lack any coherent internal organizational principle, either chronologic or thematic. Nevertheless, these volumes do demonstrate to some degree Lawrence's practice of linking poems to create a scene or tell a story.

Amores offers something of an exception to the casualness apparent in the initial ordering of *Love Poems, New Poems,* and *Bay* and further supports the intimation of *New Poems* and *Bay* that Lawrence thought of all his poems, not just those in *Look! We Have Come Through!* and *Birds, Beasts and Flowers,* as sequences rather than individual entities. Quite a few of the *Amores* poems retain their original ordering as they are incorporated into *Collected Poems,* especially those focused on the death of Lawrence's mother, Lydia Beardsall Lawrence (*Am* 26–29, *CP* 66–69; *Am* 30–36, *CP* 71–77). Lawrence inserts only one poem, "Reminder" (*LP* 8, *CP* 70), in the midst of this sequence, which he calls the crisis of volume 1 in the note to *Collected Poems*. The poems that begin what Lawrence terms in the note "the long haunting of death in life" also form a block of related verse in both *Amores* and "Rhyming Poems." "Liaison" (*CP:* "The Yew-Tree on the Downs") through "The Enkindled Spring" (*Am* 39–43, *CP* 81–85) and "In Trouble and Shame" through "The Mystic Blue" (*CP:* "Blueness"; *Am* 56–60, *CP* 103–7) compose double sets of five poems each that join with other poems from *Amores* and *New Poems* to make the core of "Rhyming Poems." Even in their earliest manuscript form, these poems tend to create clusters distinct from the other poems in the collections.[11] Indeed, "Troth with the Dead" in manuscript 5 is a proto-poem that develops into "Troth with the Dead" (*Am* 40, *CP* 82), "Dissolute" (*Am* 41, *CP* 83: "At a Loose End"), and "The Enkindled Spring" (*Am* 43, *CP* 85). (See app. I.1.) *Amores* has, then, an incipient narrative structure; and as his correspondence shows, Lawrence was conscious of it. In respect to the poems in the *Amores* manuscript, Lawrence wrote to Lady Ottoline Morrell that "they make a sort of inner history of my life, from 20 to 26."[12] Thus, the *Amores* poems supply an archaic structure upon which Lawrence can reconstruct the definitive history of the old self in the first volume of *Collected Poems*.

3. The Chronologic, Thematic, and Mythic Structure of "Rhyming Poems"

The chronological arrangement of "Rhyming Poems" covers a period of some twelve years, beginning about 1905–6[1] and ending with the approach of peace at the conclusion of World War I. "The Wild Common" (*Am* 2, *CP* 1), which opens the volume, is set in the late spring or early summer, as is the second poem, "Dog-Tired" (*LP* 24, *CP* 2). "War-Baby" (*Bay* 17, *CP* 142), one of the last poems in the volume and dedicated to Catherine Carswell and her newborn son, establishes the closing year of 1918; and "Autumn Sunshine" (*NP* 41, *CP* 146), the final poem, establishes the season. In its manuscript versions and in an earlier published form (*The Egoist*, 1 April 1914), "*Autumn Sunshine*" was set in the spring; but Lawrence changed the setting for *New Poems* and made it the penultimate poem. Both the season and the position of "Autumn Sunshine" in *New Poems* and "Rhyming Poems" effectively signal the end of things, most importantly the end of the old self. A seasonal cycle that moves from vegetative rebirth to decline and a time span that, while it begins with a poem about personal awakening, ends with poems describing a war that involved most of the Western world, provide a framework for "Rhyming Poems" that extends Lawrence's experience beyond the strictly personal. The seasonal orientation of the volume and its broad chronological organization reinforce its thematic and mythic structure.

I should note here that one obvious violation of the chronology of *Collected Poems* is that all the material relating to Lawrence's elopement with and subsequent marriage to Frieda von Richthofen Weekley appears in volume 2, "Unrhyming Poems," of *Collected Poems*. For the most part published in *Look! We Have Come Through!*,[2] this material covers the period 1912–17 and reprsents a significant omission from "Rhyming Poems." Lawrence justifies this anachronism in the note to *Col-*

lected Poems, saying that these poems begin a new cycle. He ignores the obvious: that chronologically the old self of "Rhyming Poems" coexisted with the unfolding new self of *Look!* By lifting the *Look!* poems out of their proper chronological sequence, Lawrence emphasizes the achronological nature of the new self, which, as he makes clear in the note, transcends time, place, and circumstance. In this instance, at least, thematic and mythic concerns dominate chronology, even though Lawrence explicitly identifies in the note to *Collected Poems* only his chronological structuring of experience.

A more subtle question of chronology arises as one tries to ascertain whether Lawrence does, in fact, as he says in the note he will, "arrange the poems, as far as is possible, in chronological order." By chronological order, Lawrence explains that he means both the order in which he wrote the poems and the order of experience they represent; "the order of time . . . is the order of experience," he writes. Of course, the phrase "as far as is possible" implies that Lawrence allowed himself leeway as he arranged the poems, presumably because he had at times forgotten the exact date of composition of a poem relative to the others or else because he chose to position a poem achronologically for some reason. Clearly, while the order of composition often corresponds with the order of experience, as in the case of his poems on his mother's death,[3] a good many of the earliest poems that Lawrence includes in *Collected Poems* were almost totally rewritten (e.g., "Virgin Youth"), so that one can question how closely the date of composition corresponds to the order of experience the poem depicts. Moreover, it was Lawrence's usual practice to revise poems from the early notebooks as much as ten years after he had first written them, at times only slightly changing them to fit a new context (or "experience"). Such is the case of "Bombardment," which appears in manuscript 5 as "Spring in the City" and in a revised form in *Bay,* here presented as part of the war experience. Lawrence also divides a poem in manuscript, creating two or more new ones, of which one may be placed relatively early in *Collected Poems,* the other, late (e.g., "The Inheritance" [*Am* 33, *CP* 74] and "The Noise of Battle" [*NP:* "*Apprehension,*" 1; *CP* 126], both of which form a single poem, "The Inheritance," in manuscript 5).

Looking at the distribution of poems from the early volumes in volume 1 of *Collected Poems*, one sees that the date of publication of the various poems in books and periodicals bears no certain correlation with the time at which Lawrence actually wrote them, although he does group many of the poems from *Amores, New Poems,* and *Bay* together in "Rhyming Poems," especially in the last half of the volume (see app. B). A poem such as "Little Town at Evening," published in *The Monthly Chapbook* in July 1919 and reprinted in *Bay*, exists as "Eastwood Evening" in manuscript 1, most probably the earliest of Lawrence's notebooks, written while he was still a student at Nottingham University College. That Lawrence places this poem early in *Collected Poems* (no. 17) supports his claim that he followed the order of composition in arranging *Collected Poems*. Yet one has only to realize that the last three poems in "Rhyming Poems": "Dreams Old and Nascent: Nascent," "On That Day," and "Autumn Sunshine," are among the earliest that Lawrence wrote, all appearing in the early manuscripts 1 and 5, and it becomes plain that Lawrence was willing to sacrifice the chronology of composition and experience to larger structural concerns.

While it is impossible to date precisely the composition of most of Lawrence's verse,[4] an examination of the contents of the early notebooks again supports Lawrence's claim to a basic observance of chronology "as far as is possible"—in other words, whenever it is convenient or important for Lawrence to observe it, or seem to observe it. Lawrence's ordering in *Collected Poems* of the poems from *Bay*, a book published in 1919 but containing poems from early manuscripts as well as new or extensively revised poems, provides a useful example of Lawrence's chronological ordering of his material. He arranges four poems from *Bay* early in "Rhyming Poems": "The Little Town at Evening" (*Bay* 2, *CP* 17), "Last Hours" (*Bay* 3, *CP* 19), "Guards!" (*Bay* 1, *CP* 34), and "After the Opera" (*Bay* 5, *CP* 42). The first three of these appear in the early notebooks, but are extensively rewritten by the time of their publication in *Bay*. Other poems from these notebooks: "On the March" (*Bay* 7, *CP* 131), "Ruination" (*Bay* 14, *CP* 132), "Bombardment" (*Bay* 8, *CP* 135), and "Rondeau of a Conscientious Objector" (*Bay* 15, *CP* 136),[5] revised neither more nor less than the poems mentioned earlier, remain with the new compositions from *Bay*

at the end of *Collected Poems*. Furthermore, a poem such as
"Bombardment," originally written to describe Lawrence's ex-
perience of a spring morning, depicts a vastly different experi-
ence when it is juxtaposed with the other poems from *Bay*. For
Lawrence, then, the illusion of chronology takes precedence
over the actual date of composition of a poem, and, at times,
over the nature of the experience described.

Aware of these fundamental ambiguities in the chronologi-
cal structure of "Rhyming Poems," one can more astutely ex-
amine the chronological "stages" of the volume that Lawrence
outlines in the foreword to *Collected Poems*. These are stages of
his life, defined by both internal experiences and external
events, and stages of poetic composition. Based on his detailed
description of each stage in the foreword to *Collected Poems*, I
find it helpful to a discussion of the structure of "Rhyming
Poems" to identify eight distinct stages, or phases, in this vol-
ume and to assign specific poems to each of these divisions.
Doing so enables one to perceive more readily the thematic and
mythic stages fundamental to the book.

The first stage, according to Lawrence, consists of the sub-
jective poems, such as "The Wild Common" and "Virgin
Youth"; the Miriam poems; and the first poems to his mother.
This stage includes poems 1–19 in "Rhyming Poems." The sec-
ond stage, poems 20–50, depicts the initial separation from
home and the experience of teaching and of London. Next come
the poems to Helen, along with more school poems, numbers
51–63. The break with Miriam, the long illness and subsequent
death of his mother, and the final collapse for him of his rela-
tionships with the two other important women in his life: Helen
and the Betrothed (his name in the poetry for his fiancé, Louie
Burrows), compose the central fourth stage, poems 64–99. The
fifth stage evokes what Lawrence calls "the haunting of death in
life," a state that continues through the serious illness of late
1911 that causes Lawrence to resign his teaching position (po-
ems 100–16). The sixth chronological stage, poems 117–29,
shows the world slowly coming back—but "another world," as
he puts it. He tranposes the seventh stage of *Look!* to volume 2
of *Collected Poems*, for reasons discussed above, leaving for the
final phase the war poems from *Bay*, numbers 130–43, because
according to the foreword they represent "the end of the cycle

of purely English experience, and death experience." Three ear-
lier poems actually conclude "Rhyming Poems," however:
"Dreams Old and Nascent: Nascent," originally published in
Amores but almost entirely rewritten for *Collected Poems;* and
"On That Day" and "Autumn Sunshine," the poems that close
New Poems. Although they violate the chronological structure
of *Collected Poems,* these poems provide the thematic and sym-
bolic conclusion to volume 1.

These chronological stages also cohere thematically, as
Lawrence's description of them in the foreword suggests. The
first stage presents the basic relationship of the individual or
"subjective" self to nature and to other people in the context of
nature. A peculiarly Lawrencean world emerges from these po-
ems, one familiar to the readers of the novels. The essential
feature of nature, including human nature, is its dualism. Spirit
and flesh, male and female, subject and object, day and night—
indeed, all light and dark—creation and destruction resist each
other in universal tension. Out of this tension springs the divine,
precipitated by rare moments of perfect relation, such as the one
described in "The Wild Common." In that instant, the self un-
derstands that "all that is God takes substance." For the most
part, however, the self remains alienated, sometimes longing for
union with another (as in "Dog-Tired," "Virgin Youth," or
"Last Hours") but at other times reflecting the tendency toward
isolation and separation inherent in all nature (as in "From a
College Window," "Discord in Childhood," and "Love on the
Farm"). Lawrence insinuated the fictional and dialect poems
here and throughout volume 1 as they reinforce his themaic
arrangement. For example, even though these are two of his
earliest compositions, Lawrence included "Love on the Farm"
and "The Collier's Wife" in the first stage of "Rhyming Poems"
for other than chronological reasons (indeed, he asserts in the
note that the fictional poems have "no necessary chronological
sequence"). He placed them where he did for two reasons: they
re-create the worlds of Miriam and of his mother, respectively,
for whom he said he wrote poems 1–19; and they emphasize
thematically the conflict implicit in duality.

The second stage focuses on the illusion of a different
world that change can bring. The reality beneath the illusion,
however, periodically stuns the inexperienced, sentimental self[6]

with its at times brutal indifference to human needs and emotions. This theme finds expression diversely—in the desire for the safety of memories and past dreams that "Dreams Old and Nascent: Old" ironically depicts; in the deep religious scepticism that emerges from "Weeknight Service"; in the bitter realizations of the female speaker of the fictional poem "A Man Who Died"; and in the uncertainty of the bride in "Wedding Morn." The shams that thwart the real needs of the self are exposed in such poems as "Violets," "Lightning," "Whether or Not," and "Last Lesson of the Afternoon." In this second stage, the two "Letters from Town" initiate a contrast that runs throughout most of Lawrence's writing: the north as a tainted, yet nostalgia-provoking Eden, a soporific paradise of static innocence, and the south as a hellish crucible where experience frits the soul. Old life, with its attachments, binds one to the north (as in "End of Another Home Holiday"); new life draws one to the south (as in "Morning Work" and "Transformations"). Illusion veils life in its immediate intensity, yet never completely; it reveals itself fitfully, as it will. Lawrence wrote in "Michael Angelo": "strange and fain / Life comes to thee, on which thou hast no claim; / Then leaves thee, and thou canst not but complain!" To reinforce his theme, he revised "Michael Angelo" and its companion poem, "Corot," replacing earlier reference in *Love Poems* to God and love with a single word, "life."

The poems to Helen and the school poems grouped with them take as their theme the failure of old life, including old attachments, to sustain the self—a theme introduced glancingly in the second stage of "Rhyming Poems." Each self stands isolate; attachment that does not recognize the harmony possible in separation destroys, as "Discipline" and "Coldness in Love" reveal. Whoever would cherish his isolation, however, resisting new ideas (as "Prophet" maintains most people do) or new experiences (as Helen does and the speaker of "Forecasts" predicts her lover will do), invites sterility.

In "Dolour of Autumn," Lawrence makes explicit the theme of the fourth phase of volume 1 of *Collected Poems:* "All my life, in a rush / Of shedding away, has left me / Naked." "Death" in this phase of "Rhyming Poems" becomes a metaphor for the casting off of old forms and connotes both destruction and renewal. The effluvium of the old self exudes corruption, as in "Dolour of Autumn" and "Malade." In "Come Spring, Come Sorrow," however, we see that the new self, which from a conventional point of view represents an "anti-self," constantly comes into being from the "fiery surplus of life," emanating essence. Stripped of old illusions, the self can penetrate the heretofore hidden side of things; this new perception is the son's "inheritance" from his dead mother, as the poem of that name suggests. Through the power of his new insight, he understands that sex, as one continuation of the death experience, offers a way to renewal. He sees now how he has failed Miriam, confessing in "Last Words to Miriam" that he has not had "fire" (i.e., physical passion) enough to offer her the sort of reduction he has experienced through his mother's death. When he looks to Helen and the Betrothed for the healing passion he needs, both disappoint his desire, each in her own way, by imposing mental and moral constraints on physical response. Such restraints, according to Lawrence, breed a kind of madness. "Song of Another Ophelia" lays bare the unwholesome obsession that results from repressed sexuality.

All, then, that remains for the self is the desire for physical death expressed in the fifth stage of the evolution of the self, particularly in two poems, "In Trouble and Shame" and "Call into Death." As the anti-self takes over, the usual world reverses itself; darkness becomes the source of all fire, all light, and all life, as in "Blueness." Two fictional poems, "A Passing Bell" and "The Drained Cup," suggest the passage beyond physical bounds, the former pathetically emphasizing the bewilderment of parents whose son has passed beyond their reach into the silence and darkness of death; the latter comically revealing the bewilderment of a young man completely emptied out by a week-long marathon of love-making with a woman whom he has jilted for another. A series of poems (i.e., "Parliament Hill in the Evening," and the two "Embankment at Night" poems, "Charity" and "Outcasts") describe the state of those who have passed beyond society's bounds, the derelict men and women who inhabit the bowels of London. In "Sickness," Lawrence describes his own confrontation with death during his serious illness of December 1911. Here, the self stands at the edge of life, beyond which lies the ultimate reduction of death. The last step must be taken, yet the self still believes that a woman can become the alternative to, and perhaps the substitute for, actual death as a way into the unknown—an idea explored in the new cycle of *Look! We Have Come Through!*

In the sixth stage of "Rhyming Poems," that in which Lawrence says the world slowly "came back" for him, but a world changed by both his vicarious and his personal experience of death, Lawrence develops thematically the precariousness of new life, which must be lived in the present moment, threatened by the pull of past and future dreams. Out of the corrosion of the past, he says, the new life of the future must emerge, nurtured in the "terra incognita"[7] of the present instant. He begins this segment of "Rhyming Poems" with "In Church," a poem whose central images evoke the changed perception that the intimate experience of death brings. Death, as the initiate eye of the anti-self can see, tinges all, even those things we consider exempt. "Piano" and "Twenty Years Ago" show the power of past reality to pull one from the present; "The North Country" and "Reading a Letter" reveal the ease with which the future can overcome the present moment. "Love Storm" emphasizes the terror of life lived in the "terra incognita," while "Passing Visit to Helen" and "Two Wives" stress that life lived in the flesh, which recognizes only the present moment, is paradoxically the one means of escaping solipsism. In "Seven Seals," Lawrence plays with the symbolism of The Book of Revelation, representing the moment of closing rather than unclosing. In this poem, the female speaker tries to prevent her lover from living the fleshly life, hoping with her love to shield him from others and possess him completely. She wishes to arm him against the death he seeks, just as the dark wife of "Two Wives" has tried to do for her lover. The only death worth fearing, says this poem, comes from the renunciation of the darkness of "touch"—that is, the physical reaching out through desire of one creature for another.

"Noise of Battle," "At the Front," "Reality of Peace, 1916," and "Narcissus" provide a transition to the war poems of *Bay*. The individual will to the destruction of the old self mirrors concavely the desire of England and of the whole of Western Europe for destruction, manifested in the World War of 1914–18. The first of these poems, "Noise of Battle," originally called "Apprehension," is interlined with "The Inheritance" in manuscripts 5 and 20.[8] This poem, much rewritten before its publication in *New Poems,* evolved from a contrast between time's menace to the town (and humanity in general) and its consolation to the emerging new self, who sees in the crash of day into darkness a sign of hope. In the version included in both *New Poems* and *Collected Poems,* emphasis rests on the uncomprehending anxiety of most mortals facing time and the inevitable annihilation it portends. "At the Front" voices the death-wish that Lawrence sees in himself and other Englishmen. "Realty of Peace, 1916" represents through the metaphors of decay the anguish of reduction of the old self (the old "fruit" of the poem) to the soul, or Holy Ghost (the "seed" and "blue grain of eternal fire"), out of which new life may spring, but not yet, for lonely suffering (the long winter) still lies ahead. "Narcissus," through the metaphor of myth, inserted only in late revisions of the poem for *New Poems,* expresses the desire for transformation, which leads out of the prison of the old self to otherness. The woman, "my soul's last school," whom the self addresses here, reminds us of the way to otherness explored in the next stage, i.e., the poems in *Look!* Lawrence titles the poem "Neckar" in manuscript 26, obviously wishing to evoke through the reference to a river in the Black Forest the days spent there in 1912 with Frieda Weekley. The poem goes back much further, however; as "Dim Recollections," it exists in manuscript 1 as a Wordsworthian paean of praise to nature as companion and teacher. In its final version, the poem focuses on the self who would look past his own "shadowy face" in "heaven's other direction," to the watery other, underworld. In various ways, all of these poems explore aspects of the individual and societal need and desire for transcendence, a theme that Lawrence shares with his artistic progenitors, the Romantic poets.

The final stage of "Rhyming Poems" consists of all except four of the poems published in *Bay,* reordered with one exception: "Nostalgia" ends both sequences. Lawrence includes in the volume a number of poems written specifically for it, as he tells Lady Cynthia Asquith, to whom he dedicated it, and as he says in the note to *Collected Poems.* He also implies that he has altered earlier poems to fit into the thematic context of *Bay.*[9] The war theme predominates without often becoming explicit in the poems themselves—the titles remind us of the connection more than the verse does. Lawrence's interest lies, rather, in exploring the position of one who has reached the chaos of immediate experience, a reduction that takes one past culture and mental constructs of all kinds to a state akin to the primitive ("Town in 1917" evokes this condition) and to the instinctual or archetypal (embodied in the experience depicted in "The Attack"). War becomes a metaphor for mortal man obliged to face the inevitable realities of change and death, which have him at bay. New life, whether in the species (as in "War-Baby") or in the individual (as in "Nostalgia," which asserts the necessity of forging into the new and unknown) provides the one victory of which humankind is capable.

Thematically, the final three poems of volume 1 of *Collected Poems* underscore the need for new life. "Dreams Old and Nascent: Nascent," extensively rewritten for *Collected Poems,* focuses on the collective need of modern man to break out of dreams of the past to a new awareness of life in the flesh— i.e., in the present moment—which will lead to new revelations of the self in always new "blossomings." "On That Day" looks ahead to the time when the new self, the subversive anti-self, will finally throw off the old and proclaim itself supreme. "Autumn Sunshine" represents a plea to all mortal men to take up the cup of life and burst the bonds of a dead world by realizing that the seed of a new cycle of renewal lies sleeping in the old.

The mythic structure of "Rhyming Poems" emerges most clearly at the end of that volume. For the first time in *Collected Poems,* Lawrence refers explicitly to Persephone, the hell-queen. She has, however, been implicitly present throughout most of the volume in the person of Lawrence's mother. The connection between the two surfaces in the last two poems of volume 1, "On That Day" and "Autumn Sunshine." In the former poem, Lawrence writes of his mother's grave, paradoxically insignificant, and promises to reveal her true status and power—that of queen—when he, the son, fully discovers his own. In its early versions, the poem focuses on the mother's birthday and remains an elegy for her. In the much revised version in *New Poems,* which is essentially the same as that in *Collected Poems,* the focus has shifted to the "insurgent day" of the son. His rebellion will bring his mother the recognition she deserves. The proximate poem, "Autumn Sunshine," explores the nature of the mother's kingdom and the son's insurgence. Through metaphor, the crocus flowers that have bloomed in the late autumn sunshine and have filled with dew become the cups of Persephone, who supplies the "invisible heroes," i.e., those of the unseen world, not yet manifest to others, with a drink that will bind them to overthrow what an earlier version of the poem in manuscript 26 calls "eternity: the has-been and will-be" in order to establish the "life between": that of the present moment.[10]

One of the earlier poems of "Rhyming Poems," "The Bride," also represents Lydia Lawrence as Persephone-like, carried off to the underworld by a terrible bridegroom. The ironic central image of the bride whose consummation is death invites analogy not only with Persephone but also with Eurydice, killed on her wedding day. This analogy strengthens when one discovers that Lawrence first ended the poem with these two lines: "And her dead mouth sings / O God, of the agony the bridegroom brings." Taken like Persephone in autumn (as "Reminder" makes clear), the mother leaves behind the husk of the year: a "sunken world." The only hope of renewal for the son who remains is the course adopted by Demeter (as well as by Orpheus, who lost his bride, and Dionysos, who lost his mother, Semele, to the underworld): descent into hell in pursuit of the beloved.

The perilous descent is adumbrated in the fourth and fifth stages of volume 1 of *Collected Poems.* The imagery of "Troth with the Dead" makes sense only if the son, who speaks the poem, considers himself one with the dead. His is a living death, a hell on earth, until the mythic call into the underworld, represented in "Call into Death," which Lawrence renamed for *Collected Poems* (in *Amores,* this poem, otherwise unchanged for *Collected Poems,* is called "Elegy"). "Grey Evening" and "Firelight and Nightfall" show the world fading away: the departure of the loved one has entailed the loss of all emblazonment. The son divorces himself from the pale, blighted world that remains and espouses "Darkness abundant, which shaken mysteriously / Breaks into dazzle of living," as Lawrence writes in "Blueness" (*Am:* "The Mystic Blue"). He presents the experience of hell in two poems: "Late at Night" (*NP:* "Phantasmagoria") and "Next Morning." Built on a device that Lawrence frequently employs, a

technique of metaphor by mistake,[11] "Late at Night" takes shape
in a basic confusion of realities which the reader as well as the
speaker of the poem must sort out. Is what the poet sees only the
"trees' / Large shadows from the outside street-lamp blown?"
Or is it a "throng of startled beings suddenly thrown / In confu-
sion against my entry?" Is it, in fact, the "Tall black Bacchae of
midnight"? The metaphor takes us through the veil of physical
reality to a realm equally real but beyond it. Yes, we are in the
speaker's bedroom; yes, we are also in the depths of hell. There,
presented in "Next Morning," the essential confrontation takes
place, that of the individual with himself. It is represented sym-
bolically by his coming unexpectedly upon his own reflection, or
rather, in the language of the poem, by his reflection "hungrily
stealing" upon him. The poem ends with the freighted question,
"Why am I in hell?" "Winter in the Boulevard" suggests an
answer: judgment.[12]

The subsequent poems, "Parliament Hill" and the two
"Embankment" poems, extend judgment beyond the personal:
London is judged an "unreal city," its inhabitants dead souls,
damned to "discord, misery, and revelry." The decisive moment
explored in "Sickness" represents the crisis not only of physical
illness but, symbolically, the crisis of the poet's underworld ex-
perience: what if one remains lost in the chaos of immediate
experience? What if return proves impossible? As Lawrence tells
us in the note, the end of the death experience—its integration
by the self into all aspects of life—forms the subject of the rest
of volume 1 and the first part of volume 2 of *Collected Poems*.

Many lesser motifs ramify the essential mythic structure
outlined above. The central figure of the virgin goddess assumes
several related forms throughout this narrative, which is subja-
cent to the historical, or chronological, one. Embodied by Lydia
Lawrence, she assumes the semblance not only of Persephone or
Eurydice but also of the Virgin Mary, as in "The Virgin
Mother."[13] Embodied by the other females in Lawrence's life,
she frequently appears as any of the three incarnations of the
moon: Selene, the remote moon goddess; Artemis, her earthly
manifestation as virgin huntress and queen of nature; and Hec-
ate, the moon in her dark phase, during which she rules the
underworld. The images that Lawrence uses to describe Miriam,
particularly those found in "Aware," "Pang of Remembrance,"

and "White Blossom," associate her with passionless Selene. The Betrothed, always described in nature images, such as those in "Snapdragon," emerges as a manifestation of Artemis. Helen suggests Hecate, with whom the dark imagery of "Red Moon-Rise" and "The Yew-Tree on the Downs" (*Am:* "Liason") unites her.

Elsewhere, the virgin goddess appears as Cybele, the "magna mater," mother of gods, who conceived by putting a ripe almond or pomegranate in her bosom, according to legend. Her son and lover, Attis, celebrates with her the rites of spring upon the vernal equinox; mourning and rejoicing alternately mark the festival, for Attis both dies and rises in the course of it. One of the rites commemorates his voluntary self-mutilation. This castration, symbolized by the violets of the spring, which grow from his sacred blood, prepares the way for his resurrection in the new vegetation.[14] A sequence of seven poems depicts this cyclic vegetation myth, using the symbols sacred to the Attic rite, which took place in the holy forests of Phrygia each March amidst wild celebration, accompanied by song, love-making, and the voluntary mutilation and even death of many of the followers of Attis. This sequence includes "A Man Who Died," "Letter from Town: On a Grey Morning in March," "Letter from Town: The Almond Tree," "Wedding Morn," "Violets," "Lightning," and "End of Another Home Holiday." The hero moves from death (represented in the first poem of the sequence); through preparation for the celebration at the equinox, the so-called Day of Blood (depicted in the two "Letters"); through the impregnation of the virgin goddess by the life energy in the severed genitals, usually ritualistically represented by the ripe pomegranate (a rite suggested by the poem "Wedding Morn"); followed by the symbolic burial of a likeness of the hero (the symbolic situation described in "Violets"); to the nocturnal resurrection of the hero admidst terror and sacrifice (presented in "Lightning"). The cycle ends with "End of Another Home Holiday," with the hero preparing to undergo the cyclic death once more.

Lawrence holds that art is a kind of subterfuge; one may protest that this sequence of poems is subterfuge, indeed. A study of the early manuscript versions of these poems reveals the extent to which Lawrence was conscious of their mythic content and, in fact, often chose to deemphasize it in their final versions. We see,

for example, that Lawrence retitled the first poem of the se-
quence five times. The earliest title, "Nils Lykke Dead,"[15] be-
came "A Woman and Her Dead Husband" for its publication in
Poetry in January 1914. In manuscript 26, Lawrence projects
two titles: "Choral Ode of One Woman" and "Voice of a
Woman," both obviously in line with his early plan to entitle
New Poems Chorus of Women. The title of the poem in *New
Poems,* "Bitterness in Death," Lawrence changes to "A Man
Who Died" for *Collected Poems,* the last title almost identical to
the euphemistic alternative for *The Escaped Cock,* his mythic tale
of death and resurrection, written around the same time that he
was working on *Collected Poems.* In an earlier version of the
poem in Manuscript 26, Lawrence refers to the dead man as the
"cosmic groom," a mythic reference reinforced in the last stanza
of this version by the woman speaker's words to the dead man:
"Sun of a universe / Have you gone cold?"

In a similar way, Lawrence changes another title in the
series to point the way to the poem's mythic meaning. The
poem entitled "Letter from Town: The City" in manuscript 1
becomes "Letter to the North" in manuscript 26 and "Letter
from Town: On a Grey Evening in March" in *New Poems.*
Lawrence changes only the time of day for "Rhyming Poems,"
in keeping with both the Day of Blood ritual and the vernal
equinox, which is determined by the sun's position. The title of
the second letter from town, "The Almond-Tree," remains more
or less unchanged throughout its several versions,[16] although
Lawrence revises the poem itself extensively. He apparently rec-
ognized and intended the mythic dimension of the poem from
its inception, for he develops an early version of the poem in
manuscript 1 around the Persephone myth, the first stanza of
which reads:

> You promised to send me violets—have you forgot?
> White ones and blue ones from under the orchard
>   hedge?
> You said you would be my Persephone
>   You would not
> Persephone has passed through the town, fasten-
>   ing her girdle-knot.

The poem then continues much as it does in *Collected Poems.* Even in manuscript 1, Lawrence includes a second version of the first stanza that eliminates any specific mythological reference. Curtailing the overt use of myth in favor of the evocative symbol appears to be Lawrence's early tendency, perhaps because of his apparent difficulty in subordinating the myth to the larger purpose of the poem. An early poem, also in manuscript 1, called "The Songless: 1. Tonight" (which later becomes "Hyde Park at Night: Clerks") illustrates this danger; the mythic analogy breaks the poem in two instead of unifying it, as the mythic references in *Last Poems* unify many of the poems collected there (see app. C).

In the manuscript 1 version of "Lightning," Lawrence refers to the face of the woman as "pale as a dead god," a description that parallels the religious imagery of the final version of the poem in "Rhyming Poems." The religious language and imagery of the poem generate the tensions between death and life, impotence and power, and sacrifice and consecration that are approriate to the Attic rite of death and resurrection. As this and the following poem, "End of Another Home Holiday," illustrate, the only consummation possible for Attis and Cybele is a symbolic one. Cybele's love asks but cannot give; thus, she is known as the cruel goddess. She absorbs the power of the male and generates life on her own terms, separate and complete in herself. The male longs for escape from the endless natural cycle that, as the speaker of "End of Another Home Holiday" protests, "unweariedly, unweariedly" persists in "Asking something more of me, / Yet more of me." Yet the cycle that appears at times a prison to the dying self promises renewal to the emerging self. Volume 1 of *Collected Poems,* which begins in the spring with a poem of awakening, ends in autumn, underground, in the kingdom of Persephone, land of the "invisible heroes," who will rise once more.

Lawrence uses the myth of Attis and Cybele, as he uses the entire mythic structure of "Rhyming Poems," to underscore and enlarge his personal myth of individual growth and change. It also reveals symbolically the mystery central to the old self: his relationship with his mother and her surrogate, Miriam. This relationship, very much like that of Attis and Cybele, both annihilated and fulfilled him. While it castrated him sexually, it made him productive as an artist.

Judging from the early manuscript collections of Lawrence's poems, one can say with certainty that myth attracted him from the start of his career as a way of lending resonance to his verse. The skillful integration of myth in his poetry came slowly; he eliminated most of the specific mythological references from the early poetry, keeping, however, the mythic symbols and imagery intact. The connection between his experiences and those limned in myth remained in the early verse to be revealed, often by means of revised titles and the juxtaposition of thematically related poems, when Lawrence collected his poetry in 1928.[17] At approximately the same time that he was revising and arranging *Collected Poems,* Lawrence was working on the poems published posthumously in *Last Poems,* where myth becomes explicit.

4. The Scope of the Revisions for "Rhyming Poems"

In the note to *Collected Poems,* Lawrence says that he rewrote many of the early poems "to let the demon say his say." Referring to the poems to Miriam, the foreword is more explicit: "It is not for technique these poems are altered: it is to say the real say." Thus, Lawrence disclaims any attempt on his part to overhaul the formal elements of most of the early verse (he does, however, say that he will revise the form of the poems he classifies as fictional when necessary). He implies that he limited the extent of the revisions made in the early verse, allowing imperfections to remain unless they interfere with his plan for *Collected Poems.* In no way, then, did Lawrence refashion all his early verse, exerting his mature skill on the creation of his youth (although by the time of his revisions for *Collected Poems,* he had in fact already revised most of the early poetry). Rather, Lawrence would have us understand, a desire to clarify the essential meaning of *Collected Poems* as the biography of the true self prompted most revisions. Of course, any change in content will inevitably produce technical changes, and indeed Lawrence made many minor technical alterations in the poetry without hesitation—any number of revised poems differ from their earlier published versions in only a single word or punctuation mark—yet in the forword Lawrence repeatedly emphasizes that the primary thrust of the revisions is conceptual.

When Lawrence refers to the "real say," he presumes a theoretical base for the ideas expressed in certain of the poems. As I have previously indicated, any assessment of the ideological revisions of volume 1 and, furthermore, any determination of how they relate to Lawrence's design for *Collected Poems* as a whole, depend upon our knowledge of what Lawrence signifies by the demon and how the concept functions in the poet's view of physical and human nature. Lawrence articulates this view in

several books of essays: *Reflections on the Death of a Porcu-
pine* (collected in 1925), which contains the cosmology that
Lawrence developed over a decade or more, and *Psychoanalysis
and the Unconscious* and *Fantasia of the Unconscious* (pub-
lished in 1921 and 1922, respectively),[1] which set forth princi-
ples of human psychology from a Lawrencean point of view.
These volumes provide a system that allowed Lawrence to re-
formulate the ideas implicit but not yet fully developed in many
of the early poems so that they would be consonant not only
with his mature thought but also, just as importantly, with his
thematic and mythic plan for *Collected Poems*.

A study of the extant versions of the twenty-five or so
poems that Lawrence had extensively rewritten for "Rhyming
Poems" generally supports Lawrence's implication that he re-
wrote for *Collected Poems* those poems that express philosopi-
cal or psychological ideas, especially those that neither concisely
nor consistently reflect his later, well-formulated ideas on
"blood knowledge"[2] and the demon, or "demi-urge," who
creates both man and nature.[3] As he describes in the foreword,
Lawrence revised most extensively those poems he classifies as
"subjective" (i.e., those introspective poems that contemplate
the connection between the conscious individual and unconsci-
ous nature), and the socalled fictional or imaginative poems
(which often explore the same connection objectively). He also
revised poems of the sort I shall call dedicatory, because he
wrote them to or for a particular person, whom he often di-
rectly addresses in the poem (e.g., the "Miriam poems," to
which he refers in the foreword as one type of poem he had
revised for *Collected Poems* and which comprises the sort of
poem that frequently explores the unconscious motivations of
both the speaker and the spoken to in the poem and thus relates
to Lawrence's later psychological formulations). In contrast to
these, the poems that Lawrence left unchanged, by and large,
are those descriptive ones that characterize a person or re-create
a scene or an emotional situation without attempting to make
an ideological statement about it. Lawrence's poems about the
death of his mother, for example, are essentially vivid descrip-
tions of the dead woman herself or of a particular phenomenon
that triggers the poet's grief over her death. As a general rule,
such poems undergo very few changes for *Collected Poems*.

What Lawrence does not tell us that becomes apparent as we study his revisions for "Rhyming Poems" is that, with very few exceptions, he emended only the poems first published in *Love Poems* and *Amores,* leaving those from *New Poems* and *Bay* much as they were in the earlier volumes. The poems from *Love Poems* and *Amores* he consistently and often painstakingly reworked, at times adding long sections (as he did for "The Wild Common"), at others deleting sections just as long (as from "The Best of School"), and occasionally rewriting poems almost entirely (as in the cases of 'Virgin Youth," "The Drained Cup," and "Dreams Old and Nascent: Nascent"). Why did Lawrence focus his revisions almost exclusively on poems from these two volumes? Any consideration of Lawrence's revisions for "Rhyming Poems" must begin with this question.

During his stay in England during World War I, Lawrence began systematically articulating what he called his doctrine.[4] In particular, the period that he spent in Cornwall from December 1915 through the fall of 1917 was a significant one in his intellectual growth; he experienced an intense preoccupation with philosophic issues, judging from his letters of the time. For example, he wrote his friend Mark Gertler on 1 April 1917: "We are busy gardening, and I am writing short essays on philosophy. The pure abstract thought interests me now at this juncture more than art. I am tired of emotions and squirmings and sensations. Let us have a little pure thought, a little perfect and detached understanding. That is how I feel now."[5]

In this period, Lawrence worked on many of the essays published only later in final form. He produced those that comprise *Studies in Classic American Literature,* including the essay on Whitman; "The Reality of Peace"; "Love"; "Life"; "Democracy";[6] and a lost philosophical work entitled *Goats and Compasses.*[7] Out of this prevailing interest in theoretical subjects grew the later essays on nature and psychology, some of which are revisions of drafts and of published articles written during the Cornwall years and the time just preceding it.[8]

In spite of what Lawrence says in the note to *Collected Poems,* he in large part prepared the the manuscripts of both *New Poems* and *Bay,* as well as *Look! We Have Come Through!,* during his residence in Cornwall.[9] Few of the poems from these three volumes undergo revision for *Collected Poems.*

True, many of the poems from *New Poems* and *Bay* are descriptive, carefully observing a scene (e.g., "From a College Window," "Suburbs on a Hazy Day," or "Little Town at Evening") or an emotional situation (e.g., "Piano" or "Going Back"). As previously noted, Lawrence did not spend much time revising this sort of poem for *Collected Poems*. Yet even the poems that do depend on Lawrence's philosophical or psychological ideas show little revision between *New Poems* or *Bay* and *Collected Poems*. For example, "The Attack" and "Shades" (Lawrence substituted this title, with its mythic connotations, for the Christian title "Pentecostal" in *Bay*), both of which develop Lawrence's idea of the Holy Ghost, evidence only minor changes for "Rhyming Poems." Nor did Lawrence revise for this volume many of the early poems from manuscripts 1 and 5 that appear in *New Poems* and *Bay,* although these account for fully three-quarters of the poems in the former book and almost one-half of those in the latter. Indeed, the only major revision for *Collected Poems* of a poem from either book is of "Two Wives," which is one of Lawrence' fictional poems. As he did with most others of this type, which he said he would revise for form, if necessary, Lawrence revised, first of all, to clarify the ideas that shape it and, secondly, to increase its dramatic effect.

Even though few have been revised for "Rhyming Poems," most of the poems from *New Poems* and *Bay* exist in several manuscript versions and, quite obviously, have been thoroughly revised by the time of their publication in these books. These extant versions, in particular those in manuscript 26, witness that Lawrence carefully reworked almost every one of the early poems for these collections.[10] Consequently, any complete study of Lawrence's poetic development, a study unfortunately outside the scope of this one, must take into account these revisions. Like those for *Collected Poems*, they reveal a mature poet at work. He remained content with these changes at the time of *Collected Poems,* most likely because, in addition to the nature of the poems themselves and his careful rewriting before their initial publication, Lawrence prepared them at a time when his doctrine was crystallizing. His thinking at the end of the Cornwall stay and in the intervening period before he left England for Italy, while still developing to some extent, was far more fixed and definite, and thus more like his thinking at the time of

Collected Poems than it was for the proximate *Amores* volume, prepared early in 1916.[11]

More than three-fourths of the fifty-eight poems printed in both *Amores* and volume 1 of *Collected Poems* betray some sort of revision for *Collected Poems* other than punctuation or title change. Lawrence's most drastic revisions are of poems from *Amores*—poems such as "The Wild Common," "Virgin Youth," and "Dreams Old and Nascent: Nascent"—which he almost entirely rewrote for "Rhyming Poems." Such extensive revision cannot be attributed only to the large number of poems from manuscripts 1 and 5. We must look for other reasons to explain Lawrence's apparent dissatisfaction with the poems from *Amores*.

The most plausible explanation for the many revisions of the *Amores* poems for inclusion in *Collected Poems* lies in the haste with which he had originally prepared them for publication. He can have spent little more than three or four weeks revising and arranging the poems for *Amores*, as opposed to the year or more he spent on *New Poems* and *Bay*.[12] This haste betrays itself in the similarity of many *Amores* poems to their early manuscript versions ("Virgin Youth" provides a good example of such similarity), which give credence to the contention that Lawrence revised comparatively little for *Amores*, especially considering the ten years that elapsed between the composition of the earliest poems, such as "The Wild Common," and their publication in *Amores*. Haste also shows in Lawrence's tendency to revert to early manuscript drafts of poems when he felt discontented with later manuscript or published versions of them (one has only to compare the *Amores* version of "Dreams Old and Nascent: Old" with its earlier drafts to be convinced of this tendency).

A further explanation of Lawrence's frequent revisions as he incorporated *Amores* into "Rhyming Poems" lies in the very nature of *Amores*. This is the early "inner history" of Lawrence's young manhood,'[13] and the quasi-philosophical/psychological content of many of the poems exacerbates Lawrence's need to rewrite them in the light of his later ideas. Individually and collectively, the poems tend to center on manifestations of the divine in human life. In depicting such encounters in the *Amores* poems, Lawrence relied on traditional Christian ways of talking about God or on emotion-charged hyperbole. In hindsight, Lawrence realized that the true subject of much of this verse was what he had come to call the ghost or the demon, who manifested himself to the unfolding self through the duality in nature, love, and death. As we have seen, Lawrence began developing this concept only around the time of the *Amores* volume and, consequently, before its publication rewrote little in these poems in the light of his incipient theories. These poems, also, as Lawrence later realized, frequently portray the psychological tension between conscious and unconscious will, which he was at that time beginning to consider in a systematic way in *Studies in Classic American Literature,* although he used the concept artistically in the novels of this period (particularly *Women in Love,* completed in Cornwall in 1916)[14] as well as in the verse.

Lawrence assembled the *Amores* collection at the very start of the Cornwall period, before any concentrated attempt to formulate his philosophic thought. By the time of *Collected Poems,* views that he had just begun to explore while he was collecting *Amores* were articulated, inviting him to clarify what seems to have been only half-said earlier. No wonder, then, considering this and the other factors bearing on Lawrence's dissatisfaction with the *Amores* poems, that he rewrote many of them for "Rhyming Poems."

All of the thirty poems that appear in both *Love Poems* (Lawrence's first published collection of verse, issued fifteen years before *Collected Poems*) and *Amores* were revised to some degree, and all except four or five of them manifest extensive revision. When manuscript versions of these poems in *Love Poems* exist, comparison of them with the printed text indicates they were little revised before publication. Although this reason alone need not have compelled Lawrence to revise *Love Poems* as thoroughly as he did for "Rhyming Poems"—for example, he scarcely touches "Bei Hennef," which first appeared in *Love Poems* and which he includes in volume 2 of *Collected Poems*—the sorts of poems contained in the volume tempted Lawrence to recast them. Here, in goodly numbers, are fictional poems, including many dialect poems; subjective poems; and what Lawrence called the "Miriam poems": in short, the three categories of poetry that Lawrence admits in the foreword to having revised extensively. These poems, as he says specifically of the last group, required alteration because "sometimes the hand of the commonplace youth had been laid on the mouth of the demon."

Thus, any discussion of Lawrence's revisions for "Rhyming Poems" must center on the poems from *Love Poems* and *Amores*. His extensive revision of these poems was owing not only to their being examples of his earliest published verse but, more important, because of the kinds of poems they are—poems that can be broadly classed as subjective, fictional, or dedicatory. Most often he revised them for one or more of the following reasons:

> 1. they form the keystones of his design for *Collected Poems;*
>
> 2. they are conceptually or imaginatively incomplete in the light of his later ideas on nature and man;
>
> 3. they contain formal or rhetorical elements that are inappropriate to the content of the poem.

As a general rule, Lawrence seemed satisfied to allow the form of a poem to stand unless it somehow hindered the expression of the principal idea or the force of its dramatic impact. When he altered form, as he did most noticeably in "Dreams Old and Nascent: Nascent," "Virgin Youth," and "Baby Running Barefoot," it is frequently in the direction of most of the early verse, toward rhyme, rather than in the direction of the later free verse. In all likelihood, Lawrence made this change so that these poems would correspond with the form of most (though not all, by any means) of the other poems in "Rhyming Poems," thereby further suggesting the presence of the old self, more easily recognizable in conventional terms.

In the following examination of key revisions for *Collected Poems,* I have taken into account all the available extant versions of a poem in order to assess what they reveal about Lawrence's method of poetic creation and his development as a poet. As mentioned earlier, he often incorporated in the final version of a poem elements of its earlier manuscript drafts. Thus, what appears to be a new element in a poem when we study only its published versions may prove to be primary in its unpublished forms.

5. Revision of the Subjective Poems for "Rhyming Poems"

Although many of Lawrence's poems present a subjective view of reality, what he has named the subjective poems focus on a first-person speaker whose "body of mere man" belongs to the historical Lawrence. Such poems generally start with a description of the external scene and move inward to explore the speaker's reflections on it and the associations it prompts. The conclusion of the poem communicates the speaker's consequent discovery, revealing his insight into himself, man, or nature. These poems, as do many of the dedicatory poems, resemble what M. H. Abrams has called the greater romantic lyric, a descriptive-reflective-exploratory poem practiced by English romantic and Victorian poets (Wordsworth's "Tintern Abbey" or Coleridge's "Frost at Midnight" are good examples of this type of lyric).[1] This mode becomes dominant in *Look! We Have Come Through!* and also characterizes *Birds, Beasts and Flowers,* exhibiting, as one would expect, Lawrencean peculiarities.

This category of Lawrence's poetry includes not only reflections touched off by a natural setting, as do "The Wild Common," "Virgin Youth," and "End of Another Home Holiday," but also those that occur in the classroom. Both "Dreams Old and Nascent" poems are of this sort, as are most of the other poems based on Lawrence's teaching experience. Among these, "Best of School," "Last Lesson of the Afternoon," "A Snowy Day in School," and "Discipline" are the most extensively rewritten. As one can see from the following analyses of key subjective poems, their coherence depends heavily on Lawrence's doctrine; consequently, he judged them incomplete until he had revised them in the light of his mature ideology.

"The Wild Common," the first poem in the collection, provides an excellent example of Lawrence's approach to the revision of his early verse, and specifically of the subjective poems, for *Collected Poems.* He called attention to its revision in both the note and the foreword to *Collected Poems,* pointing out what anyone familiar with the poem as published in *Amores* can see immediately: it has been "a good deal rewritten." As with the other subjective poems, he rewrote it in order to clarify its essential message, not fully expressed in its earlier form. A close study of the changes Lawrence made in this poem in its three extant versions reveals much about his developing idea of the demon and its relation to the true self, which culminates in the design for *Collected Poems* (see app. D). It also shows clearly Lawrence's maturing poetic style. Here, through a single subject, addressed first by a nineteen-year-old Lawrence, next by Lawrence at thirty, and finally by Lawrence at forty-two, the poet's artistic development visibly reveals itself.

When in the foreword Lawrence speaks of "The Wild Common" as a very early poem, he refers not to the longer, rewritten version of the poem published in 1916 in *Amores,* but to a much earlier version preserved, at least in part, in the University College notebook in which he began copying his verse around 1906 (i.e., manuscript 1). The poem begins at the equivalent of line 13 of both the *Amores* and the *Collected Poems* versions. Beginning as the poem does at the top of a page on the right hand side of the notebook, without a title, it seems likely that the page containing the first part of the poem has been lost. As it presently exists, the poem contains six four-line stanzas (see app. D.1.) The form established in the first draft of the poem remains much the same through all its versions, substantiating Lawrence's claim that his revisions were not aimed at the technical aspects of the poems. In all three versions, the basic rhyme scheme is *abab;* the rhythm is irregular, although short and long lines consistently alternate, the former usually consisting of three or four and the latter of anywhere from five to seven strong stresses.

In manuscript 1, the poem begins with a sentence fragment, which would support the hypothesis that its first part is lost; however, the punctuation in *Amores* also leaves the thirteenth and fourteenth lines of the poem a fragment, unlike the *Collected Poems* version, which links the third and fourth stanzas syntactically. The poem as it stands opens with the speaker at the old sheep-dip. The three stanzas that in *Amores* and *Col-lected Poems* describe the wild common are missing from manu-script 1. We have, of course, no way of knowing whether an equivalent of these stanzas existed at the time Lawrence rewrote the poem for *Amores* or, if they did, how much he changed them for this volume.

With the exception of its second stanza, which Lawrence cut altogether from later versions of the poem, what remains of the manuscript 1 version bears marked similarity to the last five stanzas of the *Amores* poem (see App. D.2), reflecting the tendency of the *Amores* poems to resemble closely their early drafts. Both stress the interdependence of body and spirit, in spite of the soul's misunderstanding of its actual relation to the flesh. Through a protracted metaphor, by which shadow and soul are identified with each other and with a "passionate woman," Lawrence develops the notion of the interdependence of matter and form in the poem, using an Aristotelian view of being as the basis of his comparison. A series of images suggest the universal lovemaking, or potential union, of all things immaterial with all things physical. Even as the flowers and songs of the wild common depend on "pulsing waters," so the poet's blood supports both body and soul. When the soul rec-ognizes this truth, turning back "to the man she scorned," the "warm, clinging air" confirms the universality of the need of spirit for matter by kissing the speaker's body. Wind confers with blood. In a final conceit, Lawrence extends the metaphor of the woman to the water, which becomes her blood, claim-ing the body of the young man in a union at once physical and spiritual.

Incipient here is the idea of "blood knowledge" or "blood consciousness," which Lawrence first articulated in a letter to Ernest Collings dated 17 January 1913, and takes up in a letter to Bertrand Russell dated 8 December 1915.[2] The concept is systematically developed in *Psychoanalysis* and *Fantasia*. In the manuscript 1 and *Amores* poems, as in the letter to Russell, Lawrence connected this sort of knowledge with sexuality; con-sequently, he developed his idea through a metaphor that equates the soul with a woman (he only a later defined the soul as the unconscious;[3] in this poem, the soul as woman suggests the quality of otherness without any psychological associations).

By the time of *Fantasia,* however, Lawrence denied the sexual motive as primary, replacing it with the "religious or creative motive."[4] Knowledge, Lawrence maintained consistently, is more than mental. Only later did he see it as more than sexual.

Although he may have expanded the length of "The Wild Common" (assuming that what we have of the manuscript 1 version of the poem is all that he wrote), Lawrence condensed its language for *Amores,* eliminating the repetitive second stanza and rewording the diffuse third stanza of the manuscript 1 version. His revisions for *Amores,* however, were chiefly technical, just the sort he eschewed in *Collected Poems.* They do not affect in any way the central metaphor upon which he constructed the poem nor the underlying concept of being and knowledge it conveys.

When he revised "The Wild Common" for *Collected Poems,* Lawrence concentrated on precisely those elements of the poem that he ignored in the *Amores* revision (see app. D.3). Lawrence not only expanded the poem from eight four-line stanzas in the *Amores* version to ten in *Collected Poems* but also, after the fourth stanza, created a poem very different from its predecessors, particularly in the metaphors with which he chose to develop its thematic content and in the implicit metaphysical view on which they are based.

As is the case with much of Lawrence's rewritten verse, the beginning of this poem remains substantially unrevised in *Collected Poems.* Having the chance to make technical changes, he could not resist the opportunity; however some of these changes support the conceptual changes in the new conclusion of the poem. For example, he altered the last line of the first stanza both for the meter and for the sense of the line, regularizing the anapestic pentameter in this long last line in order to stabilize the highly erratic meter of the first two lines (imitative of the short, unpredictable glints of sunlight that are his subject) and to confirm the hesitating movement of the third line toward anapestic regularity. Here, the longer, more regular beat creates in the reader a sense of the image depicted, in this case the flight of the peewits. The new poetic figure, which has the birds (or possibly the "quick sparks," or even the "gorse-bushes" themselves, so ambiguous is the context) triumphing again over the ages, remains as vague as, or even vaguer than, the old personification of the birds as "lords of the desolate wastes of sadness."

Yet Lawrence's changes here, minimal though they were, did allow him to develop images in the concluding stanza of the poem that support his revised idea for it. Knowing something of Lawrence's later tenet that "ideal and material are identical,"[5] one understands that the figure of speech suggests the identity of the concrete and the abstract, a concept supported later in the poem by the peewits' cry, "I am here! I am here!" in stanza 7 and refined to suggest the in-dwelling of everything abstract in the concrete as finally, in the last stanza of the poem, he describes the "ages" as immanent in the peewits: "Wings and feathers on the crying, mysterious ages, peewits wheeling!" The idea of immanence controls the thematic and metaphoric content of this version of the poem, leading us ultimately to Lawrence's final affirmation in stanza 10, which can well serve as the theme of Collected Poems, "All that is right, all that is good, all that is God takes substance!" Often in Lawrence's revisions, technical changes functioned in this way, ultimately serving meaning.

The changes that Lawrence made in the next three stanzas of "The Wild Common" are mainly limited to diction and punctuation; they typify his approach to technical revision of the poems, including the fictional poems, whose form he admitted revising in "Rhyming Poems." He had no aversion to attending to detail in the construction of his verse. He consistently searched for the more precise word or phrase, the more coherent image, or the more appropriate rhyme or meter as he wrote and rewrote his poetry. Thus, as Lawrence searched for greater precision, "grass" in line 2 of stanza 2 became "turf" (whose sound, incidentally, combines more interestingly with the sound of "mournful," which precedes it); and in the last line of this stanza, "Move my arms" became "Lift my arms." To break the static symmetry of the third line of this stanza in the Amores version ("Are they [the rabbits] asleep?—are they alive?"), Lawrence substituted "living" for "alive," introducing a far subtler metrical play in the line. Meter also dictated the replacement of "There the lazy streamlet pushes / Its curious course mildly" with "His bent course mildly" in Collected Poems. The two strong stresses of "bent course" slow the verse, better supporting the logic of the sentence. The exclamation point at the end of the stanza brings additional energy to the imperative voice of the sentence; just as the change in punctuation at the end of the third stanza, where Lawrence eliminated the period in the *Amores* poem, allows greater syntactic clarity by combining third and fourth stanzas into a complete sentence. These revisions, nevertheless, are relatively minor; quite clearly, Lawrence was willing to make do with what he found in the early poetry, refining diction and punctuation here, improving meter there, until he encountered a conceptual difficulty in the poem. Then he quite often wrote a new poem.

The fifth stanza of the *Collected Poems* version of "The Wild Common" begins as it does in *Amores,* but the poems soon diverge and, indeed, never really parallel each other again. The revised imagery and syntax of this stanza manifest the speaker's exploration of conscious and unconscious nature that the earlier versions of the stanza belabor without truly developing. Three questions now point the way to the thematic matters to be considered in the poem (and, more broadly, in *Collected Poems* as a whole): What is the consequence of individual death? How does the source of life relate to its particular manifestations? How does spirit relate to flesh and conscious to unconscious realities? The last question introduces the way to a poetic resolution of these concerns: the image of the white shadow of the poet, cast on the surface of the pond, and its metaphoric connection to a leashed dog. Lawrence developed this metaphor far more coherently yet far more suggestively than that of the passionate woman in the manuscript 1 and *Amores* poems. In place of the elaborate conceit in which soul, shadow, woman, water, and blood murkily merge, the images of shadow and dog work together cogently to connote a rich variety of relationships, not only those of body and soul and, perhaps, conscious and unconscious minds, which one finds in the first two versions of the poem. Lawrence hit on two images that mythically depict the soul: the animal and the shadow, with its companion image, the reflection of the individual in water. Moreover, as Frazer, in *The Golden Bough*, points out, the dog, specifically a white dog, frequently represents the spirit of the god of vegetation, with whose various manifestations Lawrence identified throughout the entire *Collected Poems*.[6]

Through this complex image, we have a sense of the many manifestations of the self. Lawrence's revised imagery also suggests the Jungian concept of the shadow, or anti-self, of which Lawrence was surely aware, referring often to Jung in *Fantasia*. It connotes as well the two types of knowledge, mental and blood, that Lawrence tried to distinguish in the early versions of the poem. As he saw later, the concept goes beyond sexuality. Knowledge, according to Lawrence in *Psychoanalysis*, "is always a matter of whole experience, what Saint Paul calls knowing in full, and never a matter of mental conception merely."[7] Using the same metaphor that he used in "The Wild Common" to explain his idea, Lawrence continues, "This is indeed the point of all full knowledge: that it is contained mainly within the unconscious, its mental or conscious reference being only a sort of extract or shadow." By the "unconscious," Lawrence signifies "that essential unique nature of every individual creature"—that which cannot be conceived mentally, only experienced. In traditional terminology, this is the soul. As we have seen, Lawrence's usual term for soul, both in man and nature, is ghost and, later, demon.

Through the presentation of the soul (equated in this version of the poem with the total person) as master and the mind as dog, and through the subsequent images of the sun as "yellow water-blobs" and the ages as winged and feathered, Lawrence conveyed quite specifically his metaphysics. He not only did not deny a spiritual principle in nature, he affirmed the omnipresence of the divine in the world. It manifests itself, however, only in substance. According to Lawrence, the ideal in any form exists only as a projection, or shadow, of the real. At the point at which the young man immerses himself in the water, uniting with his shadow, the mind fully knows itself. "No longer shadow!" murmurs the water, consecrating the youth in a celebratory baptism into life.

Lawrence created for us a momentary vision of the world in "equilibrium"—the world manifesting the demon in an instance of pure relation. How to sustain the insight of that moment and enter into pure relationship with a living universe becomes the quest of the self in *Collected Poems*. His is a religious quest, a search for God in his many manifestations in a changing world. The mature Lawrence realized what the younger Lawrence of nineteen or even thirty did not: that "The Wild Common" represents the poet's first conscious, even though fleeting, recognition of his "daimon," both in the order of experience and in the order of creative composition. The poem itself, in its revised form, communicates what Lawrence maintained is the "real say" about man, nature, and God.

Another poem that demands consideration as one studies Lawrence's design for *Collected Poems* is "Dreams Old and Nascent: Nascent," which like "The Wild Common," is a subjective poem. Lawrence violated the chronological structure of "Rhyming Poems" in order to place it near the end of that volume. In separating it from its companion poem, "Dreams Old and Nascent: Old,"[8] which he places early in "Rhyming Poems," Lawrence establishes the poles of experience depicted in the biography of the old self. "Dreams: Old" describes the context of the old self; "Dreams: Nascent" envisions that of the new self. Particularly interesting in a study of Lawrence's poetic development is the evolution of both of these poems from a single poem in manuscript 1 entitled "A Still Afternoon in School," through many intermediate versions, to the separate poems of *Amores* and the widley separated poems of volume 1 of *Collected Poems*.

Lawrence was consistently dissatisfied with "Dreams: Old" and "Dreams: Nascent," if one judges by the continuing revision to which he submitted them. His comments about the latter poem in the foreword confirm such a judgment: he declares that he was "always uneasy" about it. Even though manuscript 1 contains for the most part fair copies of the poems—Lawrence seems to have intended it as a receptacle for more or less finished poems, not as a workbook, as such—it contains two drafts of "A Still Afternoon in School," the second of which has more emendations than most others in the book. Moreover, one draft follows the other immediately, showing that Lawrence quickly and thoroughly rewrote the poem; this draft also betrays continuing revision (see app. E.1). He interlined whole stanzas with alternative renderings, most likely because he had not yet decided which to use. He rejected other stanzas by scoring them out and added still others by squeezing them into margins. This discontent continued through two more drafts of

the poem, now divided into two parts (see app. E.2). Lawrence
wrote these, no doubt, before Jessie Chambers sent off a copy of
the poem, along with several others, to *The English Review* in
June 1909.[9] Following its publication, Lawrence revised the
poem again (see app. E.3). By the time of its publication in
Amores, as two distinct poems that he arranged to be read con-
secutively, Lawrence has once again revised both (see app. E.4).

The final revision for *Collected Poems* of "Dreams: Old"
and "Dreams: Nascent" produced still more thoroughgoing
changes in both poems. For this volume, Lawrence almost en-
tirely recast "Dreams: Nascent," arranging it third from the last
poem in volume 1. "Dreams: Old," far less changed, remains
early in the volume, among the poems about Lawrence's experi-
ence of teaching and of London.

What do the final versions of these poems reveal about
Lawrence's plan for *Collected Poems?* "Dreams: Nascent" is a
visionary poem, describing a self and a society just coming into
being. "Dreams: Old" presents an anterior view of time and
experience. Looking back to earlier times experienced anew
through imagination and memory, the soul metaphorically ex-
plores its personal and cultural past, delighting in the conscious
mind. Luxuriating in their daydreams, both the speaker and his
students experience the languid, seductive charm of a region
that exists only in the mind. Indeed, as the third stanza of the
poem makes plain, these daydreams alter one's perception of
external reality, reducing it to a dreamlike projection of one's
experience. For the time of the dream, which like a shunting
engine diverts life from the present moment, the speaker can
escape from the storm of living, which "Dreams: Nascent" ex-
plores. "Dreams: Old" sympathetically portrays the thrust of
the old self, which romanticizes and sentimentalizes real life by
converting it into purely mental experience. In sharp contrast to
this view of reality, "Dreams: Nascent" shows the charming
dreams of the old self multiplied through an entire society and
reveals them as they appear to the self reborn: they conceal,
confine, and smother new life.

In "Dreams: Nascent," the new self, or demon, speaking
more clearly through the poet, expresses his condemnation of
the deathly world of the old self and prophesies the coming of a
new order. Taken together, as their similar titles invite the

reader to do in spite of their separation in *Collected Poems,* "Dreams: Old" and "Dreams: Nascent" stand as contrasting descriptions of the self. They represent opposite approaches to experience, the first describing the allure—and failure—of life lived vicariously or in the past, through the mind; the second suggesting the liberation of life lived in the flux of the present moment, through the teeming blood. By placing the two poems as he does in *Collected Poems,* one at the beginning and the other near the end of volume 1, Lawrence erects the poles of experience that he represents in this volume. The nascent dream, which produces the new self, comes out of the death experience represented in "Rhyming Poems" and points the way to the new life of "Unrhyming Poems." By expanding the image of the railway workers until it becomes the unifying force in the poem, Lawrence finds a concrete way to represent the concept underlying the poem. The workmen symbolize the "demi-urge," a word that in Greek literally means "workman" and refers to the universal creative force. This force, acting through man, will renew human life, says the poem.

The many early versions of "Dreams: Old" and "Dreams: Nascent" show how persistently Lawrence tried to express this idea but was unable to do so completely, because of the lack of any developed idea of God or His relationship to the world. Even in the earliest drafts of these poems in manuscript 1, their energy comes from the tensions that remain in their final versions: the tension between old and new dreams, between the conscious and the unconscious mind, and between passivity and activity. In the *Collected Poems* version of "Dreams: Old," these tensions depend on the overall structure of volume 1, which contrasts the old with the emerging new self, and on the already mentioned implied contrast with "Dreams: Nascent," signaled by the similar titles, even though the poems are widely separated in this volume. Nevertheless, even though these broad contrasts exist in "A Still Afternoon in School" (in the first manuscript 1 draft), they are not yet sharply defined. Old and new dreams mingle in the verse, hardly by design but because of Lawrence's lack of any systematic approach to the proper relation of conscious and unconscious minds and of old and new experience. In 1908 or 1909, when this draft was probably conceived, Lawrence had not yet worked out his theory of mental versus blood consciousness, nor had he expressed his attitude to the past, which he first did to Catherine Carswell in a letter dated 16 July 1916[10] and later developed in *Movements in European History*. Consequently, the reader experiences confusion when trying to sort out what the poem says about knowledge and experience. The ideas, particularly in the last half of the poem, are incoherent. How do the dreams represented by the Palace, Dora Copperfield, and Norwood Hill differ from the dreamful world commanded by the men moving along the railway? How does the "dream-stuff" that is "molten and moving mysteriously" relate to the "fixed and finite dreams"? Even more importantly, how does the consciousness that caused the speaker to realize that he is Life relate to the "unconscious rapture that moves unthought with Life"?

These ideational difficulties prompt Lawrence's second attempt at the poem, that of the second manuscript 1 draft. Lawrence adds a subtitle to the original title, "A Still Afternoon in School": "Dreams Old and Unborn," emended to "Nascent." Extensive revision begins at the end of the fourth stanza (as usual, Lawrence remained content with the opening stanzas of the poem) and continues to its conclusion. At the end of stanza 4, Lawrence introduces the metaphor of the soul as an explorer, which prepares the way for the related figure, developed as an alternative for stanza 5 of the past years as a sea on which the soul sails. Lawrence repeats in stanza 6 part of the original lines of stanza 5, which contain the image of the world as a painted fresco. He thereby saves the reader from a confusion of images in the long fifth stanza, even though, typical of his early verse, a plethora of images still plagues the poem taken as a whole. Although neither extended metaphor is present in the first draft of the poem, the germ of each is there. (Lawrence referred to "dream-tossed years" in both manuscript 1 drafts, striking out the phrase in the second draft, and describes the past as "visible like a picture" in the first.)

Even though Lawrence shifted phrases and reworded lines, the last half of both manuscript 1 drafts share a similar difficulty. The last portion of the poem depends upon exclamation about, and abstruse reference to, an undefined entity presented as physical (it is a force akin to light and heat) yet described also in conventional religious terminology (it is the "Creator," the "unseen shaper," "The One," and a "Great Thing"). Its effect on the speaker is to produce rapture, ecstasy, and terror. Lawrence thus obliquely referred to God or a godlike power in these drafts, but he resisted any direct reference to Him, wishing perhaps to avoid the idea of a personal presence who can be distinguished from His creation. He did not balk at referring directly to God in other poems of this period (e.g., "Corot" and "Michael-Angelo"), even though, judging from his later elimination of most of these references, he felt uneasy about doing so. Clearly, Lawrence had not yet articulated the idea of the demon which he began to do only around 1915. In these early poems, Lawrence groped for language, and particularly images—which depend upon a clear idea of the entity described—through which to present his intuitions of God. He arrived at an organic image of the bud of life becoming the fruit, or flesh, of the world, but in general, images and language remain vague in these two drafts of the poem.

What appear to be further revisions of the manuscript 1 poem exist in a second surviving college notebook, which Carole Ferrier dates somewhat later than manuscript 1; and in an untitled fragment of three poems that appeared with only slight changes in the November 1909 issue of *The English Review*.[11] Lawrence had by this time divided the poem into two major sections, "Old" and "Nascent." Each of these is subdivided into various parts, a tacit admission by Lawrence of the imperfect unity of the poem. At this stage of its development, the poem suggests a collection of fragments, not only formally but stylistically, as Sandra Gilbert points out.[12] Lawrence shifted the parts of the poem, apparently arbitrarily, from one version to the next. This disunity of theme and image repeats itself in the form of the poem. The basic *abab* rhyme scheme of its first half, which consists mainly of four-line stanzas, disappears altogether in the unrhymed stanzas of indeterminate length in the last half of the poem.

Lawrence has tried to temper the fustian tone of the manuscript 1 versions of the poem by replacing the exclamatory sentence fragments that mark the syntax of the last part of the poem with declarative sentences that attempt to describe the godlike force through controlled similes and metaphors. Apparently despairing of rendering coherently the contrast between conscious and unconscious minds, Lawrence eliminated all reference to them, cutting the final six lines (five in the second manuscript 1 draft) of the original poem.

The version of "Dreams: Old and Nascent" that exists among poems sent by Lawrence to Edward Garnett in 1911 (designated as manuscript 19) stands in time between the versions of the poem published in *The English Review* and *Amores*. [13] In "Old," this poem closely resembles the former version, although Lawrence expanded the fifth stanza from ten to sixteen lines, in spite of making the individual lines more concise. His revision of Manuscript 19 reflects an experimental expansion of the comparison of the soul with a boat and an effort to regularize the meter of the lines, refashioning most of them into tetrameter. "Nascent" follows *The English Review* version through the equivalent of Part 8 of the published text, returning thereafter to the second manuscript 1 draft to reintroduce the distinction between conscious and unconscious life.

A return to the manuscript 1 drafts of the poem also marks "Dreams: Nascent," now an independent poem in the almost identical manuscript 26 and *Amores* texts. "Dreams: Old" in these versions differs from *The English Review* poem only in minor details of punctuation and phrasing, with one notable exception. Part 4 of the poem as it appears in *The English Review* has been eliminated from "Dreams: Old" and serves as the opening stanza of "Dreams: Nascent" in manuscript 26 and *Amores*. These later forms of the poem acknowledge the shifts in subject, tone, and imagery that follow the fifth stanza of "Dreams: Old." Lawrence did away with all interior divisions of the poem, apparently judging that the shift from sea to fresco imagery was too jarring for a single poem to accommodate, no matter how it was divided internally. Having made this decision, Lawrence essentially completed his revision of "Dreams: Old." For *Collected Poems,* he changed only occasional words or phrases of the *Amores* version, mostly for the sake of the sound of the lines, not their meaning. Specifically, he cleared out some of the accumulated short syllables that plagued his early verse, chiefly by eliminating adjectives, as in the case of the last lines of the second stanza of the poem.

Unlike "Dreams: Old," which assumed its essential shape as early as the second manuscript 1 draft (even though its relationship to the last half of the poem took Lawrence a long time to work out), "Dreams: Nascent" continued to present difficulties through the *Amores* version. Although he used certain phrases from *The English Review* version in the *Amores* poem, Lawrence essentially returned to manuscript 1, as he was wont to do when preparing poems with problematic sections for *Amores*. Lawrence depended upon the second manuscript 1 draft for the second, fourth, eighth, and ninth stanzas of the *Amores* poem, and unmistakably incorporated elements of the first draft of the poem into its third, fifth, sixth, and seventh stanzas. In fact, this poem became a patchwork of all preceding versions, with the two drafts from manuscript 1 dominating. (A study of the revisions of this poem demonstrates the dangers that lie in any assessment of a poet's development when only published material is available.

Perhaps the spontaneity and energy of "A Still Afternoon in School" appealed to Lawrence, viewing the notebook drafts after an interim of several years. Certainly, compared with *The English Review* version of the poem, they generate a sense of unconstrained activity—unfortunately through an absence of discipline in the verse. The lack of focus on any developed theme or image, and the free flowing, at times unruly, form that caused Lawrence to rewrite these drafts for *The English Review* persist in the *Amores* version. As the various versions of the poem show, its parts are altogether too interchangeable, betraying a lack of internal logic or even predictable association among them; and readers have the same unanswered questions with which earlier versions of the poem had left them. The *Amores* poem testifies to the speaker's experience of the inexpressible without supplying his readers with any means by which to understand or experience it for themselves.

The most obvious change that Lawrence made in "Dreams: Nascent" for *Collected Poems* is that he cast it in regular verse form. It seems odd that Lawrence, by this time a master at creating cadenced 'verse, as *Birds, Beasts and Flowers* amply demonstrates, should return in his revision of this poem to the rhymed verse of his youth. One critic suggests that he used the four-line stanza (generally rhymed *abab*) in an effort to do precisely that—i.e., be consistent with his early practice, thereby de-emphasizing that this poem is a new creation.[14] This is not the only poem that Lawrence recast in rhyme for *Collected Poems:* "Virgin Youth" and "Baby Running Barefoot," formerly unrhymed, became rhyming poems in their final versions. Lawrence, however, did not consistently change all the unrhymed poetry of volume 1 to rhyming verse. Although he rewrote "Malade" in other ways, he did not alter its form, nor did he change that of "In Trouble and Shame," "Embankment at Night, Before the War: Charity," or "Sorrow." Even more convincing as an explanation of why Lawrence rhymed "Dreams: Nascent" for *Collected Poems* is that rhyme offered him a means of organizing and unifying what had proved to be difficult subject matter.

Even though "Dreams: Nascent" in 'Rhyming Poems" begins with a slightly different form of the four-line stanza that begins the *Amores* poem, it soon takes its own direction, returning thereafter only briefly to earlier versions for a phrase or line. This is a new poem, yet one whose origin remains clear in more than an unchanged title. Lawrence has deleted all reference to the classroom, in which the discoveries of the earlier versions of the poem occur, but the railway workers who initiated the vision in all of them remain in *Collected Poems,* assuming a more developed role in the poem. These figures embody the creative life force, or demi-urge, which is the subject of the poem. Lawrence had now worked out the characteristics of this force and had no need to rely on generalizations. It is dualistic, creating a new order through destruction of the old. It works through humankind, by means of active bodies in touch with the "secret" stirring in their limbs—i.e., "the blood of the live world," as stanza 17 reveals. It frees them to relate to reality immediately, through the senses, ultimtely leading them to find new words to describe new experience. Lawrence can now distinguish between the dreams that imprison him and his entire society in mental constructs, abstractions, such as money, power, and prestige; and the vigorous dream of emerging life that looks to the present instead of the past.

In its new shape, "Dreams: Nascent" expresses poetically the doctrine expressed in *Reflections on the Death of a Porcupine.* To Lawrence, this doctrine was "amusing" and "gay," something to be delighted in rather than taken solemnly.[15] The concluding image of the final version of "Dreams: Nascent," the vital rose-tree with life shooting out of its roses and delicate smell—and thorns—reminds us of Lawrence's prickly humor, which could lighten even his most polemical poems.

The other subjective poems, almost all of which Lawrence thoroughly revised for "Rhyming Poems," follow the pattern of revision that emerges from a careful analysis of "The Wild Common" and "Dreams: Nascent." "Virgin Youth," which Lawrence mentions in the note as much rewritten, is, like "Dreams: Nascent," a new creation in *Collected Poems* (see app. 7). The *Amores* version is almost identical with the manuscript 1 draft, betraying less revision for that volume than "The Wild Common." For *Collected Poems*, Lawrence expanded the poem from twenty-two to sixty-two lines, divided into thirteen stanzas of either four or five lines each. The free verse of the early poem becomes rhyme, as in "Dreams: Nascent," although no rhyme or metric scheme predominates. The *Amores* poem echoes Lawrence's earlier mentioned letter to Bertrand Russell in its description of the experience of blood knowledge. The eyes of the virgin youth, on which depends the "ordinary mental consciousness," go dim. Superseding mental consciousness, according to Lawrence, is "the blood-consciousness, with the sexual connection holding the same relation as the eye, in seeing, holds to the mental consciousness. One lives and has one's being in the blood, without any reference to the nerves and brain. This is one half of life, belonging to the darkness."[16]

The body in the *Amores* version searches for connection through sex with the woman, who will bring new knowledge analogous to the mental knowledge transmitted by the eye. In the revised poem, the two centers of consciousness confront each other. Mental consciousness, which in the words of the speaker "looks through my eyes / And quivers in words through my mouth," faces off against what he calls the "lower me" that communicates itself through the penis, personifed as a "homunculus." The lower self is a godlike entity, for the phallus is "the great old symbol of godly vitality in a man, and of immediate contact."[17] Sex, myth, and religion merge in the language and imagery of the poem, much as they do in a poem such as "Snake," particularly in lines like these, which describe the little man who overcomes the upper identity.

> How beautiful he is! without sound,
> Without eyes, without hands;
> Yet, flame of the living ground
> He stands, the column of fire by night.
> And he knows from the depths; he quite
> Alone understands.

The poem expresses the yearning of the body for blood knowledge. Mental consciousness, helplessly uncomprehending before the force with which it has to deal, can only lament over, desire, and apologize for what society denies them both—full knowledge and renewed purposive activity through complete sexual self-expression. Unlike the early poem, which sets the mind against the body, the revised poem recognizes, as does the revised version of "The Wild Common," the body as total self. Opposed here are modes of consciousness, equally physical, equally vital, equally valid, divided by propriety, which the young man allows to alienate him from himself.[18]

The figures that bring the poem to life, the rhythm of the lines, and the syntax itself all contribute to the development and expression of the ideas in the poem. In one simile, Lawrence compares the erect phallus to a lighthouse with night churning round its base. Its "dark light rolls / Into darkness and darkly returns." This figure communicates the power, the terror, and the incomprehensibility of blood consciousness, which seems like darkness to the mind. The role of the sexual organ as beacon for and guide into the unknown becomes clear through this image. Lawrence expresses the sensuous, immediate nature of the understanding of the lower consciousness through the incremental rhythm of lines such as these:

> And then
> My unknown breasts begin
> To wake, and down the thin
> Ripples below the breast an urgent
> Rhythm starts, and my silent and slumberous belly
> In one moment rouses insurgent.

Through the recurring questions addressed by the mind to the blood, Lawrence makes apparent the bafflement of mental consciousnes in any attempt to understand blood consciousness. Furthermore, language and images work together to carry the reader beyond ideas, into the experience of the numinous. The mind, which claims the body as its own (the poem, spoken from the point of view of mental awareness, speaks of "my mouth," "my breast," "my belly"), recognizes the penis as other and addresses it in the third person singular or the prayerful "thou." The "I" of the poem addresses the "homunculus" as "thou lustrous one," and compares him to a "column of fire" and a "dark, ruddy pillar"; expresses a desire to worship him; and confesses to him, begging for forgiveness. Lawrence creates a poem whose elements combine to convey the concept and the emotion that the earlier poem adumbrated. The demon is explicitly revealed in one of his many manifestations.

So, too, the school poems express more coherently in their revised versions the ideas and emotions implicit in their precursors. All are constructed on the introspective model of "The Wild Common." "Best of School," "Last Lesson," "Snowy Day in School," and "Discipline" were much changed for *Collected Poems,* no doubt because in their early forms they struggle to express sophisticated insights into the psychology of the student-teacher relationship. Some of these insights, Lawrence also explored in the sections of *The Rainbow* devoted to Ursula's teaching experience, but not until the essays on psychology did Lawrence formulate in any systematic way the role of the will in human relationships.[19] In the light of this later doctrine, Lawrence rewrote the school poems, clarifying the nature of the students' alternating dependence on and struggle against their teacher and situating it in a cosmic context of creative flux.

These changes follow the pattern of revision in "Dreams: Old." Lawrence altered them to clarify the fundamental concept on which they depend. Doing so enabled him to simplify images, sharpen language, and generally tighten the form of the poems. In every case, the early versions of these poems strike the reader, particularly when compared with their revised versions, as wordy and unfocused, as though the poet were thrashing about in search of what he wanted to say rather than how he wanted to say it.

For "Rhyming Poems," Lawrence pared away the last half of "Best of School," simplifying the image of the boys as growing vines supported by the tree of his life by simplifying the idea conveyed: that independence need not preclude vital connection. The revised "Last Lesson of the Afternoon" clarifies the nature and consequences of the dual struggle of will between students and teacher. The last lesson now unequivocably is that taught the teacher: one must conserve energy for vital conflict, not squander it on futile carping. In a similar way, Lawrence sharpened the meaning and, consequently, the imagery and phrasing of "A Snowy Day in School." In its final form, he shows the wrangle of individual wills against a cosmic background of silence, in which things compel attention unconsciously and effortlessly.

"Discipline," the most extensively revised of the school poems, exists in many versions, although like "Dreams: Old" and "Dreams: Nascent," only three distinct versions of the poem precede the one in "Rhyming Poems."[20] One of these appears in manuscript 1, a second in *The English Review* for November 1909, and a third in *Amores* (see app. G). A comparison of the four versions demonstrates dramatically how Lawrence's evolving thought could dictate successive, massive revisions of a poem. Seen in the context of periodic revisions, certain of Lawrence's extensive alterations for *Collected Poems* seem anything but an anomaly. Rather, they follow from his usual practice of reshaping his verse to fit his changing ideas.

The first version explains that the speaker's classroom discipline has come from tearing out "the roots" from his soul to fashion a whip with which to discipline his students. His class is a cosmos, of which he is a god. Even though he would prefer to be a merciful god, he must establish the law of Jehovah, the punisher.

The first two stanzas of *The English Review* version closely resemble those of the manuscript 1 poem. Thereafter, Lawrence alters both images and meaning. The rope of discipline, for example, is here formed from "the easy roots that bear the leaves of pity," no longer threatening the speaker's identity. One presumes that Lawrence had gained distance from the painful experience that prompted the original poem. He uses as justification of his harshness the universal pattern of suffering and bitterness set by God, unlike the manuscript 1 poem, which emphasizes the suffering of a god who must subordinate love to law. In this poem, the speaker represents himself as a prophet rather than a god. Later versions of the poem eliminate both suggestions, although Lawrence published the fourth stanza of this version as an independent poem, "Prophet," in both *Amores* and *Collected Poems.* Like the manuscript 1 draft of the poem, *The English Review* version stresses the brutality implicit in life, especially in love, where inceased vulnerability invites brutality. A similar idea pervades Lawrence's fiction of the period, as in the case of *The White Peacock* and *The Trespasser.*

The *Amores* version of the poem expands the imagery of the opening stanzas in order to depict a primeval struggle of wills in the under darkness between student and teacher. It also introduces the notion that opposition exists not only in nature and between individuals but within the individual himself, between his conscious and unconscious wills. This is the Lawrence of the period of *Women in Love* and *Look! We Have Come Through!* Through the metaphor of a flower whose light warms the amicable but burns the hand of the potential violator, the poem expresses the stance of the vulnerable soul, once wounded and now defensive. In doing so, the poem veers away from its initial affirmation of opposition, ending in a self-pitying complaint of the wounded ego. The speaker appeals to his beloved to comfort him. If she will comply, to her alone will he expose his sensibilities. This version, contemporaneous with *Look!,* turns to the woman for restoration, affirmation — and escape.

The final version of "Discipline" seeks no justification for conflict in a harsh god, nor does it desire refuge from a cruel world in a woman. Lawrence eliminates the self-righteous quality of the manuscript 1 draft, the apologetic note of *The English Review* poem, and the whining tone of the *Amores* poem. It becomes a lesson in human growth and development, whose theme is that one shall not thwart nor be thwarted in the dark struggle of the self to unfold. His stance here, as in *Fantasia,* is that self-fulfillment through power is good, but must be kept within limits by discipline. Love tolerates and asks too much, weakening the autonomy of the developing person, depleting the will of the developed self. Love can only exist between two independent souls. The poem ends with the speaker's affirmation that he will henceforth discipline himself as well as his students, loving only where and when it is appropriate. The struggle for control has cost him much — he is like a "plant in winter"—but it has given him knowledge and a sense of his own resources. In its final version, the poem boldly affirms the struggle of wills as not only necessary but good, a message that earlier versions of the poem avoided and that the *Amores* poem betrayed.

Two other interesting revisions of subjective poems for "Rhyming Poems" are those of "Troth with the Dead" and the poem called "Blue" in *Amores,* from which Lawrence struck the last seven stanzas, renaming the shortened poem "The Shadow of Death" in *Collected Poems* (see app. H.1). His only other changes in "The Shadow of Death" are punctuational. No doubt Lawrence eliminated these stanzas because they closely parallel the six-stanza poem called "The Mystic Blue" in *Amores,* re-named "Blueness" in *Collected Poems.* Early manuscript versions of these poems reveal that Lawrence divided the stanzas of early single drafts of a poem called "Blue" into the two *Amores* poems. Essentially, the last seven stanzas of "Blue" and the six stanzas of "The Mystic Blue" represent variants of a single poem. While Lawrence changed the phrasing of the early drafts, the images remain the same (see app. H.2). He wisely eliminated this duplication in *Collected Poems* by shortening "Blue" and renaming both poems.

"Troth with the Dead" was also a much longer poem in its early manuscript drafts. Lawrence divided the ten stanza poem called by this title in manuscript 5 into three poems for *Amores:* he rewrote its first four stanzas to form "Troth with the Dead"; changed its fifth and sixth stanzas to form the first two of "The Enkindled Spring"; altered its last two to the shape of "At a Loose End"; and eliminated most of the seventh and eighth stanzas of the draft. In its final version, Lawrence rewrote the poem that already had undergone several drafts before its publication in *Amores,* struggling with the central image of the poem to clarify the relationship of the speaker to the dead mother. A comparison of the versions of the poem illustrates Lawrence's increasing ability to handle imagery in a symbolic way (see app. I). Manuscript 5 establishes the basic image upon which Lawrence constructed the poem: that of the half moon, which suggested to him a pledge of his fidelity to his mother. He presents the moon as his mother's half of the "coin of troth"—it has risen from her grave, where he planted it; his own half seems literally to be a coin—he presses it in his pocket against his thigh. In *Amores,* to simplify the compelling but problematic image, Lawrence makes the moon a sign for the living of their troth with the dead; the moon's other half remains underground, with the speaker's dead mother. The image loses force, as does the entire poem, in this version, as its last stanza shifts to dual images, quite conventional, of death as sleep which is like waves. As this version of the poem confirms, Lawrence at the time of *Amores* still had difficulty controlling his tendency to proliferate images, although he was clearly aware of it, dividing as he did the manuscript 5 version of the poem into three separate poems, primarily because he had despaired of accommodating so many images in a single poem.

Lawrence focused the final revision of "Troth with the Dead" on the problematic third stanza of the poem, increasing the symbolic resonance of the image by suggesting that two coins exist: one, symbolic of the troth all the living are pledged to keep with the dead; the other, of the speaker's personal troth with the dead woman. Thus, the visible half-moon becomes an outward sign of the "weird and blue" half-moon beneath the speaker's heart, both connecting with unseen moons in the dark land of the dead. This eerie image now fully conveys not only the ideas of the connection between the living and the dead that Lawrence had been stuggling toward in the earlier versions, but also creates a powerful impression of its strangeness and mystery. By means of this revised image, Lawrence invested the speaker of the poem with a mythic identity. He is one who is in connection with the land of the dead, an interpreter of its secrets. In this small but effective way, Lawrence used his revision of this poem to further his plan for *Collected Poems,* even as he strengthened the poem itself.

As we shall see, Lawrence's other revisions for "Rhyming Poems" adhere to the general patterns that emerge from a close study of selected subjective poems. What most concerned him was clarification of the ideas upon which the poems are constructed, which usually entailed that he wrestle with the images in which the poems are cast. Whether Lawrence's revision led to his rewriting entire poems, adding long sections to them, or eliminating a major part of them, his aim was consistently the same: to tell the truth about the demon as he had come to understand it.

6. Inclusion of the Fictional, Dedicatory, and Descriptive Poems in "Rhyming Poems"

Although Lawrence's most extensive revisions for "Rhyming Poems" are of subjective poems, he also greatly modified many of the fictional, or imaginative, and dedicatory poems for this volume. As mentioned earlier, he usually allowed the descriptive poems to remain unchanged as he transposed them into the *Collected Poems,* although many of these poems have several earlier versions that afford valuable insights into Lawrence's poetic development. Also bearing on any study of the design for *Collected Poems* is a consideration of those poems that Lawrence deleted from "Rhyming Poems," even though they were previously published in one of the books that compose that volume.

The fictional, or imaginative, poems collected in "Rhyming Poems" are of three kinds. The first, which includes the largest number, seeks to create a view of experience other than the poet's own but dramatically presented, either through dialogue (as in the case of "A Passing Bell") or, more frequently, through Browning-like monologue (as in "Love on the Farm," "Wedding Morn," or "Seven Seals"). The second kind closely resembles the first, but the monologue or dialogue is presented in dialect (as in "The Collier's Wife," "Violets," "Whether or Not," and "The Drained Cup"). The third kind combines narration with spoken dialogue (as in "Two Wives").

As Lawrence mentions in the prefaces to *Collected Poems,* he revised the fictional poems to "make the 'fiction' more complete" and also to improve the form of these poems by taking out the "dead bits." What this revision amounts to, in most instances, is that Lawrence did one or more of the following. He cut out repetitive stanzas, as in "The Collier's Wife"; he rephrased parts of poems, especially endings, as in "Wedding

Morn" and "Love on the Farm"; and he rendered the dialect more authentically and consistently. Lawrence did, however, thoroughly revise several of the fictional poems, reformulating the intellectual premises on which they are based or redesigning the structures of the poems for greater dramatic effect. The rewritten endings of "Violets," "Whether or Not," "The Drained Cup," and "Two Wives" increase the drama of the situations portrayed by clarifying the causes or natures of the antagonisms presented, resolving them less conventionally, and in certain cases restructuring the forms of the poems. Lawrence took this opportunity to deepen the psychological insight so important to these poems, particularly in "The Drained Cup." In its *Love Poems* version, this poem treats of a young man's sexual and psychological overmastering by a socially inferior older woman. Rewriting the last seven stanzas of the poem (the revision of the poem's first five stanzas consists mainly of technical improvements of the sort mentioned above) allowed Lawrence to sharpen the perceptions of the woman speaker of the poem, thereby increasing our interest in her and in the young man being addressed. She now explores his psychology in depth, revealing her own as she does so. Lawrence's doctrine emerges from the woman's dialogue as she exposes the nature of their sexual relationship and the young man's dilemma, torn as he is between mind and blood.

"Two Wives," the only poem from *New Poems* that Lawrence revised in any substantial way, provides an interesting study of the poet's revision of the fictional poems. Here, he revised not only for "the say," " but also for the form, returning to that of an early manuscript draft of the poem. Here, again, this poem clearly demonstrates the importance of the manuscript drafts to an analysis of Lawrence's revisions. Futhermore, it gives one an appreciation of how Lawrence's developing ideas, in this instance on the physical and spiritual dimensions of human sexuality and its connection with the divine, shape each version of a poem and unite it with other writings of a particular period.

The earliest form of "Two Wives," entitled "White," is preserved in manuscript 19, written around the time of the first drafts of *Sons and Lovers* (see app. J). Its setting, plot, and imagery are basically the same as in later versions, with some interesting differences. A young man's wife, always associated with pale images, and his mistress, described as dark, reveal their contrasting natures and ways of loving before his corpse in the bedroom where he has just died. In this version, unlike the later ones, the young man speaks before he dies. He repents, in her presence, of having wed the pale wife in pride, rejecting to do so his first love, to whom his soul belonged. He promises that in heaven he will register his dark love as his true bride. After his death, the dark wife comes to claim her husband. Her claim consists of the Christ-like suffering she endures to initiate him into the eternal mysteries of life and death through sex. Her sexuality, like that of Miriam in *Sons and Lovers,* has been a crucifixion. As in the romantic tradition, the consummation of her love is death, and death reunites the lovers. The poem in manuscript 19 concludes with an exchange between pale and dark wives. The former proclaims her physical triumph over the dark wife: she bears the dead man's living child within her. In reply, the dark wife admits her failure to preserve or even satisfy her lover physically, nonetheless asserting that she has borne the "dream" of him, which she maintains has superior vitality. Hers is the last word in the poem.

Lawrence has designed this poem to reveal constrasting approaches to sexuality. Much as in *Sons and Lovers,* spiritual and carnal expressions of sexuality oppose each other, but this contest lacks the force of the one in *Sons and Lovers.* Here, the Miriam-like woman triumphs with little effort. The poem leaves us in no doubt: were the man less base, he would have mated with the dark wife long before. Death, which ennobles him, allows real marriage, a marriage of the spirit, to take place.

For *New Poems,* Lawrence changed the poem by considerably shortening it, cutting out the superfluous deathbed confession of the man as well as the reply of the pale wife. Not only does the dark wife have the last word, she has the only word in the poem. Yet the pale wife becomes more sympathetic in this version—her husband dies of a war wound, not some mysterious illness for which her love seems vaguely responsible, and her husband's attraction to her appears to have stemmed from affection rather than pride. Correspondingly, the dark wife becomes more sinister—her entry is described as "ominous" and her manner of asserting her claim on the dead man strikes the reader as cold and self-righteous. Nevertheless, the former is impotent in the face of death, while the latter is in her element. In this version of the poem, the dark wife represents what Lawrence in "The Crown" calls the "Source and the Beginning."[1] Her sexuality leads beyond the temporal and represents a way into the eternal, where duality vanishes. During the war years, Lawrence was concerned with the relationship between the temporal, which at that time he thought involved constant struggle, and the eternal, which promises peace. Although a hint of this idea exists in the manuscript 19 poem, Lawrence emphasizes it here by focusing entirely on the dark wife and her otherwordly claim. He revised the manuscript 19 poem to show in *New Poems* the attraction of death, the point at which "duality and polarity is transcended into absorption."[2] The dead man has achieved perfection of a sort incomprehensible to the pale wife. The dark wife's sexuality, however, has allowed her to transcend the ephemeral, a transcendence that unites her and her alone to the dead man.

In his revision for "Rhyming Poems," Lawrence completely reverses the impact of the poem. He added two new parts, or a total of six stanzas, to the version in *New Poems,* leaving the first part of the poem unaltered. In other words, Lawrence did not change the words of the dark wife, allowing her approach to love and her view of death as expressed in *New Poems* to stand. Now, however, far from being displaced by the dark wife, as she is in both earlier versions, the pale wife roundly rejects the claim of the dark wife as a solipsistic dream, as insubstantial words, and as lifeless abstraction. In contrast, she affirms life in the flesh, including mortality. Her sexuality has united her with the dead man and with the eternal in the only way that counts—in the here and now. The dark wife has known mental connection only, and its insubstantiality nullifies any real claim she has on the dead man. Lawrence distinguishes between death as abstraction and death as physcial reality, an intrinsic part of the vital process of nature. Consequently, light and dark images reverse their significance in this poem. The dark wife now represents the denial of life rather than the dark power of the spirit; the pale wife, instead of suggesting the weakness of the flesh when confronting mystery, manifests the bright reality of all things physical.

The form of the final version, which combines narration with spoken debate, represents a return to the earliest form of the poem. It greatly enhances the dramatic force of the poem, even while it provides Lawrence with a convenient way of supplementing its message. The pale wife's ideas are those which, by 1924, Lawrence was exploring in "On Human Destiny." In this essay, Lawrence writes the following, which sums up the pale wife's argument: "I live and die. I ask no other. Whatever proceeds from me lives and dies. I am glad, too. God is eternal, but my idea of Him is my own, and perishable. Everything human, human knowledge, human faith, human emotions, all perishes. And that is very good; if it were not so, everything would turn to cast-iron. There is too much of this cast-iron of permanence today."[3] Similar thoughts run through the essay "Reflections on the Death of a Porcupine," as well as the posthumously published *Apocalypse*. When Lawrence revised for *Collected Poems*, his developed theories prompted him to carry a poem like "Two Wives" to what he now saw as a complete expression of ideas only half expressed before. As with the subjective poems, most of Lawrence's extensive revisions of the fictional poems were of this sort.

The third type of poem that Lawrence was wont to rewrite for *Collected Poems* can be classified as "Dedicatory." In this category fall the poems to Miriam, some of which Lawrence says in the foreword "had to be altered, where sometimes the hand of the commonplace youth had been laid on the mouth of the demon." Also included are the poems to Helen and the Beloved, as well as a few of the poems to Lawrence's mother. Like the school poems, these concern themselves with the subtleties of human relationship, in this case between male and female.

As on other subjects, Lawrence's ideas on this topic developed over many years, which is not to say that they ever reversed themselves or even changed markedly. On this topic, they became more nuanced and elaborate, as did his ideas on blood knowledge, for example. *The Study of Thomas Hardy*, which Lawrence wrote in the autumn of 1914, although it was not published in *Phoenix* (1936)[4] until after his death, contains Lawrence's first developed discussion of the relationship of male and female, a topic he returns to consistently in the essays as well as in the novels and poems. He considers the subject at length in *Psychoanalysis* and *Fantasia,* exploring the idea of the woman as representative of the other (i.e., the "not-me," which in true relation with the self can give birth to the ghost); in *Reflections,* developing the idea of woman as a reducing agent that can bring forth the essential self; and in *Assorted Articles,* attacking what he sees as the aberrations of modern females.

In general, all these essays regard male and female as opposites, particular manifestations of a male and female principle that, in turn, reflects the duality of the cosmos. Man and woman experience that which they are not through each other, bringing forth newness and ultimately leading each other toward God. In relating to the opposite sex, the individual can seek either the consummation of union, in positive desire, or, negatively, what Lawrence calls "a frictional reduction." In the latter case, "it is his mind, his conscious self he wants to reduce. He wants to dissolve it back. He wants to become infantile, like a child, to reduce and resolve back all the complexity of his consciousness, to the rudimentary condition of childhood."[5] Reduction can destroy the weak-willed, but in the case of the strong-willed, it can lead to the "final and utter reduction": death. "And in the brush with death," writes Lawrence, a man may be "released again into positive life" by reducing his soul to its elements, breaking down its egoism so that it can experience life anew.[6] In either case, Lawrence maintains, relationship between the sexes is our only hope for getting back in touch with the rhythm of the cosmos, from which modern life too often disconnects us.

His increasingly well-formulated ideas on the nature of sexual relationships, as well as his larger experience of women and sexuality and his distance in time from the emotional relationships depicted in these poems, allowed Lawrence to alter the content and tone of the dedicatory poems as he revised them for "Rhyming Poems." As a general rule, any formal or technical revisions of these poems follow from conceptual changes.

The form of these poems, I should mention, often resembles that of the subjective poems, taking the shape of an interior monologue in which the historical Lawrence, his memory triggered by some external event or object, reflects on aspects of his relationship with the woman to whom the poem is dedicated.

Such is the form of "Scent of Irises," for example.[7] The dedicatory poems can also assume other shapes. Some share the form of the fictional monologues and dialogues, in which the poet addresses the woman directly (e.g., "Last Words to Miriam") or enters into discussion with her (e.g., "Lilies in the Fire"). Others take the form of "Two Wives," combining narrative and dialogue (e.g., "Snap-Dragon"). Still others share the form of the descriptive poems (e.g., "Hands of the Betrothed" and "A Love Song"); these, as one would expect, evidence little revision for "Rhyming Poems."

"Last Words to Miriam" is a good example of Lawrence's revision of the dedicatory poems. The Collected Poems version of the poem shows that Lawrence has clarified its content, both by being more explicit about the nature of the relationship between him and the woman and by refining his analysis of its failure (see app. K for the three versions of this poem). He also alters the tone of the poem, adopting in its final version a more objective point of view in comparison to the Amores version, which strikes the reader as self-centered. Finally, he tempers his choice of diction and imagery, which in the earlier versions tends to emotionalism and imprecision.

By adding a stanza between the second and third stanzas of the Amores poem and refining the two central metaphors in the poem, Lawrence conveys more clearly why his relationship with Miriam failed; it failed because, while he sought otherness through Miriam, his passion lacked the strength to unite with her. Instead, consciousness intervened, resistance developed, and the ego assumed control, preventing the transformation that true sexual union initiates.[8] By developing the double metaphor implicit in the earlier poem, Lawrence furthers his idea of failed transcendence. He draws the first metaphor from the passion of Christ and the other from the craft of metal casting, connecting them through the shape of flames, which resemble thorns. These metaphors connote the idea basic to Lawrence's sexual theory, that apparent destruction of the egocentric old self through physical union with or frictional reduction against the other can lead to new life, to purification, and to transformation into the numinous new self. This process has stopped short of its final end in their case. Her flesh, instead of rising anew, has remained inert; instead of emerging pure from the fire, it has hardened in an imperfect cast. Theirs is a mutual failure, as the imagery of the final version of the poem emphasizes: Lawrence changes the confused imagery of the first and second stanzas of the manuscript 1 and *Amores* poems to present her early love as intense but insubstantial by comparing it to sunshine. His love he portrays as receptive and passive, like the response of the growing flower to the sunshine. Consequently, we are prepared to understand that when Miriam must incarnate her love and he must put his into action, both fail.

By adjusting the point of view in the second and fourth stanzas of the poem, in particular, Lawrence clarifies the role of each in the relationship, shifting the emphasis from his perception of events and his effect on her to their mutual participation in the love affair and their consequent mutual failure. He deletes the smug, "I knew your pain and it broke / My fine craftsman's nerve," from the third stanza of the *Amores* version, replacing it with a more objective statement of their physical relationship in the equivalent stanza four in the final version of the poem. No longer does his pity undo them. Making explicit the implication of the first metaphor in the poem, he strikes at the heart of their difficulty: her body failed him and his will failed her. The impartial tone of the final version eliminates any note of self-pity. The last lines of the poem in the revised version maintain this tone as they underscore the joint reponsibility for the failed relationship. No longer does the speaker bemoan his eternal responsibility for this failure. As we have seen, by the time of *Collected Poems,* the idea of eternity had lost importance for Lawrence. Much more consistent with his ideas at the time of the final version of "Last Words to Miriam" is his emphasis on the failure of relation in the present moment, which might have re-created them and incarnated the divine.

Lawrence's revision of "Last Words to Miriam," altering as it does tone and imagery in order to communicate concepts more subtly, serves as a paradigm of his alteration of other dedicatory poems. In its successive versions, "Scent of Irises," another poem that reflects on the failure of the love relationship with Jessie Chambers, gives an increasingly broader perspective on the relationship, markedly affecting the tone of the poem. The version of the poem that exists in manuscript 5 concludes with the speaker obsessed by the memories triggered by the smell of the flowers. They poison his blood as well as his thoughts. The poem printed in *Amores* registers relief that the immediate clash of their passion is finished, even though its consequences linger like the scent of the flower. In its final version, the tone of the poem has become distanced, even philosophic. Healing has commenced; soon even their memories will fade like the scent of irises.

So, too, Lawrence modifies the tone of another Miriam poem, "A White Blossom," by altering its last phrase. In *Love Poems,* the imagistic poem reads as follows:

A tiny moon as white and small as a single jasmine flower
Leans all alone above my window, on night's wintry bower
Liquid as lime-tree blossom, soft as brilliant water or rain
She shines, the one white love of my youth, which all sin
    cannot stain.

It evokes the inviolate purity of his first love and tacitly reveals the guilt she provokes in him. An earlier manuscript draft of this poem makes the guilt explicit. Identical after revision with the *Love Poems* version, the manuscript 14 draft reveals that Lawrence struck out "my" as a modifier of "sin" in the last line of the poem.

For *Collected Poems,* Lawrence changes the poem to read:

A tiny moon as small and white as a single jasmine flower
Leans all alone above my window, on night's wintry bower
Liquid as lime-tree blossom, soft as brilliant water or rain
She shines, the first white love of my youth, passionless
    and in vain.

Here, Lawrence conveys to us not only the purity and remoteness of the woman but also the sterility of the love between them. Instead of guilt, the tone of the poem suggests the speaker's ironic appreciation of the beauty of the love and the woman, even while he rejects her and her love as fruitless.

Lawrence revised dedicatory poems such as "Last Words to Miriam," "Scent of Irises," and "A White Blossom" as much on the chronological, or experiential, level as on the thematic or mythic. He wanted to portray the relationships depicted not as the wounded ego has perceived them but as the anti-self, or demon, does. In this sense, the changes for *Collected Poems* are quite literally re-visions. His thematic and mythic concerns, however, dictated his revision of certain others of the dedicatory poems. He revised "Red Moon-Rise," for example, a poem that David Garnett has judged the best in *Love Poems* and complete as it was,[9] in order to supplant references to God as a creative force in the earlier poem with womb imagery that explicitly pictures the universal creative urge that the moon, still bloody from birth, and the bedded lovers manifest. Lawrence extends the metaphor not only by substituting it in place of references to God but also by expanding various sections of the poem to develop more completely his idea that the whole of the world, even the world of the mind, sends off sparks of the "seed of life incarnate." In its final version, the poem expands upon and illustrates the theme of *Collected Poems* as introduced in "The Wild Common:" "All that is God takes substance!" It also adds to the mythic content of the book by revealing yet more of the habits of the demon, who through the seed of life unites us with a living cosmos. These revised lines of the poem certify such a message:

> And the same fire that boils within this ball
> Of earth, and quickens all herself with flowers,
> Is womb-fire in the stiffened clay of us:
>
> And every flash of thought that we and ours
> Send suddenly out, and every gesture, does
> Fly like a spark into the womb of passion,
> To start a birth, from joy of the begetting.

Lawrence revised many of the poems to Miriam and Helen for the same reason he revised "Red Moon-Rise": to further the thematic and mythic message of *Collected Poems*. Thus, he revised the images and phrasing of "Release," "These Clever Women," and "Come Spring, Come Sorrow" to communicate more pointedly the necessity of love incarnate in human relationships. The body emerges as the only way to consonance with the universe. His extensive changes in the images of "Lightning," "Lilies in the Fire," and "Repulsed" define more sharply the destructive opposition of the male and female who refuse to allow the demon to "step through [their] loins in one bright stride" because their ego-consciousness sets one against the other in deadly hostility. They willfully distort the creative opposition from which the demon springs. Lawrence develops the same message by shifting the focus of "Yew-Tree on the Downs" from the speaker's personal need for sexual union in the *Amores* poem to a universal need for mythic experience in "Rhyming Poems."

Although Lawrence did not as a rule extensively revise any of the poems to Louie Burrows, the Betrothed, for *Collected Poems*, most likely because her psychology (and consequently his relationship with her) was less complex than that of Miriam or Helen, he did revise to some extent "Kisses in the Train." This revision offers an example of how even a small change in an image can be explained by Lawrence's desire to correct a point of doctrine. The last stanza of the poem reads as follows in *Love Poems:*

> But firm at the centre
>   My heart was found;
> Her own to my perfect
>   Heart-beat bound,
> Like a magnet's keeper
>   Closing the round.

For *Collected Poems,* Lawrence reversed the pronouns of the third line of this stanza. Why did he make this change, almost the only one in the final version? He realized that the *Love Poems* version is inconsistent with his idea, expressed in *Study of Thomas Hardy,* that the woman provides for the man a "center and swivel, . . . the axle, compelling him to true motion."[10] His revision for "Rhyming Poems" brings the final image of a poem describing sex as the center and still point of a turning world into line with his theory of the male-female relationship.

As in the case of the poems about Louie Burrows, few of the poems that center on Lawrence's mother show much revision for *Collected Poems*. Many of these, especially those that portray the circumstances of her death or the son's grief, are, as mentioned earlier, descriptive poems. Even those that belong to the fictional and dedicatory categories, however—for example, "The Collier's Wife" and "Monologue of a Mother" in the first and "The Virgin Mother" in the second classification—exhibit few changes in their final versions.

These poems, however, are much revised before the time of *Amores,* the book that contains most of them. Apparently, Lawrence achieved for that volume an artistic representation of his relationship with his mother that continued to satisfy him, something he was unable to do until much later in the case of Miriam and Helen. This conclusion is supported by comparison of the three versions of "Brother and Sister," a dedicatory poem addressed to his sister Ada that Lawrence did not much change for *Collected Poems.* In its manuscript 5 version, the poem bears the title "To Lettice, My Sister"; it portrays the conspiracy of a brother with his sister to win their mother back from death. Its tone is one of desperate longing for the departed woman. By the *Amores* version, however, the tone of the poem becomes one of acceptance; the brother counsels the sister: "Let us not cry to her still to sustain us here, / Let us not hold her shadow back from the dark." The dramatic shift in attitude from early to later versions of this poem suggests a corresponding shift in Lawrence's attitude to and acceptance of death as well as the loss of his mother.

Lawrence did not often revise for *Collected Poems* what I have called the descriptive poems, probably because they did not depend on his doctrine in any substantial way. Moreover, because they tend to be short, their early defects are painfully obvious; Lawrence often reworked these poems several times before their publication in one of the four volumes collected in "Rhyming Poems." As a general rule, these poems characterize a person, as do "Gipsy," "Flapper," and certain of the poems about Lawrence's mother and betrothed; observe a place or scene, as do many of the London poems; or evoke a mental image of an emotional situation, as do "Discord in Childhood," "Cherry Robbers," and "Piano." As with the poems in other classifications, study of the early drafts of these poems lends valuable insight into Lawrence's poetic development. Even though these are not, strictly speaking, the subject of this book, a brief consideration of the several versions of a representative descriptive poem can deepen our understanding of Lawrence's growth as a poet. "Sorrow," whose subject is the poet's grief over the death of his mother, demonstrates not merely his growing control of the technical aspects of poetic composition but also his increasing ability to transform personal experience into art.

The first of two drafts of the poem, preserved in manuscript 1, reads as follows:

Why does th [is, e] thin grey strand
Floating from between my fingers
Where my cigarette burns forgotten
Why does it trouble me.

Ah, you will understand—
When I carried my mother downstairs
A few times only, at the beginning of her brief sickness
I would find on my coat, floating, a loose long grey hair.

The second stanza of this draft is not poetry, but a record of the external phenomenon that triggers sorrow in the speaker of the poem; it does not touch us. The language in which the description is couched does not involve us in his experience by recreating its emotional impact. Indeed, the image itself confuses: how can a hair found on a coat be floating? Lawrence realizes that he must parallel the drifting grey smoke with the grey hair in order to establish the mental association that leads to the emotion of sorrow, but he has not yet found a convincing way to do so.

The second draft of the poem in manuscript 1 shows vast improvement, even though the long last line spoils the final emotional impact of the poem.

Why does the thin grey strand
Floating up from the forgotten
Cigarette between my fingers
Why does it trouble me?

Ah, you will understand—!
When I carried my mother downstairs
A few times only, at the beginning
  her
Of Δ soft-foot malady

I should find, for a reprimand
To my gaiety, a few long grey hairs)pressed(
On the breast of my coat,)which(and one by one
I would let them float, grey strands,)towards(into the
  dark chimney.

In this revision, Lawrence has improved the poem by sharpening the image of the cigarette in the first stanza (and coincidentally improving the phrasing) as well as hitting upon the evocative "soft-foot malady" in the second as a subsitute for the banal "brief sickness." He adds a third stanza in order to develop the tension implicit in the first stanza between forgetfulness and recollection, specifically of sorrow, and to carry to completion the correspondence between cigarette smoke and the floating grey hairs of his mother. The internal rhyme of the last stanza ("gaiety" / "chimney" and "coat" / "float") give the reader a sense of completion, but the long last line violates the concision of the rest of the poem, robbing it of its punch, allowing it, like the hair it describes, to drift off instead of verbally inducing sorrow.

Lawrence published a version of this poem called "Weariness" in *Poetry: A Magazine of Verse* in December 1914. With the exception of a few punctuation changes, he kept the first two stanzas as they appear in the second manuscript 1 draft. The last stanza, which follows, and in particular the last line of the poem, continues to elude him.

> I would find for a reprimand
> To my gayety, a long grey hair
> On the breast of my coat, and I let it float
> Grey strand, towards the dark chimney.

Even though he shortened the last line of the poem considerably, it still goes flat; and the internal rhyme of the third line of this stanza, coming so close together, produces an effect too flippant to be suitable to the subject. The single strand of hair, floating towards the chimney, lacks significance, as, on a smaller scale, does the repetition of the word "grey."

By manuscript 26, however, Lawrence gave the poem its final shape, which it kept through subsequent publication in *Amores* and *Collected Poems*. Altering a few punctuation marks only, he allowed the first two stanzas to remain as he wrote them in the second manuscript 1 draft. He resolved the problem of the last stanza by making the following revisions:

> I should find, for a reprimand
> To my gaiety, a few long grey hairs
> On the breast of my coat; and one by one
> I watched them float up the dark chimney.

Here, the last two lines of the poem link not only with the image of the first stanza but also with its mood. The sorrowful memory prompted by the cigarette smoke has been previously triggered by the grey hairs found on his coat. One imagines the speaker deliberately letting go, strand by strand, of the troublesome hair, brooding in his sorrow, relinquishing his mother bit by bit to the darkness. In its final form, language, image, and mood unite to convey starkly the emotion that prompted the poem.

A comparison of the various versions of the descriptive poems from *New Poems* and *Bay*, very few of which show much revision for "Rhyming Poems," reveals that in almost every case intensive rewriting preceded their publication in one or the other of these volumes. Whether or not a poem had already appeared in print made little difference to Lawrence. Some of his most vigorous revisions were of poems published in various periodicals or anthologies. In general, an analysis of these revisions yields much the same conclusion as does the study of his revision of "Sorrow": Lawrence was a mature poet by the end of the war years, in possession of considerable poetic skill.

As we have seen, Lawrence's revisions can be full of surprises. He sometimes reverts to the earliest extant version of a poem in a final draft or composes an entirely new poem, in whole or in part. He may halve a poem or double its length. He may simplify images or complicate them. In arranging volume 1 of *Collected Poems*, Lawrence included a number of poems that he condemned as conventional (e.g., "Flapper") or that he had admitted disliking (e.g., "Love on the Farm"),[11] while he excluded others, albeit only three, that he had collected previously and two of which he had allowed to be reprinted in *Selected Poems*, published the same year as *Collected Poems*.[12] Why did Lawrence, with no explanation, exclude "Song-Day in Autumn," "Disagreeable Advice," and "Restlessness" from *Collected Poems*, the first of which had been previously published in *Love Poems*, the other two of which appeared in *Amores*? Of course, one can only theorize about his reasons for deleting them. Paul Delavenay suggests that Lawrence omitted "Restlessness" from "Rhyming Poems" because his revision of "Virgin

Youth" rendered it superfluous.[13] This explanation seems as good as any, especially in light of Lawrence's revision of "Blue" (i.e., "The Shadow of Death" in *Collected Poems*) which eliminated half the poem because it duplicated "The Mystic Blue" (i.e., "Blueness" in *Collected Poems*). I would like to suggest that he eliminated "Song-Day in Autumn" and "Disagreeable Advice" for the same reason.

"Song-Day in Autumn" depicts a Persephone-like female figure, innocently seductive, who is "scared in her play" as she wanders in the fields. The last of autumn loveliness fades even as she watches and frightens her with its initmations of death. The poem subtly imparts the maiden's fear of sexuality: when a "trembling flower" encloses an ecstatic bee, she turns away from her walk, confronting, ironically, the lover who seeks out her "heart of dismay."

In "Autumn Sunshine," Lawrence had not only already made the thematic connection between autumn and death suggested in "Song-Day in Autumn"; but had also made it in a similar manner, through the presence of a mythic figure as well as through the use of imagery. He had also presented the virgin's terror of sexuality more compellingly in "Snap-Dragon" and more originally in "Ballad of Another Ophelia." Thus, because "Song-Day" merely duplicates elements already fully developed and would not further his design for *Collected Poems,* he no doubt decided to eliminate it from "Rhyming Poems."

So, too, "Disagreeable Advice," in its earlier versions called "An Epistle from Arthur," repeats a number of elements from the two "Letters from Town." Duplicated are the spring imagery, the image of dancing girls, the contrast in emotion (i.e., delight and bitterness) and in setting (i.e., blossoming orchards and barren wastelands), and the form of the poems (all three, at least as Lawrence originally conceived them, are letters). As has been discussed, the "Letters from Town" are essential to the mythic structure of "Rhyming Poems." "Disagreeable Advice," a simple description of the beauty and cruelty of spring and of love, was apparently nonessential to the design of *Collected Poems,* and in fact must have seemed superfluous to Lawrence as he arranged "Rhyming Poems."

Out of the four books of verse that are included in volume 1, only these three poems plus one poem from *Love Poems* and two from *New Poems* that Lawrence put in "Unrhyming Poems" are excluded. Based on his thorough revisions for volume 1 of *Collected Poems,* chances are good that Lawrence would have salvaged these poems if they had served in any way his chronologic, thematic, or mythic structure for this volume. We can only assume that they did not, and that he therefore discarded them when it came time to assemble *Collected Poems.*

One last question must be considered in connection with Lawrence's extensive revisions for "Rhyming Poems." Did Lawrence improve the individual poems by revising them? In her review of the American edition of *Collected Poems* in *Poetry,* Harriet Monroe voiced her disapproval of Lawrence's changes in the early poems. Some she calls "a desecration, almost a crime." "None is an improvement," she maintains, claiming that by revising the poems "Lawrence has ruined their poignancy and spontaneity."[14]

Lawrence's view of poetry as expressed in "Poetry of the Present" invites such criticism, for the poet seems to posit spontaneity as one of the cardinal features of vital verse. "We can break the stiff neck of habit," he writes. "We can be in ourselves spontaneous and flexible as flame, we can see that utterance rushes out without artificial foam or artificial smoothness."[15] Yet one has only to examine Lawrence's exhaustive revisions of most of his verse to realize how mythic this description is when applied to his own manner of composition. Lawrence comes closer to depicting his own attitude and practice when he asserts in the same article that in poetry of the present, nothing is finished.[16] As I mentioned earlier, publication of a poem never deterred him from revising it when he saw something that could be improved.

Lawrence's comments about his verse should never be taken out of the context of the verse he was writing: verse that was increasingly experimental and increasingly unappreciated by the critics who reviewed his books. (The very volumes he revised for *Collected Poems,* namely *Love Poems* and *Amores,* are the only two that received general praise from reviewers. No wonder Harriet Monroe felt outrage at his revisions!) Consequently, Lawrence frequently used his poetic theory to validate his own verse. When he wrote "Poetry of the Present," probably sometime in 1919, he knew that his ideas were still unfolding, as was his poetic style. The unconventional poetic form that even in his earliest verse violated the expectation of ears attuned to the Romantic and Victorian poets was continuing its eccentric development, as *Birds, Beasts and Flowers* would shortly verify. Lawrence fostered the myth of spontaneity to gain time and acceptance for his experiments in verse, much as Wordsworth and Coleridge had done before him, and to claim the freedom to concentrate on aspects of poetry other than rhyme and meter.

As he emphasizes in both the note and the foreword to *Collected Poems,* Lawrence aims his revisions not at improving the verse per se but at communicating mythically the way to a new self, not only for the individual but also for the race. The understanding upon which this myth of regeneration depends took most of Lawrence's lifetime to emerge. From its inception, Lawrence's verse tended towards the philosophic, as "The Wild Common" witnesses. His poetry depends upon mental conceits as much or more than that of his contemporaries. Not falling heir to a tradition, either philosophic or poetic, that he could accept readily, Lawrence had to invent both for himself and, moreover, communicate them to the readers of his work. One cannot say that his ideas about nature and poetry or the novel changed over the years so much as that they developed, given direction by expanding experience and wide and eclectic reading. When he revised for *Collected Poems,* as we have seen, Lawrence gave his full attention to the poems, or to the parts of the poems, that are philosophically incomplete rather than formally or technically imperfect. On the infrequent occasions when he did permit himself to rewrite primarily to improve form and clarify images, as he did in "Baby Running Barefoot," Lawrence was capable of producing a polished sonnet with subtle rhymes and carefully observed images. Yet he allowed what Sandra Gilbert calls the "greeting-card rhymes and pseudo-romantic images" of "Transformations" to remain,[17] even though he revised the content of the poem's last stanza in order to communicate the notion of revolutionary transformation.

Thus, we can conclude that Lawrence's revisions for "Rhyming Poems" were motivated by a large shaping vision that relegated to secondary importance the shape of any particular poem. In this context, the question of whether his revision of a particular poem improved it is not as important as whether it enhanced the mythic, thematic, or experiential message of the book.

Even so, one cannot entertain much doubt after a careful study of the revisions of poems such as "The Wild Common," "Dreams: Old" and "Dreams: Nascent," "Virgin Youth," and "Two Wives" that Lawrence did improve them by clarifying their core ideas. From such fundamental clarification, as I have tried to show, more precise, yet frequently more evocative, imagery, diction, and form followed. As Harry Moore rightly pointed out, critics and general public alike have come to accept the text of Collected Poems as the final form of Lawrence's poetry.[18] Consequently, using criteria intrinsic to the poetry, such as coherence, or extrinsic to it, such as reader acceptance, Lawrence's revisions for Collected Poems improved the individual poems. Had Harriet Monroe realized the extent to which Lawrence's final revisions of the poems were only the last in a long line of such changes, she might have been able to view them, not as the result of Lawrence's tampering, but of his intellectual and artistic integrity.

7. The New Self Emerges: The Assimilation of *Look! We Have Come Through!* into *Collected Poems*

In a letter dated 9 February 1917, Lawrence wrote his friend S. S. Koteliansky from Higher Tregerthen, Cornwall, "I have got together my final book of poems. It seems like my last work for the old world. The next must be for soemthing new."[1] About the same time, he wrote Catherine Carswell, "As a sort of last work, I have gathered and shaped my last poems into a book. It is a sort of final conclusion of the old life in me—'and now farewell,' is really the motto."[2]

Lawrence refers in both these instances to *Look! We Have Come Through!*,[3] a collection begun when he and Frieda eloped to the Continent in the spring of 1912 and augmented periodically through the intervening five years of their peripatetic existence. As his letter to Koteliansky reveals, the book contains what Lawrence hopes will be his last expression of European existence. Even as he wrote Koteliansky, he daily expected the approval of his and Frieda's passports, which would enable them to begin their search for Rananim, the community of friends that Lawrence hoped to establish somewhere in America. Only three days later, however, on 12 February, he wrote Lady Cynthia Asquith in despair that his application had been denied.[4] Lawrence would be, in fact, condemned to remain in the Europe he detested for five more years. At the time he finished *Look!*, he regarded it as a final expression of the old Lawrence who had come through to a new existence, an existence that he hoped, quite literally, to spend in a new world.

Nonetheless, describing these poems in the note to *Collected Poems*, Lawrence perceives them as the beginning of a "new cycle" of experience. He declares that they thematically portray the new self, brought to birth through his intimate relationship with a woman and paradoxically emerging in the context of an old world marked by death and destruction. Mythically, as the foreword indicates, *Look!* records the phase when "the demon had a new run for his money." His various comments indicate that Lawrence came to regard *Look!* as pivotal in his description of the self. On the one hand, it represents the old world (and the old self that it has produced) that is only gradually passing away; on the other, it treats of the process of individual renewal through the destruction of the old self, which can serve as a model of regeneration for others. The emerging new self is at once the consequence and manifestation of a larger creative force moving through human life. Thus, *Look!* goes beyond the "death-experience" depicted in "Rhyming Poems" to the sloughing off of the conventional old self in the first sustained experience of otherness through sexual union.

Much on Lawrence's mind through the five-year genesis of *Look!* was the male-female relationship. It dominated not only his personal life but also his creative one. He explores the subject in the two novels written during these years, *The Rainbow* and *Women in Love,* and also philosophically examines it in *Study of Thomas Hardy,* first written in the fall and winter of 1914 but rewritten four times during the next three years.[5] The *Study,* as mentioned earlier, explores the role of sexuality in the experience of the other and, ultimately, the divine. Lawrence outlines two universal principles, Law and Love, which combine to create all things. In Christian terms, Law is represented by the Father, Love by the Son, and the relation between them by the Holy Ghost.[6] This duality exists in all nature, inanimate as well as animate. In mankind, it exists in the female, who manifests "the Law, the Soul, the Senses, the Feelings"; and in the male, who displays "the Love, the Spirit, the Mind, and the Consciousness."[7] When they seek each other, male and female aim: "to recognize and seek out the Holy Spirit, the Reconciler, the Originator, He who drives the twin principles of Law and Love across the ages."[8] Any true relationship between male and female furthers the creative purpose of life, both by sowing the seed of new life and, even more importantly for Lawrence, by bringing each individual to the full achievement of self.[9]

Upon this framework of ideas, Lawrence constructed *Look!* in 1917, organizing it into a sequence of poems that he intended

us to read as "an essential story, or history, or confession, un-
folding one from the other in organic development."[10] Unlike
the books that compose "Rhyming Poems," he allowed the
order of *Look!* to remain almost unchanged as he incorporated
it into *Collected Poems,* forming as it already does a chrono-
logic, thematic, and mythic unit. As he mentions in the note, he
had not much rewritten *Look!* for *Collected Poems,* although
he had inserted in the original sequence several poems published
in other books because they belonged to the new cycle. In other
words, they would enable him to tell his "story," or "history,"
more completely. Lawrence situated "Bei Hennef," first pub-
lished in *Love Poems,* at the start of the new cycle. This poem,
which is in all probability the first that he wrote about his love
for Frieda, describes the man's feeling for the woman in terms
of the external landscape: in the early spring, next to a rushing
river, he can see his love "whole like the twilight." Chronologi-
cally, thematically, and mythically, it initiates the story of how
the self experiences otherness and, consequently, new life
through love.

In the midst of a series of poems concerned with the diffi-
culties of loving well, Lawrence inserted a poem first published
in *New Poems,* "Everlasting Flowers," in its final form subtitled
"For a Dead Mother." This poem records the speaker's grief
that he cannot share his new experiences with his dead mother,
affirming nevertheless his enduring memory of and ghostly
union with her. Placing the poem as he does, Lawrence develops
the theme that the source of the lovers' problems lies in the
inability of the old self to leave the past behind and enter fully
into a relationship in the present moment. The man's maternal
tie—analogous, in fact, to the woman's—hobbles him as he
struggles for freedom.

Lawrence also included in the *Look!* sequence "Coming
Awake," the first and in manuscript the title poem of the vol-
ume that became *New Poems.* He arranged it among the poems
that conclude the sequence, all of which portray thematically
and mythically the regeneration that can follow a true marriage
of opposites.

Finally, Lawrence reunited with the poems originally pub-
lished in *Look!* "Song of a Man Who Is Loved," which the
publisher, to Lawrence's dismay, eliminated from this collection

before its first publication. Lawrence says in the foreword that the mixture in the poem of love and religion caused its omission. He, however, did not take the opportunity provided by the publication of *Collected Poems* to restore to the sequence "Meeting Among the Mountains," which the publisher also struck from *Look!* Although many students of Lawrence have expressed surprise that he left this poem out of "Unrhyming Poems," one has only to read the letter to his agent Pinker in which Lawrence discusses these two poems, to realize that he had no special attachment to "Meeting Among the Mountains."[11] Furthermore, Lawrence had subsequently used the figure of the wayside Christ crucified in both *Women in Love* and *Twilight in Italy*. He may very well have decided that he had used too often the central image in the poem.

The layered structure of *Look!*, which forms the first section of "Unrhyming Poems," follows that established in "Rhyming Poems." Lawrence used chronology, theme, and myth to organize the continuing story of the self. In all likelihood, as I shall consider later, Lawrence designed volume 1 of *Collected Poems* along the lines suggested by *Look!* and *Birds, Beasts and Flowers*. Incorporating these two books into *Collected Poems* with minimal changes, he no doubt extended their form to *Love Poems, Amores, New Poems,* and *Bay,* in which chronologic, thematic, and mythic form had not yet been made explicit. In any event, Lawrence's design for "Rhyming Poems" continues to apply to *Look!*

A rather well-defined chronology forms one level of structure of *Look!* The note, as does the original foreword to the book, invites us to read these poems as a sequence dependent upon the particular circumstances of time and place in which the events first occurred. Lawrence attached place names to a good many of the poems so that the approximate date of the composition of a poem, or at any rate the date of the occurrence depicted in it, is relatively easy to ascertain. In fact, in the note, Lawrence specifically dates the composition of the first and the last of the cycle, "Bei Hennef," written "in May 1912, by a river in the Rhineland"; and "Forest Flowers," the last of the cycle, which he says he wrote "in Cornwall, at the end of the bitter winter of 1916–17."

The first of the poems, those which describe the end of the

death-experience, encompass the six- to nine-month period before the young man of the verse, quite obviously the historical Lawrence, meets and elopes with a married woman, without doubt Frieda Weekley. Lawrence set the second poem of the series in Eastwood, suggesting his last vacation there at the end of the summer of 1911. "Martyr à la Mode" he places at Croydon, most probably in the autumn or winter of the same year, when serious illness put an end to his teaching and kept him an invalid for more than one month. Lawrence identifies "The Sea" with Bournemouth, where he went to convalesce in January and February 1912. "Ballad of a Wilful Woman," the last poem of the old cycle, he sets in the Rhineland, at Trier, where he waited on 11 May 1912 for Frieda to join him, leaving her family behind.[12]

"Bei Hennef" records the moment in early May 1912 when Lawrence made clear to himself and to Frieda, the nature of his attachment to her. He celebrated the moment in both poetry and prose; one sees in the following letter the prose equivalent of the poem (see app. L).

> Now, I am in Hennef—my last changing place. It is 8:30—and still an hour to wait. So I am sitting like a sad swain beside a nice, twittering little river, waiting for the twilight to drop, and my last train to come. I shan't get to Waldbröl till after 11:00—nine hours on the way—and that is the quickest it can be done. But it's a nice place, Hennef, nearly like England. It's getting dark. Now for the first time during today, my detachment leaves me, and I know I only love you. The rest is nothing at all. And the promise of life with you is all richness. Now I know.[13]

The place names on the poems that follow "Bei Hennef," through "Everlasting Flowers," trace Lawrence's wanderings with Frieda through Germany and Austria from the end of May to September 1912, when they reached Italy. He violated chronology obviously only once, when he included "A Doe at Evening," a poem written at Irschenhausen, where Lawrence and Frieda stayed in the summer of 1913, among the German poems written one year earlier. Why did he do so? The answer becomes apparent when we compare the sequence of the *Look!* poems with an actual record of Lawrence's travels during this period. He maintained only the illusion of chronology in *Look!* He actually arranged the poems, much as he did those in

"Rhyming Poems," according to thematic and mythic consid-
erations, sacrificing chronology whenever it hindered his larger
design.

Although in reality Lawrence and Frieda made several trips
to Germany during the years 1912–14, even returning to En-
gland in the summer of 1913 in an attempt to see Frieda's
children, Lawrence consolidated the poems set in Germany into
one series within the larger sequence of Look!, even as he did
the poems set in Italy and England that follow. Thus, the verse
depicts only one continuous Italian sojourn. "Spring Morning,"
set at San Gaudenzio and probably written during Lawrence's
stay there in April 1913, just before his first return to En-
gland,[14] provides a transition to all of the poems set in England.
The years 1913–14 merge in the poems "Wedlock," "History,'
and "Song of a Man Who Is Loved," just as the autumns and
winters spent in Italy during 1912–14 merged in the poetry.

In the remaining poems, Lawrence observed a more or less
accurate chronology. He set "One Woman to All Women" in
Kensington, where the Lawrences lodged in the summer of 1914,
following it with "New Heaven and Earth," placed at Greatham,
where they lived in the winter and spring of 1914/15. "Mani-
festo," set at Zennor, in Cornwall, dates from sometime in 1916.
We know that "Frost Flowers" was written at the end of winter
in 1916/17, as "Craving for Spring" must also have been.

We can see, then, that what appears to be a faithful
chronological account of the first two years of Lawrence's rela-
tionship with Frieda was significantly altered by Lawrence,
presumably to further his artistic ends. As in "Rhyming Po-
ems," art skillfully, silently, and often extensively reshaped
Lawrence's experience without appearing to do so.

The thematic structure of Look! is also well-defined. Law-
rence printed at the beginning of "Unrhyming Poems" a modi-
fied version of the Argument with which he introduced Look!,
as follows: "After much struggling and loss in love and in the
world of man, the protagonist throws in his lot with a woman
who is already married. Together they go into another country,
she perforce leaving her children behind. The conflict of love
and hate goes on between the man and the woman, and be-
tween these two and the world around them, till it reaches some

sort of conclusion." He eliminated from this version the last seven words of the original, which declare that the couple transcended "into some condition of blessedness." Apparently, by 1928, Lawrence had altered his estimate of the role of sexual union in self-transcendence. He now seemed content to regard it as what he calls in the foreword a "phase" in the development of the new self rather than its ultimate cause or conclusion.

Like its chronological organization, the thematic arrangement of *Look!* falls roughly into four parts. The first of these, which presents the husk of the old self and the old world, opens with a poem in which nature points the way to rebirth. The form and the setting of the poem, however, suggest the old order. The Keatsean "Moonrise," cast in blank verse, metaphorically connects sexual consummation with individual fulfillment. Like the other poems that introduce the *Look!* sequence, this poem is set at night, in a darkness broken only by the occasional moon. The speaker looks "beyond the grave" (i.e., to eternity), for self-realization. The self of "Elegy" and "Nonentity," plagued by the romantic dilemma of self-consciousness, longs for annihilation. He at once fears and hopes that self-transcendence may lie in his reabsorption into the world around him through death.

Lawrence followed these poems with a Swinburnean address to God as sleep, describing the self as a dream of grief. His martyrdom is ordained by laws of existence outside his ken. Both "Don Juan" and "The Sea" continue the cosmic setting of the earlier poems, all of which examine human life against vast natural forces that dwarf its significance but magnify its propensities. For example, the sea, like the self, is "all unloving, loveless"; it is "celibate and single, scorning a comrade even"; yet it takes "the moon as in a sieve" and rolls "the stars like jewels in [its] palm." "Hymn to Priapus" adopts a similarly vast perspective, presenting the self in the context of earthly existence and also the mythic world of the dead woman of the poem (who walks "the stark immortal / Fields of death") and Orion (who stands "looking down" from the constellations on the homeward journey of the speaker). Past, present, and future are equally present in the poem; the dying woman's "last long kiss," the dance at the Christmas party, the cold walk home, and the "stream of life in the darkness / Deathward set" occur simultaneously. So, too, "Ballad of a Wilful Woman," similar to some of Tennyson's ballads, defies conventional presentations of time and space as it follows the figure of the virgin mother on a series of fantastical journeys during which she tries out various mythic forms.[15] In the end, she renounces her privileged status to minister to the needs of one man, a beggar, sacrificing herself to him. "I give, whoever denies," she announces cryptically as she chooses the beggar over not only husband and children but her own dreams. With this symbolic choice of the real over the ideal, the new cycle of *Look!* can begin.

The second part of the sequence, that set in Germany, addresses thematically the struggle of two individuals to meet each other in the body in the present moment. The feeling of connection with each other and with nature is fleeting, as the poems "First Morning" and " 'And Oh—That the Man I Am Might Cease to Be —' " disclose. The past acts as a magnet to pull one away from the reality of the present, an idea that "She Looks Back" makes plain. In "Frohnleichnam," Lawrence presents the approach to union of the two lovers as a dance that moves "Out of indifference . . . / Out of mockery . . . / Out of sunshine into the shadow, / Passing across shadow into the sunlight, / Out of sunlight to shadow."

Moments of trust in and pure desire for the other (e.g., "On the Balcony") alternate with overwhelming fears: the fear of the unknown, glimpsed through the other (as in "In the Dark" and "A Young Wife"); the resistance to final commitment ("Mutilation"); and the hopelessness of life without the other, when even death offers no consolation ("Humiliation"). Yet the ecstasy of union, quite apart from "ulterior motives," such as the possiblity that one can discover a new world and a new self—indeed, even create new life in the form of a child, is enough to impel one towards the other, past all inhibition, as "Green" and the following cluster of "rose" poems demonstrate. The philosophy expressed here reflects that of the *Study of Thomas Hardy:* blossoming is all.

A further complication, however, exists in that the self must come into proper relation not just with the other, in this case the woman, but also with all nature. The self realizes his alienation from nature and his need to participate in its rhythms in "Song of a Man Who Is Not Loved," but cannot get past the immensity of the world: "How shall I flatter myself that I can do / Anything in such immensity? I am too / Little to count in the wind that drifts me through," he says in this poem, speaking for all men who have fallen out of relation with the universe. In "Everlasting Flowers," in a denial of the present moment, the self turns back to old loves, away from the new self to the old.

The third section of *Look!*, that set for the most part in autumn and winter in Italy, limns the dark fight for union: the prolonged, necessary battle of will and desire that occurs between individuals forging new life, existing as part of a universal pattern of purification through reduction. As the first poem in the series, "Sunday Afternoon in Italy," suggests, certain males and females are "fated" to be singled out for such a confrontation. They stand as champions for the race. Hate and love war in them and through them in a battle charted in the next three poems: "Winter Dawn," "A Bad Beginning," and "Why Does She Weep?" "Giorno Dei Morti" and "All Souls" show life balancing death in mysterious equilibrium. "Lady Wife" and "Both Sides of the Medal" show hate balancing love in analogous opposition. In the passionate friction between opposites, each of whom lusts for absolute power over the other, each self defines itself apart from conventional moral categories, reducing itself to its essential elements in a process similar to dying. Lawrence attempts to develop this parallel through the figures of the sacrificial dove in "New Year's Night" and the snared rabbit in "Rabbit Snared in the Night." The renewal that occurs is presented in terms of a new creation, where woman is born of man, her opposite (as in "Birth Night"), and man is delivered by woman from the "womb of time" (in "Elysium"). The pain of passion has fused the mind "down like a bead" and remoreseless hate has reduced the self to "calm incandescence," allowing male and female to reenter paradise on their own terms in "Paradise Re-entered." This dark flight has brought them through a ritual death to new individual life ("Spring Morning") and perfect union ("Wedlock").

The final series of poems from *Look!* is set in England during the war years. Lawrence juxtaposes poems describing the mating of opposites—male and female, love and hate—which results in "glorious equilibrium" and the experience of another world, with poems depicting an enervated England filled with unrealized selves. "Manifesto" expresses the speaker's philosophy and offers a challenge to all men to "detach themselves and become unique" so that we may all move "in freedom more than the angels, / conditioned only by our own pure single being, / having no laws but the laws of our own being . . . / We, the mystic NOW." In "Craving for Spring," the last poem in *Look!*, Lawrence questions whether the horror of the war raging in Europe may be the first throes of the fight for renewal, the stirring of new life in the "rotten globe of the world." If so, he says, "Oh, if it be true, and the living darkness of the blood of man is purpling with violets, / if the violets are coming out from under the rack of men, winter-rotten and fallen, / we shall have spring." Thematically, individual rebirth points to the possibility of the regeneration of all human society.

This theme is furthered by the pervasive light and dark imagery of *Look!* As mentioned earlier, the darkness that permeates the verse of the first part of the book does not lift until the second part, with the twilight of "Bei Hennef" and the dawn of "First Morning." Darkness symbolizes the desire for singleness and death in these poems; light signifies vital connection.[16] Continuing this symbolism, the remaining poems set in Germany, when the lovers veer between misery and ecstasy, occur in uncertain light. Those situated in Italy, portraying as they do the long fight that leads to union, begin and end in daylight, with all of the intervening poems set in profound darkness, lit only by fires that connote passion. In the English setting, Lawrence contrasts the dark, artifically lit external world of "People" and "Street Lamps" with the otherworldly light of the lovers in "New Heaven and Earth" and "Elysium." In "Craving for Spring," the speaker, aware of his own renewal, prays for a parallel regeneration of the world, forming his supplication in images that by this point in the sequence powerfully convey his message: "Let the darkness turn violet with rich dawn. / Let the darkness be warmed, warmed through to a ruddy violet, / Incipient purpling towards summer in the world of the heart of man."

As in the case of the chronologic and thematic structure of *Look!*, Lawrence also intimates its underlying mythic structure. He has organized the book on a cyclic, seasonal plan that begins in spring (after a few poems that end the old cycle, which are appropriately set in autumn and winter) and ends in winter. The last poem in the sequence, "Craving for Spring," which anticipates universal rebirth in society and nature, then serves as the transition to the final section of "Unrhyming Poems," which explores the way to transcendence. As the lover's struggle for union progresses, the seasons depicted in the poems shift, reflecting as they do the mood of each stage in the development of the relationship. The affair begins in spring and develops in summer in the German section of *Look!*; the bitter struggle in Italy occurs in autumn and winter. Rebirth occurs in spring as the couple leave the south to return to England, where they are wed in summer. The love matures in autumn. The death-experience of England is presented in a poem set in winter, with the speaker longing for spring.

The seasonal orientation of *Look!* continues that of "Rhyming Poems," which begins in spring and ends as winter approaches. It situates the maturing relationship of the lovers in a natural cycle of creation and destruction where renewal, growth, decay and dormancy regularly succeed each other in fruitful opposition. As in "Unrhyming Poems," Lawrence uses the seasonal cycle to suggest a mythic level in the verse. In *Look!*, however, appropriate to the increasingly manifest demon, Lawrence makes more apparent the parallel of the male and female with their mythic counterparts. Indeed, the male figure gains in stature as the sequence progresses. At its start a worldly Don Juan, the speaker nevertheless traces his inconstancy to a mythic origin: "Isis the mystery / Must be in love with me." He implies an incipient identification with Osiris, the brother, husband, and son of Isis, but makes clear that he is condemned to hell, without hope of resurrection. In the poem "Hymn to Priapus," originally called "Constancy of a Sort" in the version published in *The English Review* in September 1917, the speaker identifies with the vulgar Priapus, a lesser god of fertility in the Greek pantheon who presides over gardens and human genitalia. Heavy with grief over the death of his beloved, he is nevertheless capable of enjoying a "ripe, slack country lass" and of grinning and chuckling over his despair at his own faithlessness. "She Looks Back" draws the parallel between him and Lot/Orpheus. He would rescue his wife from the deathly past, but she resists, never quite turning herself in his direction. In "Mutilation," the speaker walks among the "broken wheat," his ache like "the agony of limbs cut off." This poem suggests the likeness of the lover cut off from his mate to the figure of Attis and the other vegetation gods, Adonis, Dionysos, and Osiris, in particular, whose sacrificial mutilation is part of the spring ritual that assures new life. We remember, as well, Christ, whose suffering and mutilation are preludes to his resurrection.

The group of rose poems in the second part of *Look!* connotes the figures of Adonis and Aphrodite, whose love is responsible for the red rose, according to legend.[17] (Thematically, the rose is reminiscent of the rose-tree that symbolizes new life in the final stanza of "Dreams: Nascent.") "A Youth Mowing," like many of the poems in this section, makes the connection basic to the worship of the vegetation gods: that between the corn harvest and human fertility. The youth, like the speaker of "A Doe at Evening," is identified with the stag, symbol of proud masculinity. As if to humble the male by making clear to him his subservience to nature and its designs, as well as to the female, who brings his seed to fruition, the female speaker of "Fireflies in the Corn" asserts the superiority of the grain to her lover. "The rye is taller than you, who think yourself / So high and mighty," she says. "O darling rye / How I adore you for your simple pride!"

In part three, the autumn and winter poems set in Italy, with their references to death and burial in "Giorno Dei Morti" and "All Soul's" and to dark, womblike enclosure in "New Year's Eve" and "Birth Night," evoke the ritual death and burial of the vegetation god, who lies dormant until spring. Lawrence implies rebirth through the comparison of the male to Adam in "Birth Night," "Paradise Re-entered," and "Elysium," and finally to the resurrected god in "New Heaven and Earth" and "Manifesto." Indeed, in the latter poem, the speaker claims to be "the son of man."

Lawrence establishes the female's mythic identity early in the *Look!* sequence, in "Ballad of a Wilful Woman." In this poem, the Frieda-like figure who eventually deserts her family tries out various identities: she is alternately Mary, Aphrodite, an angelic presence, and Cybele.[18] In the later poems, she becomes a fertility goddess wooing the corn in "Fireflies in the

Corn"; a figure like Lot's wife or Eurydice in "She Looks Back"; and a new Eve in "Paradise Re-entered." In "Lady Wife," the speaker of the poem, in a mundane mood, expresses exasperation with the mythic dimensions of his mate, as the woman has done earlier in "Fireflies in the Corn." He cries out: "Rise up and go, I have no use for you / And your blithe, glad mien. / No angels here, for me no goddesses, / Nor any Queen." Yet he himself invests her with full mythic significance in poems such as "Birth Night," "Paradise Re-entered," "Elysium," "New Heaven and Earth," and "Manifesto." The female becomes the other in all its mystery, delivering the male from "the monstrous womb / Of time from out of which I come."

In *Look!*, Lawrence uses all of the poetic forms that he employs in "Rhyming Poems." We most frequently find subjective poems, whose primary aim is self-discovery: for example, "Bei Hennef," "Mutilation," "Wedlock," and "New Heaven and Earth." Many of the poems are dedicatory, often similar to the subjective poems in their reflective tone but different in that they address specifically another person and explore the love relationship. "Rose of All the World," "Frohnleichnam," "Everlasting Flowers," "All Souls," and "Spring Morning" fit comfortably into this category. Lawrence also includes several fictional, or imaginative, poems in *Look!* As in "Rhyming Poems," they advance the thematic and mythic structure of the collection: consider, for example, "Ballad of a Wilful Woman," "A Youth Mowing," and "Sunday Afternoon in Italy." Poems such as "Fireflies in the Corn" and "One Woman to All Women," which are essentially monologues of a female speaker, can also be classified as fictional. In addition, Lawrence creates two dialogue poems for this volume: "In the Dark" and "She Said as Well to Me," which call to mind "Violets" or "A Passing Bell" from "Rhyming Poems." These *Look!* poems, however, have a direct connection with Lawrence's life that the latter do not share. In their exploration of his and Frieda's love relationship, the *Look!* dialogue poems are closer to the dedicatory poems of this volume.

"Green," "Gloire de Dijon," and "People" are clearly descriptive poems, although one finds this form occurring far less in *Look!* than in "Rhyming Poems," owing to the subject matter of the former. Many of the shorter lyrics, such as "New

Year's Eve" and "Autumn Rain," have a strong symbolic element of the sort found in some of the poems published in *New Poems* and *Bay*. Like "Going Back," originally published in *Bay*, these poems that on one level seem purely descriptive use a common thing like fire, rain, or a train in a verbal context that weights it with a significance far beyond its particular meaning. When Lawrence writes in "New Year's Eve," "There are only two things now, / The great black night scooped out / And this fireglow," he does more than describe a particular setting; he pronounces what seem to be elemental truths. The sequential nature of the *Look!* poems augments this symbolic aspect of the poems because a symbol tends to recur in several poems, gaining resonance each time. Obversely, the symbols themselves augment sequential unity.

As he admits in the note, Lawrence did little rewriting of *Look!* for *Collected Poems*. He—or quite possibly the printer—makes punctuation changes in some of the poems, by far the largest number of revisions for "Unrhyming Poems." A few times, he corrected an infelicitous word or phrase, as in the last stanza of "December Night," where he changed the word "feet" to "limbs" in the penultimate line: "I will warm your feet with kisses;" in the fourth and seventh stanzas, respectively, of "Paradise Re-entered," he emends "our awful embraces" to "our awed embraces" and "our earthy covers" to "our earthly covers." Such changes are infrequent and usually reveal little about Lawrence's method of composition or his development as a poet. He forgoes even the usual title changes for *Collected Poems*, perhaps because he frequently retitled poems for *Look!*[19]

When earlier versions of the poems exist, either in manuscript or published form, they usually reveal extensive revision before their publication in *Look!* Such is the case of "Moonrise" and "The Sea," which form a single poem in manuscript 19; "Martyr à la Mode"; "Ballad of a Wilful Woman"; and "People" and "Street Lamps," both of which exist in manuscripts 5 and 19 as one poem. Most often, however, early drafts of the *Look!* poems do not remain, not because they never existed but because Lawrence probably destroyed them.[20] Of the sixty-one poems first published in *Look!* (excluding the four Lawrence added to the sequence in *Collected Poems*), thirty-eight have no extant version other than the published one. Lawrence did make final changes in the proofs of *Look!*, which have been preserved, but these are not extensive revisions of the sort one always finds in early drafts of his poetry.

"People" and "Street Lamps," for example, are early poems compared to most others in *Look!*, dating from manuscripts 5 and 19, in which they form a single poem called "The Street-Lamps." Lawrence has rewritten the first and fourth stanzas of the original poem of six stanzas and given them an independent existence as "People." The remaining stanzas he forms into "Street Lamps" for *Look!* (see app. M). The revision of this early poem into the two poems in *Look!* reveals the extent to which Lawrence overhauled the early verse, not only for *Look!* but also for *New Poems* and *Bay,* the two volumes that followed its publication. Although the central image of the manuscripts 5 and 19 poems—the luminous globes of the street lights, from which issue the many metaphors of the poem—remains the same in the *Look!* poems derived from these drafts, what Lawrence makes of the image differs greatly from early to late versions. Both early poems are love poems. The street lights remind the speaker of and lead him to his beloved in various ways: in both poems, they call to mind the breasts of his beloved; they act as balloons to his desire; they swarm to her, like golden flies. In *Look!*, "People" and "Street Lamps" become social criticism. In the first poem, the street lamps reveal the deathly, meaningless faces of the passers-by on a city street. In "Street Lamps," the globes have exploded like rotten fruit, scattering luminous seeds that hold the promise of new life.

One of the few poems written specifically for *Look!* for which an early draft survives is "Elysium." Lawrence copied or composed the draft on one of the covers of a notebook that contains a draft of *Women in Love*. It demonstrates to some extent the method of revision that Lawrence employed in his composition of the new verse for *Look!* (see app. N).

Typical of the incorporation of *Look!* into "Unrhyming Poems," Lawrence revised the poem no further before its publication in the latter volume. Of course, we have no way of knowing how many drafts of this poem preceded or followed the one draft that remains. Lawrence considerably lengthened the poem for *Look!*, increasing it from eight to twelve stanzas.

The manuscript 31 version is the speaker's account of his discovery of a new world through blood knowledge. Mental consciousness, which involves the eye, in particular, plays no part in his discovery of a paradisaic world—thus the title of this manuscript, "The Blind." The poem concludes with his perfect, silent, dark union with the other, Eve. Through its first seven stanzas, "Elysium" closely follows "The Blind." Then Lawrence develops the idea of consummation, only abstractly referred to in the two drafts of the final stanza of "The Blind." In this poem, Eve acts as midwife to the speaker, delivering him from the old world and the old self through her touch.

In both these revisions, as in the others still extant, we see that the demands of Lawrence's final plan for *Look!* determines to a large extent the final form of the poem. He converts "Street Lamps" from a long, metaphor-filled love poem to two short, focused criticisms of contemporary society that further the plea of *Look!* for the regeneration of all mankind. "Elysium" goes beyond a description of blood consciousness, which Lawrence had already described in some of the *Amores* poems, to a symbolic statement of the need of the individual for a new world, to be found through new modes of perceiving and relating to reality.

Lawrence's proposed titles for *Look!* reflect an increasingly broad perspective. Lawrence replaced the autobiographical *Poems of a Married Man* with the generic *Man and Woman*, which focuses attention on the theory of sexual relationship that underlies the volume. *Look! We Have Come Through!*, unlike the earlier titles, shifts our attention to the process of regeneration being described, tempting us to theorize that as his design for the volume took shape, Lawrence saw ever larger implications in his personal experience. Exactly when the idea of organizing *Collected Poems* as the complete story of both the old and new self occurred to Lawrence, no one can say, but *Look!* gives every sign of being its prototype. Here one finds, fully developed, a chronologic, thematic, and mythic plan that, with a certain amount of ingenuity, Lawrence could extend to the rest of his poems when he collected them ten years later. Incorporating as they do a developed philosophical point of view that continues to hold good, Lawrence saw no point in revising the poems from *Look!* in any substantial way. He altered the original sequence only to insert four poems that enhance it. Conceptual, formal, and technical changes in the verse are minimal. When we consider the few changes that Lawrence made in the first part of "Unrhyming Poems," we can scarcely accuse him of tampering with his verse. Here, as in "Rhyming Poems," the primary purpose of Lawrence's revisions was to allow the demon "to have his say." The conclusion that follows from our study of the revisions for *Collected Poems* thus far is obvious: by 1917, the demon had taken over.

8. Red-Wolf Meets Star-Road: *Birds, Beasts and Flowers* as Demonic Revelation

Lawrence spent three years writing the poems published in 1923 in *Birds, Beasts and Flowers,* the book that concludes *Collected Poems.* By its position in the collection, Lawrence signaled its importance to the structure and meaning of *Collected Poems* and to his own poetic career. This book elucidates the final coil of what the note and the foreword to *Collected Poems* describe as the cycle of experience; it reveals a "life" experience as opposed to a "death" experience by presenting the new self, now fully manifest, in his proper relationship with the cosmos. This essential self shows itself through the body of "mere man," as Lawrence phrases it in the foreword, but originates in the unknown, or unconscious, forming a link between the individual and all that is other than himself. Because the demon, or ghost—i.e., the essential self—has assumed control of both art and life by the writing of *Birds, Beasts and Flowers,* the poems elicit the condition that produced them: what Lawrence has called the "third reality," or "third thing," a concept discussed more fully above, in chapter 1. It is a state generated by the coexisting realities of life and death. He explains this notion in "The Crown" in a way helpful to our understanding of *Birds, Beasts and Flowers:* "While we live, we are balanced between the flux of life and the flux of death. All the while our bodies are being composed and decomposed. But while every man fully lives, all the time the two streams keep fusing into the third reality, of real creation."[1] In this last section of "Unrhyming Poems," the poet through his poems evokes creation. In them, he explores the intrinsic condition of all that exists. Consequently, as Lawrence says in the foreword, these poems—like the creatures that form their subject matter—"are what they are": essential and unchangeable.

In a mythic manner, Lawrence thus explained why, although he has altered the first volume of *Collected Poems* extensively, he has made few revisions of the books that compose the second volume. We infer from this statement what his correspondence makes explicit: Lawrence considered these his best poems.[2] Consequently, he feels no need to alter them. The only significant change that Lawrence made as he incorporated them into "Unrhyming Poems" was to include with them the Tortoise poems, first published by Thomas Seltzer in 1921. Far from making this change expressly for *Collected Poems,* however, Lawrence had previously included *Tortoises* in the first English edition of *Birds, Beasts and Flowers,* published within one month of the American edition. One finds occasional punctuation differences between *Birds, Beasts and Flowers* and "Unrhyming Poems," as well as the correction in the latter of what appear to have been printer's errors in the original.[3] These differences do not significantly alter the verse, nor do they reveal anything about Lawrence's poetic development or his plan for *Collected Poems.* More revealing in this connection is how little Lawrence changed these poems for *Collected Poems.* The organization of *Birds, Beasts and Flowers* and, even more importantly, its content, suggest the design of *Collected Poems.* Both this volume and *Look!* no doubt served as the model and provided the impetus for Lawrence's chronologic, thematic, and mythic arrangement of *Collected Poems:* thus, the few changes needed for their incorporation into "Unrhyming Poems" and the many required for the books included in "Rhyming Poems."

Quite obviously, Lawrence arranged the poems in *Look!* chronologically and thematically. The mythic organization of the poems, although less apparent, reveals itself through the titles and juxtaposition of poems as well as through their allusions and images. Arranged as it is by subject, *Birds, Beasts and Flowers* depends far less obviously upon chronology, either of composition or experience, than does *Look!* As we shall see, however, Lawrence did arrange his poems with the dates of their composition in mind, although other considerations sometimes took precedence in the design of *Birds, Beasts and Flowers.* Indeed, not only the chronologic but also the thematic and mythic arrangement of the book easily eludes the reader. Most critics who reviewed the book upon either its first publication in 1923 or its reissue in *Collected Poems* in 1928 regarded it as a collection of descriptive poems, a "Wonder-Zoo," as one reviewer put it, and "the lighter harvest of travel," according to another.[4] In an apparent effort to correct such misinterpretations, Lawrence wrote prefaces, nine in number, for each of the groups of poems in the collection when the Cresset Press published it in 1930 in an expensive, illustrated edition.[5] These prefaces direct the reader to the thematic and mythic content of the volume.

More recent critics of Lawrence's poetry have come to realize that the organization of *Birds, Beasts and Flowers* is far less dictated by subject matter than seems to be the case, looking at the titles of the sections into which the poems are divided. That Lawrence ended the section "Fruits," for example, with poems called "The Revolutionary," "The Evening Land," and "Peace" alerts us to some other, less obvious organizational principle. George Y. Trail and Sandra Gilbert explore aspects of the chronologic, thematic, and mythic structure of the book in their respective articles, "West by East: The Psycho-Geography of *Birds, Beasts and Flowers*" and "Hell on Earth: *Birds, Beasts and Flowers* as Subversive Narrative."[6] While much of what they say supports my view of Lawrence's plan for *Collected Poems,* their consideration of *Birds, Beasts and Flowers* apart from Lawrence's earlier poetry leads to uncertainties about Lawrence's creative purpose and, at times, misconstructions of the meaning of particular poems or groups of poems. For example, Sandra Gilbert openly admits her puzzlement over whether Lawrence planned the narrative structure she discerns in *Birds, Beasts and Flowers.* "Did Lawrence actually intend *Birds, Beasts and Flowers* to have the narrative and allusive coherence I am suggesting it has?" she asks. "I think that is hard to say."[7] In fact, she does not say. Trail's interpretation also suffers from too limited a view of the poems. Taken out of the context of *Collected Poems,* he feels free to interpret *Birds, Beasts and Flowers* as a flight from the destructive feminine, which permits Lawrence to integrate psychologically the threatened and threatening masculine. According to Trail, in this book Lawrence projects himself as a "leader of men in a womanless world," moving toward a new order of civilization.[8] Knowledge of *Collected Poems,* pervaded as it is with the sub-

ject of male/female relationship, prevents one from interpreting
Lawrence's often sharp criticisms of the modern female as a
blanket rejection of the feminine, and from confusing what
Lawrence says about sexual opposition, which he regards as
positive, with such criticisms.

The scholarly work that has been done on the structure of
Birds, Beasts and Flowers, meager as it is, points to the conclu-
sion that this volume can only be rightly viewed in the context
of *Collected Poems.* Its fullest significance emerges only when
one understands that Lawrence came to see the book as the
culmination of his poetic expression and self-revelation. His
plan for *Collected Poems* sharpened his understanding of the
particular volumes contained in it, including this one. His over-
all design of *Birds, Beasts and Flowers* unfolded bit by bit, as I
shall show, gradually expanding to encompass all of his poetry
written to that point. Lawrence was still elaborating upon his
design in 1930, when he prepared the prefaces for the Cresset
edition of *Birds, Beasts and Flowers.* As Lawrence then realized,
without the earlier poems, this last volume could not be rightly
understood, just as the early verse remains incomplete when
viewed in isolation. When we see how *Birds, Beasts and
Flowers* fits into the total design of *Collected Poems,* we under-
stand both works better.

In the note to *Collected Poems,* Lawrence specifically refers
to the chronological orientation of the volume, implying its link
with the earlier poetry as the last part of the biography of the
self. He concludes the note as follows: "The poems of *Birds,
Beasts and Flowers* were begun in Tuscany, in the autumn of
1920, and finished in New Mexico in 1923, in my thirty-eighth
year. So that from first to last these poems [the entire *Collected
Poems*] cover all but twenty years." In the foreword, Lawrence
asserts that his poems "hang together in a life," stressing that
"the same me" wrote both early and late poems. Clearly, by
1928, Lawrence had come to regard *Birds, Beasts and Flowers*
as the last stage in the revelation of the self that began in "The
Wild Common."

Lawrence did not originally conceive of *Birds, Beasts and
Flowers* as a depiction of his literal and symbolic journey from
the old to the new world and from the old to the new self,
although he came to regard it as such. On 7 March 1921 he

wrote that he had just finished the book, which he had apparently divided into three sections, as the title would suggest.[9] Six months later, he asked his agent, Curtis Brown, to include three more poems in the "Beasts" section of the book, for which Brown was still trying to find a publisher.[10] By November 1921, however, Lawrence had received Mabel Dodge Luhan's invitation to go to Taos and by January 1922 had made the decision to travel to New Mexico by way of Ceylon, where his friends the Brewsters were living. The plan to extend and reorganize *Birds, Beasts and Flowers* to include the creatures he encountered in his travels as well as his further spiritual progress probably occurred to Lawrence sometime during the journey itself. In any case, within one month of his arrival in New Mexico, Lawrence was composing poems based on his American experience for inclusion in the volume.[11] Already written were "Elephant" and "Kangaroo," based on his Eastern experience. By early February 1923, he sent Seltzer the completed manuscript.[12]

If we cannot determine exactly when Lawrence decided to shape *Birds, Beasts and Flowers* around his journey from Europe to America, we can trace in his letters his growing awareness of the symbolic dimension of such a journey. Even when he first considered emigrating to America during the war years, Lawrence conceived of the move as a symbolic shaking off of the old life and putting on of the new. His ideas are far more elaborate by January 1922, when he writes to Brewster that his imminent trip to the United States is a way of embracing "the clamorous future." Only in struggle, he maintains, that is, in "the fight and the sorrow and the loss of blood," can men "fight a way for the new incarnation." This effort to flesh the gods in human form, he implies, can best be made in the United States, which is further advanced in corruption than is Europe.[13] When he alters his travel plans, deciding to go west via the east, Lawrence explains to Brewster the symbolic nature of his decision: "Probably there, east, is the *source:* and America is the extreme periphery. Oh God, must one go to the extreme limit, then to come back?"[14] Writing to Lady Cynthia Asquith from shipboard, on his way to Australia, Lawrence describes himself as a wanderer "like Virgil in the shades."[15] This mythic allusion suggests that Lawrence regarded himself as a bearer of life, the one vital man among the multitudinous dead, in search of the land of the living. By *Birds, Beasts and Flowers,* he had partially charted the journey to the new life, which he completed, as I have suggested, in *Collected Poems.*

In an essay called "New Mexico," written in 1928 at approximately the same time that he was collecting his poems, Lawrence recalls the spiritual impact of his move to the new world. What he writes about the transition from one world to another and from one self to another is worth quoting at length, if for no other reason than that it shows us that by the time of *Collected Poems* Lawrence had become fully conscious of the symbolic nature of his journey.

> I think New Mexico was the greatest experience from the outside world that I have ever had. It certainly changed me forever. Curious as it may sound, it was New Mexico that liberated me from the present era of civilization, the great era of material and mechanical development. Months spent in holy Kandy, in Ceylon, the holy of holies of southern Buddhism, had not touched the great psyche of materialism and idealism which dominated me. And years, even in the exquisite beauty of Sicily, right among the old Greek paganism that still lives there, had not shattered the essential Christianity on which my character was established. Australia was a sort of dream or trance, like being under a spell, the self remaining unchanged, so long as the trance did not last too long. Tahiti, in a mere glimpse, repelled me: so did California, after a stay of a few weeks. There seemed a strange brutality in the spirit of the western coast, and I felt: O, let me get away!
>
> But the moment I saw the brilliant, proud morning shine high up over the deserts of Santa Fe, something stood still in my soul, and I started to attend. There was a certain magnificence in the high-up day, a certain eagle-like royalty, so different from the equally pure, equally pristine and lovely morning of Australia, which is so soft, so utterly pure in its softness, and betrayed by green parrot flying. But in the lovely morning of Australia one went into a dream. In the magnificent fierce morning of New Mexico one sprang awake, a new part of the soul woke up suddenly, and the old world gave way to a new. [16]

Here, Lawrence describes in prose the process of spiritual transformation precipitated by nature that he recreates poetically in *Birds, Beasts and Flowers.*

In spite of the inwardness of many of the poems in *Birds,*

Beasts and Flowers, concerned as they are with the state of mind of the speaker and reflective as well of his mood, Lawrence called attention to the animate and inanimate existences that form the subjects of most of these poems and, moreover, situated most of them in particular places in the outside world. Why did Lawrence so carefully objectify these poems that are anything but objective? They are filled with the contentious, often mocking voice that opens the collection: "You tell me I am wrong. / Who are you, who is anybody to tell me I am wrong? / I am not wrong." It closes the book, as well:

> Is that you, American Eagle?
>
> Or are you the goose that lays the golden egg?
> Which is just a stone to anyone asking for meat.
> And are you going to go on for ever
> Laying that golden egg,
> That addled golden egg?

Indeed, far from dealing with "the otherness of birds, beasts and flowers primarily for their own sake," as Sandra Gilbert maintains they do,[17] these poems consider their subjects primarily for the speaker's sake. The answer, I believe, to the question why Lawrence points so insistently to the world outside and, in some sense, antithetical to his consciousness lies, first of all, in his desire to suggest the dynamic interaction of man with nature that can lead experientially to spiritual regeneration. It also stems from his desire to show the speaker's unfolding awareness of the cosmic context of human life, which sharpens his moral perceptions and explains and confirms his obligation to challenge the values of other men. Finally, it reflects the mythic identification of the demonic self with all that is other than the particular self. Ultimately, Lawrence uses nature to know himself, as we shall see.

Like those that end the poems in *Look!,* the place names appended to the poems in *Birds, Beasts and Flowers* suggest an itinerary of Lawrence's travels from 1920, when he first started working on *Birds, Beasts and Flowers,* through 1923, when he finished it. True, the chronology of the itinerary does not bear close scrutiny, as a comparison of it with Lawrence's letters and the diary he kept during these years discloses.[18] In his correspondence, in particular, Lawrence frequently mentions the individual poems in this volume, especially those that he was preparing to publish in periodicals—no small number: twenty-two were published before their inclusion in *Birds, Beasts and Flowers,* several in more than one periodical. Consequently, even when he did not date a poem in manuscript, a fairly accurate assessment of the date of composition of most of the poems in the volume is possible, as Keith Sagar has demonstrated.[19] Without too much effort, we can see when the order of the poems in *Birds, Beasts and Flowers* reflects the order of their composition or of the experience they depict. The poem "Humming-Bird" provides an interesting example of how Lawrence altered actual chronology to foster the illusion of it. As Trail points out, Lawrence falsified the dateline on this poem, which he wrote in Italy and published in *The New Republic* in May 1921, yet situated in Española, a town in New Mexico, when he published it otherwise unchanged in *Birds, Beasts and Flowers.*[20] Apparently, Lawrence made this change to avoid the discrepancy of placing as part of the European experience a poem describing a bird indigenous only to the Western Hemisphere. Other exceptions to the chronological arrangement of the poems are the rule in this collection. For example, "Mosquito," which Sagar identifies as the first poem in the book to be completed, stands midway through the collection. Several poems about the New Mexico experience precede others about Italy (as in the case of the last three poems in "Birds" and the first two in "Animals"), challenging even the illusion of chronology. We are compelled to conclude that chronology was not Lawrence's first concern in his arrangement of the poems in this volume. Nevertheless, as both Trail and Gilbert point out, the general arrangement of the verse unequivocally suggests Lawrence's eastward journey from Italy, by way of Ceylon and Australia, to New Mexico. This broad chronology provides indispensible support for the thematic and mythic organization of the volume.

Even though certain themes and mythic allusions are evident in the poems completed by March 1921, when Lawrence considered, if only temporarily, the book finished, the generic organization of the poems predominates. Judging from the presence in all the poems of a voice that challenges convention, the reader infers that Lawrence must have determined from its inception that the book would have certain unifying elements

beyond subject matter alone, chief among them being tone and
point of view. "The Revolutionary," among the first poems
written for *Birds, Beasts and Flowers* and the first in the book
to deviate obviously from its proclaimed subject matter, serves
as a clear indication that, even from its earliest stages, Lawrence
intended to connect the poems thematically and mythically, if
not chronologically. When he finally conceived of the idea of
connecting the poems geographically and experientially, Law-
rence no doubt realized how easily he could extend the concept
of revolution already implicit in the work to include his perverse
journey to the new world and the new self. By literally turning
his narrator the wrong way in relation to his goal, he could
underscore and indeed indicate the rebellious stance often taken
by him. In its final form, the speaker of *Birds, Beasts and
Flowers* uniformly moves against established modes of thought
and action on all levels. The geographical paradox that one may
arrive west by traveling east supports the thematic paradox that
one may discover full humanness by experiencing the inhuman,
and the mythic paradox that one may find new life by relin-
quishing the old. Moreover, it provides an image for the move-
ment of the demon in human life, which we have heretofore
only obliquely observed in "Rhyming Poems" and the first half
of "Unrhyming Poems." The demonic element in human life,
which drives one to reject conventional definitions of reality,
and in particular of the self, results, as we have seen, in the
development of a demonic anti-self who consistently rejects the
accepted way. Indeed, the demon is the quintessential revolu-
tionary who seeks always to overturn and renew life from
beneath.

   That such is the real subject of *Birds, Beasts and Flowers* is
substantiated by the prefaces that Lawrence wrote for the Cres-
set Press edition of *Birds, Beasts and Flowers*. These direct us to
specific themes and myths in the poems. Through them we can
easily identify pervasive themes, such as the necessity of strife to
the existence of all things, as well as specific themes, such as the
fundamental nature of sexual opposition or the vitiation of the
white race and its gods. Lawrence considers a wide range of
controversial topics in this book, attacking, for example, vari-
ous political systems (democracy, socialism, and communism, in
particular); female rights; industrialization; and organized reli-

gion. The prefaces also make us aware of the mythic allusions in many of the poems. Specifically, we find frequent references to the pagan underworld of Dis (Hades) and its ruler or lord Dis (Pluto). We also find explicit references to its denizens Persephone, Orpheus, and Dionysos, who descend into the infernal regions but return alive. Connected to them through his blindness, which intitiates him into a dark world that parallels Dis, is the Christian hero Samson. Opposed to these are various gods of light, for example Horus, the Egyptian god of day.

By means of these prefaces, Lawrence points as well to the influence of early Greek thought on the content of *Birds, Beasts and Flowers*. As Pinto and Roberts indicated when they reprinted the prefaces in the *Complete Poems,* they include a large number of quotations from John Burnet's *Early Greek Philosophy,* which Lawrence first read in Cornwall around 1916.[21] In its emphasis on oneness in opposition and on daimonic possession, the verse in *Birds, Beasts and Flowers* in particular and in *Collected Poems* as a whole owes a debt to Heraclitus. From Empedocles, Lawrence may have derived the core idea of *Birds, Beasts and Flowers* and the *Collected Poems:* i.e., the poet as immortal daimon. Also present in Empedocles is the emphasis on blood as the primary seat of perception as well as the idea that the indestructible elements of nature mix, unmix, and remix in eternal flux.[22] In general, the language and content of these prefaces, frequently mythic and strongly atavistic, recall the content of the earlier verse and anticipate that of *Birds, Beasts and Flowers*. Only in that which is very old, Lawrence intimates in these prefaces and poems, do we find the most new. Existence is cyclic, turning serpentlike upon itself, tail in mouth.

The preface called "Fruits" directs us to the dominant theme in this first section of *Birds, Beasts and Flowers:* the limits of sexuality as the way to knowledge; in particular, the limited role of the female as initiator of the male into new life. To understand this section, consequently, we must recall the thematic content of *Look!* as well as of certain of the earlier poems, which explore the vital role that the female does play in bringing the male to blood consciousness. Here, Lawrence qualifies this role but he does not negate it. As *Psychoanalysis* and *Fantasia* also claim, sexuality offers the first sustained experience of otherness, but one cannot stop there, making sex an end in itself. Otherwise, the soul will atrophy and die, crucified by passion. As Lawrence writes in *Fantasia:* "There can be no successful sex union unless the greater hope of purposive constructive activity fires the soul of the man all the time: or the hope of passionate, purposive *destructive* activity: the two amount religiously to the same thing, within the individual."[23]

The imagery of the poems in "Fruits" conveys a message similar to that developed by Lawrence in the penultimate chapter of *Fantasia.* The fissure in the pomegranate, peach, and fig suggest the "female part"—"the wonderful moist conductivity towards the centre." In the words of *Fantasia,* the woman, "polarized downwards, towards the centre of the earth," leads the man downwards, away from "the sun and the day's activity," toward which he is naturally polarized.[24] In the verse, this center becomes hell and the man who journeys toward it becomes an Orpheus or a Dionysos. In "Medlars and Sorb-Apples," we see the male brought into the underworld by a female but fated to find his own way out. This lonely journey, far from terrifying him, as it had in the earlier poetry, delights him. As Sandra Gilbert says in "Hell on Earth," the underworld that the speaker of this poem and subsequent ones experiences strengthens and transforms him.[25] The following lines from "Medlars and Sorb-Apples" describe the process of purification initiated by the descent into the darkness of immediate experience.

> Going down the strange lanes of hell, more and
>   more intensely alone,
> The fibres of the heart parting one after the other
> And yet the soul continuing, naked-footed, ever more
>   vividly embodied
> Like a flame blown whiter and whiter
> In a deeper and deeper darkness
> Ever more exquisite, distilled in separation.

The man must leave the woman behind as he forges into the unknown, presumably because she refuses to follow him, seeing the darkness as sufficient in itself. Now we see why the speaker of "Sickness' in "Rhyming Poems" makes no progress in the hellish underworld to which he is drawn. He looks back to the female to console him instead of making his own way into an unknown that appears to be meaningless because the mind cannot know it. In this poem, the senses lead the way into new knowledge, forbidden by the mind but embraced by the blood.

The speaker of "Figs" delivers a lecture to modern women, whose self-consciousness and self-righteousness betray them into flouting their "secret": i.e., their initiatory sexuality. Rivaling men, they seek the sun, refusing to see that the denial of inwardness means death, both for them and for men, who achieve inwardness through them. He continues his diatribe in "Grapes," eschewing "the universe of the unfolded rose, / The explicit / The candid revelation." The way into life, he says, is an inward way, the way of tendrilled touch that our "open-countenanced, skyward-smiling" age has forgotten but may be about to re-remember, if we will only let ourselves. Instead, we resist the dreams of night that the fruit of the vine brings upon us. Indeed, says the speaker, even America—the evening land— has "gone dry," prohibiting any except sterile brews, so fearful is she of the forgotten world of our ancestors. In its concluding lines, "Grapes" urges each of us to begin the hellish journey:

> Dusky are the avenues of wine,
> And we must cross the frontiers, though we will not,
> Of the lost, fern-scented world:
> Take the fern-seed on our lips,
> Close the eyes, and go
> Down the tendrilled avenues of wine and the otherworld.

To do so, says the poem, we must close our eyes, or in other words, pass beyond mental consciousness; we must take on our lips the fern-seed, or transcend sexuality, as the fern-seed, symbol of asexual reproduction, suggests; and we must cross the frontiers into the world before the floods, when dark and evasive men flourished, i.e., we must pass beyond good and evil according to conventional morality.

While both "Figs" and "Grapes" contain vivid descriptions of the fruits whose name they bear, these poems, like many of the others in *Birds, Beasts and Flowers,* are primarily social criticism, aimed here most obviously at women but no less at a society whose fault of self-betrayal they share. Thematically, these poems join with the three that follow, "The Revolutionary," "The Evening Land," and "Peace," to insist upon the need for change in all areas of human life. Donald Davie hits the mark when he calls Lawrence not only a poetical but also a political revolutionary.[26]

Still in mythic form, the demon speaks in "The Revolutionary," now in the guise of a blind Samson, who tugs at the pillars of "pale-face authority." He predicts the eventual overthrow of our civilization, product of the vitiated white race and its ideals. When our world crumbles, he will move freely, assuming his rightful role as "Lord of the dark and moving hosts." To hasten that time, the narrator of "The Evening Land" contemplates a journey to America, where a false dawn presages the real one to follow. In its advanced corruption, America promises soon to burst open, scattering the seeds that will regenerate mankind. In America, land of "nascent demon people," the demon will come into his own. As "Peace," the last poem in the section, reveals, the only way out of stagnation is nature's way: upheaval.

"Fruits" establishes the tenor of *Birds, Beasts and Flowers*. Not only does it pose the fundamental question of the volume: what way leads to new life?, but it also suggests that Lawrence will develop the answer to a large extent through myth and emblem. Assuming as does the whole of *Birds, Beasts and Flowers* the applicability of myth to all human experience and the correspondence of one part of creation to all its other parts and to the whole, the poems in the first section allude mythically to the rebellious act of tasting forbidden fruit and, as a consequence, of falling into a hellish order of existence; and the fruits that are their subjects serve as emblems of multiple orders of reality, and in particular, of human existence.

The first section, moreover, serves to introduce us to the bold voice that narrates the poems. We can recognize in this voice, more strident now, the voice that celebrates substance in "The Wild Common," delights in the homunculus in "Virgin Youth," and berates his beloved in "Lady Wife." It opens *Birds, Beasts and Flowers* with the challenge to authority in the opening lines of "Pomegranate," the invitation to opposition in "Peach," and the defiance of salubrity in "Medlars and Sorb-Apples." It instructs us in unorthodoxy in "Figs" and seduces us into immorality in "Grapes." This voice sounds through the subsequent sections of the book, expressing beyond mistaking the recusancy of the anti-self on matters involving manners and morals, but also disclosing his full participation in and assent to the natural order of life, however bewildering it may be to the mind of the ordinary self.

The form of the poems in "Fruits," as well, is typical of that of most of the poems in *Birds, Beasts and Flowers*. Lawrence uses variations on the lyric form that he has named "subjective" in the note and which I have suggested bears a close resemblance to the form that M. H. Abrams calls "The Greater Romantic Lyric." Keeping this paradigm in mind helps us to appreciate the discipline of Lawrence's approach to his material as well as his strong ties to the romantic tradition in English poetry. According to Abrams, poems in this mode

> present a determinate speaker in a particularized, and usually a localized, outdoor setting, whom we overhear as he carries on, in fluent vernacular which rises easily to a more formal speech, a sustained colloquy, sometimes with himself or with the outer scene, but more frequently with a silent human auditor, present or absent. The speaker begins with a description of the landscape; an aspect or change of aspect in the landscape evokes a varied but integral process of memory, thought, anticipation, and feeling which remains closely intervolved with the outer scene. In the course of this meditation the lyric speaker achieves an insight, faces up to a tragic loss, comes to a moral decision, or resolves an emotional problem. Often the poem rounds upon itself to end where it began, at the outer scene, but with an altered mood and deepened understanding which is the result of the intervening meditation.[27]

As Abrams goes on to point out, physical description is subordinated to meditation, which is "sustained, continuous, and highly serious."[28] The tone of the poem is usually one of "profound sadness, sometimes bordering on the anguish of terror or despair, at the sense of loss, dereliction, isolation, or inner death, which is presented as inherent in the condition of the speaker's existence."[29] This form allows Lawrence to express and explore what can best be understood as a spiritual crisis. Like Coleridge before him, he uses this lyric form to attempt "the reintegration of the divided self (of 'head and heart') and the simultaneous healing of the breach between the ego and the alien other (of 'subject and object')."[30] As in "Medlars and Sorb-Apples," the greater romantic lyric form allows the speaker free passage between subjective and objective worlds, implying a correspondence between them and permitting insights on one level to apply as well to the other.

"Fruits," then, launches both speaker and reader on the voyage to self-discovery. The preface to "Trees" expands upon the thematic and mythic content of "Fruits." It emphasizes the secret knowledge that communication with the underworld can bring, once one has tasted its fruits. Standing as reminders, or emblems, of an ancient order, trees are the creatures of hell propelled upwards by an excess of heat. They witness to us of the dark world before day was distinguished from night, i.e., before consciousness was split, if we understand "day" and "night" symbolically, as Lawrence instructs us to do in *Fantasia*.[31] Undivided in their consciousness and sexuality, trees represent blood knowledge and their fruit, our way to it.

The individual poems in this section of the book explore the secrets of trees, now almost inaccessible to modern men, communicated as they are through "dark thoughts / For which the language is lost." The poet serves as intermediary in these poems, most obviously in "Cypresses," where he invokes the "spirits of the lost" so that they may speak through him and instruct the living. Through his priestly role, he initiates us into the perverse world of the demon. In "Cypresses," we learn the secret of morality: "Evil, what is evil? / There is only one evil, to deny life / As Rome denied Etruria / And mechanical America Montezuma still." The Cypress trees, monuments to the dead Etruscans, release this secret knowledge entrusted to them by "those that have not survived, the darkly lost." On the basis of this revelation, we are left to reevaluate the morality of our own civilization as well as that of the "silenced races" with their "abominations."

In a similar way, "Bare Fig-Trees" causes us to reevaluate our ideals and institutions, as well. This tree challenges our ideal of equality and the democratic institutions common to the western world, suggesting that true democracy is "a weird Demos, where every twig is the arch twig, / Each imperiously over-equal to each, equality over-reaching itself." Like the twig on the fig-tree, the individual should regard himself as "the one and only," free to forge ahead of others as if he "were the leader, the main-stem, the forerunner." What unites these individuals in a governmental unit? The speaker suggests a solution to this "equality puzzle" of the fig-tree: the demon unites men, for he exists in and guides each member of the true democracy. The secret of good government (and here Lawrence extends his idea of correspondence to language itself) lies in the recognition of the "demon" in "democracy."

In a special way, these poems suggest, trees reveal the secrets of the universe and, in particular, the demonic plan for human life. The final tree poem, "Bare Almond-Trees," whimsically depicts the tree as a cosmic telegraph, an emblem of intercourse between opposites as it picks up and transmits messages between the heights and the depths of the universe. Furthermore, trees reveal to the initiate the way to spiritual transformation. As the last two poems of the section, "Tropic" and "Southern Night," consider, this way consists of identification with the lost or subjugated dark races, who, like the trees themselves, connect to the underworld through "the flood of black heat that rolls upward" through them. The way is a dark way, called "evil" by the white races; it is open only to those who dare be impure and risk anathema.

The preface to 'Flowers" focuses our attention on the theme of regeneration, situating human rebirth in the context of seasonal regeneration. Both "Almond Blossom" and "Purple Anemones" stress that rebirth must occur from within and beneath (i.e., from the senses and the blood, not from mental consciousness or will). Mythically, Lawrence develops this theme by telling us in both these poems that flowers, the first signs of spring, are in truth the gifts of hell. Pluto gives them to the earth, we learn in "Purple Anemones"; they are, moreover, truly hellish gifts, prompted by cruelty rather than love. Sent in pursuit of the escaped Persephone, flowers are living emblems of the demonic force that at once renews life and inevitably pursues it, always reclaiming it in the end. To understand birth properly, we must recognize the universal exchange between life and death. This exchange occurs throughout history, as "Sicilian Cyclamens" and "Hibiscus and Salvia Flowers" illustrate. In the first poem, the speaker contemplates the beginning of consciousness and of civilization as we know it. In the second, he anticipates its destruction, which he sees as necessary and inevitable according to the demonic laws of life. Assuming that the old order must be destroyed, the question how remains. Contemplating the potential of the Socialists and Communists to wreak such destruction, the speaker of the poems despairs of their ability to bring the end about cleanly, through fire, by which Lawrence means revolution. The way of slow decay, or moral corruption, is their way, he decides. Although he realizes that the "slow watery rotting back to level muck / And final humus" will suffice, he nevertheless condemns the incongruity of the emblems the Socialists wear, the vivid red flowers of the hibiscus and salvia bushes. They are indeed symbols of destruction, but of hellish destruction that consumes to "flame-clean ash."

The next section of *Birds, Beasts and Flowers,* "The Evangelistic Beasts," takes up the subject of religion, only hinted at previously in references to the pale gods of the modern world and their dark counterparts of ancient times. As the preface explains, these beasts, once powerful creations of man's religious impulse, have lost their vitality. The man, Saint Matthew, torn between spirit and flesh, is exhausted. Domesticated by his responsibility for the lamb, the lion, Saint Mark, has settled down to a comfortable existence. Self-sacrifice has emasculated the bull, Saint Luke. The eagle, Saint John, bound by an empty Word, has lost interest in soaring and wants only to hatch a new idea. Lawrence lets us know that the Christian ideal, once compelling, has lost its power. The evangelistic beasts manifest this decline. As Lawrence points out in *Apocalypse,* they represent "a process of degradation or personification of a great old concept."[32] He explains, also in *Apocalypse,* that the beasts were originally part of a grand concept, older perhaps than even God himself. "They belong to the last age of the living cosmos, the cosmos that was not created, that had yet no god in it because it was in itself utterly divine and primal." Man progressively robbed them of independent life, subordinating them first to God, then personifying them. As the preface to this section of *Birds, Beasts and Flowers* states, man has lost some of his life in robbing the beasts of theirs: "When the heavens are empty . . . sleep is empty too."

In "Creatures," however, we see the true, vital creatures of darkness, vividly contrasting with the dying evangelistic beasts of the night skies. These are the things that "love darkness," as the preface states, whether the absence of light, as with the bat; the darkness of blood, as in the case of the mosquito; or the darkness of sensation, as with the fish. Confronting them in their perfect otherness, the speaker knows his limits. As he says in "Fish": "And I said to my heart, *there are limits / To you, my heart; / And to the one God. / Fish are beyond me.*" the revulsion he feels in the presence of such otherness, which refuses personification, amounts to terror in his confrontation with the bat in "Man and Bat." Otherness may not be impinged upon, even though the speaker's first impulse is to strike out, indeed to kill, as he does to the mosquito and the fish, and is tempted to do to the bat. Yet he realizes that killing, while not wrong in itself, is no solution to antipathy. "Bats must be bats," he decides. These poems, juxtaposed as they are to "The Evangelistic Beasts," reveal that one must recognize other creatures and other gods beyond human range, for life filled only with man denies reality and robs life of the awe and majesty of the unknown. Man and the other will always be in opposition, yet from this enmity rises the demonic zest of life. Through the demon, we can learn to tolerate otherness, seeing in it the preservation of the world, even though it will always be inherently antipathetic to us. Through the demon, we can learn to relate to the other in what Lawrence calls creative opposition. Thus, in "Man and Bat," having recognized and pitted himself against the bat, the victorious speaker can choose either to kill or to release him. Releasing the bat to his own element, the darkness, the speaker can exult in his proven superiority: "*There he sits, the long loud one! / But I am greater than he . . . / I escaped him.*"

The theme of vital antipathy continues in "Reptiles," as the preface confirms. "In the tension of opposites all things have their being—" we read. "Snake" shows the speaker once again ready to kill without confrontation. Responding to the demonic voice, he hesitates; the voices of his "accursed human education" urge him on, tempting him to assert his ego and deny the antipathetic relationship which would allow serpent and man to exist in mutual recognition of each other or else define themselves in strife. Much has been made of the subconscious fear of sexual intercourse conveyed by this scene, emphasizing as it does the speaker's mingled horror and fascination as the snake enters the "horrid black hole," "the earth lipped fissure," returning to "the burning bowels of the earth." His response, I believe, arises not from the suggestion of vaginal intercourse between male and female, but of anal intercourse between males. This his educated mind cannot abide. Yet the demonic consciousness refuses to reject even this approach to the underworld. Paralleling the tension between him and the snake, the internal strife that the speaker endures is just as enriching as his recognition of the creature's otherness. Vitality arises from such elemental struggles, the poem implies. From them comes the deep awareness of self and of life.

The sequence of tortoise poems fully develops the central role of opposition, especially the strife involved in sexuality, in the experience of all animate life. According to the preface, the tortoise is "the first of creatures to stand upon his toes." The forerunner of animate life, he bears on his back the "outward and visible indication of the plan within," the chart that reveals the "foundation of the world." Life's secrets are encoded there in a kind of mystical mathematics, first interpreted by Pythagoras, that reveals itself also emblematically, as a cross.

Born to walk alone, absolute in isolation, the adult tortoise, with no apparent need of communication, finds voice in the torment of his sexuality. Observing the mating of tortoises, the speaker of the poem cries out, "Why were we crucified into sex? Why were we not left rounded off, and finished in ourselves, / As we began, / As he certainly began, so perfectly alone?" Yet, watching, he feels that "the last plasm of [his] body was melted back / To the primeval rudiments of life, and the secret." All of life begins here, he sees, with the first abandonment of the self. First comes the tearing apart, then the consequent search for wholeness, and finally the movement when that which is in part finds "its whole again throughout the universe." Sex points to the deeper secret of our need not only for strife and separation but also for connection. As these poems demonstrate, connection can be established only after suffering and an experience of individual destruction akin to death, as the deaths and resurrections of Christ and Osiris show us mythically. The irresistible search for union may begin with sex, says this poem, but it must lead us through psychic and even physical dissolution to a new wholeness. He who has mastered death, writes Lawrence in *Apocalypse*, has "final power over the powers below." He is "master of the future, and the god of the present. He gives the vision of what was, and is, and shall be."[33] In this sequence of six poems, the central mystery of *Collected Poems,* the necessity of both separation and connection, is codified.

The man who would be whole must find himself in the darkness, stripping himself of his "nervous and personal consciousness."[34] Only then will he be able to look to the sky and face the sun, the begetter of vital activity. In *Apocalypse,* Lawrence describes this process of self-discovery, depicted artistically in *The Man Who Died* and *Birds, Beasts and Flowers.*

> The sun has a great blazing consciousness, and I have a little blazing consciousness. When I can strip myself of the trash of personal feelings and ideas, and get down to my naked sun-self, then the sun and I can commune by the hour, the blazing interchange, and he gives me life, sunlife, and I send him a little new brightness from the world of bright blood . . . . There is an eternal vital correspondence between our blood and the sun.[35]

In the next section of *Birds, Beasts and Flowers,* the speaker questions the initiates of light, the birds who, as the preface to this section tells us, serve as intermediaries between the earth and sky. He contemplates in turn the turkey cock, sacred bird of the Toltecs; the hummingbird, sun-hero in Mexican mythology; the eagle, "sun-starter" and attendant of the gods; and the blue jay, self-proclaimed aristocrat of birds. Will it fall to one of these birds, he wonders, to wake the new dawn and rouse us with it? Not likely! concludes the narrator. Three perch arrogantly and complacently, unable or unwilling to soar, while the fourth, the hummingbird, has dwindled in the modern age to insignificance. The god-thrust enters them from below, not above; they are still dark, unready for dawn. The speaker concludes that birds, like men, have lost their godliness; like men, they themselves seem in need of an intermediary to bring them into connection with the living cosmos.

How can creatures get past themselves, into connection with the central mystery of life, which, in the end, lies within them but outside them, too? This central question of *Birds, Beasts and Flowers* is posed once more in the preface to "Animals." Creatures differ radically, one from another: can we do more than project ourselves onto each other? Can any creature escape the "degradation" of personification? In "Animals," the

speaker of the poems realizes that not only man has made a leap
for the sun, trying for connection and for purposive activity.
The ass has tried and failed, dragged down by "love," which
refuses to recognize opposition and change. He has capitulated
to sexuality, making of it an end, yet he cannot forget the true
end of life. For man, the ass is the emblem of "everlasting
lament in everlasting desire," the living reminder of one who
tries for ultimate connection but falls short. "He-Goat" also
provides us with a lesson for human existence: life without
enmity robs us of the ability to test our limitations and to ratify
ourselves. Without struggle, only libidinousness is left. The he-
goat shows the potential for vitality of self-will pitted against
divine will, yet, domesticated, he cannot realize his will. In one
way or another, all of the creatures that the speaker studies are
enslaved either to themselves or to others: the she-goat to her
self-conscious sexuality; the elephant to his patient, mountai-
nous blood and his unbelief; the kangaroo to her inwardness;
and the dog to his lack of discrimination. Only in "Mountain
Lion" do we catch sight of one of the animals who has success-
fully remained aloof from man and thereby avoided corruption.
Even in death—a death caused by man, "the only animal in the
world to fear"—she is beyond corruption; her bright face still
shimmers with vitality.

In each of these poems, man's corruptive influence on all
creatures is implicit, as is Lawrence's assumption that man has
ultimate power over and responsibility for the well-being of all
animals. He domesticates beasts, taming their otherness; he re-
wards their slavishness; he annihilates those that resist him and
patronizes those that do not (even the speaker caters to the
corrupted tastes of the gentle kangaroo, feeding her peppermint
drops). From these poems, we conclude that a creature who is
only a creature and a man who is only a man denies the god in
him and consequently lacks life and purpose. A world known
only by the senses or by the mind loses mystery and meaning.
Understanding this lesson, learned from nature herself, the
speaker has reached the end of understanding.

The final poem of this section, "The Red Wolf," culminates
Collected Poems. In this religious poem about transfiguration,
the poet comes face to face with the true subject of the entire
work: his demon. The speaker tells us that he followed the sun to

its final setting, tracking it "from the dawn through the east, / Trotting east and east and east till the sun himself went home." In this way, Lawrence sums up the thrust of his life and his art: his dogged denial of the expected way, his fascination with ultimates, and his exploration of the primeval origins of his personality and his culture. In the desert, the traditional scene of religious confrontation with otherness, he meets a shrouded Indian who calls himself "Old Harry" and "Old Nick," colloquial names for the devil, and observes, sitting in the Indian's shadow, a red wolf. At first, Indian and paleface resist each other, warning each other off in enmity. But, slowly approaching each other, they finally touch, accepting each other as blood brothers. As we see in the following passage, which concludes the poem, the Indian tells the speaker his secret name: Red-Wolf. The Indian then reveals his own hidden name: Star-Road.

> Across the pueblo river
> That dark old demon and I
> Thus say a few words to each other
>
> And wolf, he calls me, and red,
> I call him no names.
> He says, however, he is Star-Road.
> I say he can go back the same gait.
>
> As for me . . .
> Since I trotted at the tail of the sun as far as ever
>   the creature went west,
> And I lost him here,
> I'm going to sit down on my tail right here
> And wait for him to come back with a new story.
> I'm the red wolf, says the dark old father.
> All right, the red-dawn-wolf I am.

What the speaker confronts in the desert twilight is himself as other. This primary confrontation unites him with his demonic self and through him with all creatures, represented totemically by the red wolf. Aware now of his true identity and accepting it, he acknowledges his role of forerunner. His part is to await the new dawn so that he can wake all men to it. Unlike the royal prince in "Elephant," who desires only to serve, he will now assume the burden of leadership that the lords of life must bear.

Written around the time of *Aaron's Rod, Kangaroo,* and
The Plumed Serpent, the so-called leadership novels, the poems
of *Birds, Beasts and Flowers* share the concerns of the prose of
the period. In all of them, Lawrence makes the same point: a
leader of men must emerge, a man of vision and firm will who
dares to be more than himself in order to awaken others from
their trancelike servitude to defunct institutions and moribund
ideals. Only thus can life and the cosmos be revitalized. Does
Lawrence see himself as such a one? Is he a Don Ramón, who
dares to be the living Quetzalcoatl? *Collected Poems* leaves no
room for doubt. Of course, as the foreword to *Collected Poems*
makes clear, he does not fancy the commonplace, "ordinary
meal-time" Lawrence to be such a leader. But the demonic voice
that fumes in the poetry—can we deny that Lawrence con-
sidered him his "spark of divinity"?[36] His artistic task parallels
Don Ramón's political task, which is "to bring the great oppo-
sites into contact and into unison again."[37] The ability to act as
intermediary, according to Lawrence in *The Plumed Serpent,* is
the "god-power" in man.

"The Lords of Life are the Masters of Death," sings Huit-
zilopochtli in *The Plumed Serpent.* Lawrence has named the last
section of *Birds, Beasts and Flowers,* appropriately enough,
"Ghosts." The dead include the men of New Mexico, who
"amazed and mad with somnambulism" think that "death will
awaken something," as well as the women whom he once loved,
now dead or lost to him, whom the speaker summons home, to
his heart, desiring a final, true marriage with the feminine.[38]
"Autumn in Taos" reveals that to the man united with his
demon, the man who is more than man, the world is alive, filled
with presences. As he rides, he passes "betwixt the slopes of the
golden / Great and glistening-feathered legs of the hawk of Ho-
rus," or sometimes under the "hairy belly of a great black
bear." The poet now participates in the old symbolic mind of
the "purely religious," described in *Apocalypse.*[39] The symbolic
creatures have not yet been revivified, however. Before their
nerves can revive, the demon must lead men to new life. "The
American Eagle," the last poem in the book, appeals to Ameri-
cans to assume the leadership that is theirs and lift the "rabbit-
blood of the myriads up into something splendid." Characteris-
tically, the demon ends the volume with spiteful satire, venting

his wrath on docile, complacent men who refuse to rise to life's challenges and claim life's riches.

Birds, Beasts and Flowers, which began in autumn with "Fruits," progressed through winter in "Trees," emerged into spring in "Flowers," and sustained summer through its subsequent sections, comes full circle in "Ghosts" to conclude in autumn. Thus, the seasonal orientation of the book supports its protagonist's cyclic journey from east to west, suggesting through its form an endless succession of new horizons as well as of births, deaths, and rebirths. As we have seen, the seasonal arrangement of material also characterizes *Look!* and, indeed, the entire first volume of *Collected Poems.* No doubt, Lawrence extended a seasonal orientation to "Rhyming Poems" to stress the mythic dimension of those poems. *Birds, Beasts and Flowers,* however, is the only volume in *Collected Poems* that returns upon itself, evoking the recurring death and eternal return of the mythic hero. For the book entirely devoted to the new self, this arrangement is particularly appropriate. Yet, viewed in the larger context of *Collected Poems,* which begins in spring and ends in autumn, *Birds, Beasts and Flowers* represents the end of a linear and thus singular movement from birth to death of the "mere man" whose historical experience both books recount. In this seamless way, myth and history merge in the structure of *Collected Poems.* Life carries the "meal-time" Lawrence inexorably toward death while the demonic Lawrence lives on in the myth he has used his "god-power" to create. His art is Lawrence's bright gift of life to us. Through his art and the life that made it and moves through it, Lawrence teaches us that any vital person must make myths; they are our way to truth and wholeness.

9. The Demon at Large: His Presence in *The Plumed Serpent* Hymns, *Pansies*, *Nettles* and *Last Poems*

Collected Poems initiates us into the secret of Lawrence's art and life: his "spark of divinity." The revelation of the demonic self continues in the poetry that Lawrence wrote after that collected in 1928. Certainly, Lawrence's chronological account of his discovery of the new self ends with *Birds, Beasts and Flowers;* nevertheless, the demon appears in the thematic and mythic content of the poems from *The Plumed Serpent* and in *Pansies, Nettles,* and the posthumously published *Last Poems,* including "More Pansies."

The poems from *The Plumed Serpent,* first drafted in the months immediately following the completion of *Birds, Beasts and Flowers,* depend upon the larger structure of the novel for their full significance, just as *Birds, Beasts and Flowers* reveals its deepest meaning in the framework of Lawrence's life. The hymns are the products of Don Ramón, who writes them, then arranges for their printing and distribution. Here is a foreshadowing of Lawrence's own experience; he soon took upon himself the publication and distribution of several of his last books, including the unexpurgated edition of *Pansies.* Like *Birds, Beasts and Flowers,* the hymns of Don Ramón reveal the essence of the man who wrote them: his divine spark and godlike aspect. The identification of both men with mythic personages is conscious. They perceive themselves as apotheoses of the "god force" in humans. Unlike Lawrence, however, Don Ramón has undertaken a political and religious mission that identifies him with a particular manifestation of the divine. In the hymns, he speaks out boldly as the returned Quetzalcoatl, who has risen anew in order to exchange places with an exhausted Christ. The horrified Doña Carlota explains her husband's intentions as follows: "He wants to destroy even Jesus and the Blessed Virgin, for this people. . . . He says he wants to make a new connection between the people and God. He says himself, God is always God. But man loses his connection with God. And then he can never recover it again unless some new Saviour comes to give him his new connection. And every new connection is different from the last, though God is always God. And now, Ramón says, the people have lost God. And the Saviour cannot lead them to Him any more. There must be a new Saviour with a new vision."[1] Doña Carlota sees her husband's mission as diabolical; she is not wrong in her interpretation, although her lack of appreciation of the demonic provokes Lawrence's unwavering scorn.

In the second hymn, Don Ramón calls the resurrected Quetzalcoatl "The Lord of the Morning Star," a name that signifies that he is a new god who rules in the twilight, bridging the opposites of day and night, water and earth.[2] In "Old Archangels," one of the poems from "More Pansies," Lawrence associates Lucifer also with the Morning Star: "It is Lucifer's turn, the turn of the Son of Morning / to sway the earth of men, / the Morning Star." As is Star-Road in *Birds, Beasts and Flowers*, Quetzalcoatl, too, is the demon in one of his many forms. According to another of the hymns, he is "Lord of the Two Ways." In his demonic nature, he transcends the duality of the universe, uniting all things. "Out of the depths of the sky, I came like an eagle," Quetzalcoatl sings in one of the last songs. "Out of the bowels of the earth like a snake."

The demon's message in the Quetzalcoatl hymns is more than metaphysical. He preaches political and social revolution, similar to that advanced in *Birds, Beasts and Flowers*. If the men of Mexico refuse to purify themselves, purging their land first of all its machines and the foreign overseers who have brought them, he will destroy the Mexicans and their land. This apocalyptic message persists in the fourth hymn, "What Quetzalcoatl Saw in Mexico." Here, in a voice reminiscent of that of certain of the *Birds, Beasts and Flowers* poems and anticipatory of the satiric tone of *Pansies*, Quetzalcoatl lambasts the watery-hearted Mexicans and peons, enslaved to modern technology: "Lo! you inert ones," he warns, "I will set the dragons upon you. / They shall crunch your bones. / And even then they shall

spit you out, as broken-haunched dogs, / You shall have no-
where to die into."

Once the god has proclaimed his salvational purpose, he
manifests himself to the faithful through ritual conducted by his
avatars: Don Ramón who manifests Quetzalcoatl himself; Cip-
riano, the living Huitzilopochtli; and Kate, the living Malintzi.
Don Ramón explains to Kate the mystery of his own identity:

> "There must be manifestations. We *must* change back to the
> vision of the living cosmos; we *must*. The oldest Pan is in us, and
> he will not be denied. In cold blood and in hot blood both, we
> must make the change. That is how man is made. I accept the
> *must* from the oldest Pan in my soul and from the newest *me*.
> Once a man gathers his whole soul together and arrives at a
> conclusion the time of alternatives has gone. I *must*. No more
> than that. I *am* the First Man of Quetzalcoatl. I am Quetzalcoatl
> himself, if you like. A manifestation, as well as a man. I accept
> myself entire, and proceed to make destiny. Why, what else can I
> do?"[3]

Lawrence tells us that Cipriano embodies the mystery of the
primeval world. His is the face "at once of a god and a devil,
the undying Pan face"; his mystery is "the ancient phallic mys-
tery."[4] Kate recognizes Cipriano as her "demon lover." He
knows himself to be the living Huitzilopochtli, god of purifica-
tion and doom.

In Kate's struggle to accept herself as more than a "meal-
time" woman, more than Kate Forrester, the drama of *The
Plumed Serpent* lies. Her struggle to realize her divinity, to cast
off the old self, parallels that of the young Lawrence in "Rhym-
ing Poems." Her conscious mind resists her unconscious sym-
pathy with and understanding of the religious destiny of her
lover, Cipriano, and her friend, Don Ramón. To become Ma-
lintzi is to acknowledge her halfness—i.e., her need for the
male, which parallels his for her. "[Is] the individual an illu-
sion?" she asks herself.[5] Under Cipriano's influence, she experi-
ences the goddess in her, becoming for one night "the goddess
bride, Malintzi of the green dress."[6] Like Lawrence during the
period recounted in *Look!*, Kate finds herself caught between
two selves, "one, a new one . . . the other hard and finished,
accomplished, belonging to her mother, her children, England,
her whole past."[7] She takes the first steps towards the new self

at the close of the novel, but still has the long process of "coming through" ahead of her. Lawrence intimates that Kate, "a wise woman," will in time come through in her own way, by her own road, to new life.

The fictional depiction in *The Plumed Serpent* of the demon incarnate in the individual no doubt contributed to Lawrence's conscious recognition of the same force at work in his own life. *Collected Poems* allowed him the chance to chart its course in his personal experience. To have included *The Plumed Serpent* hymns in *Collected Poems,* however, would have been an anomaly. The hymns and the best poems in *Collected Poems* share the assumption that they are the work of the demon; the themes thus mythically presented also often resemble each other. Nevertheless, the hymns disembodied from the novel lack their full meaning, as would *Collected Poems* detached from the orienting context of Lawrence's biography.

After the composition of *Birds, Beasts and Flowers* and *The Plumed Serpent,* over five years elapsed before Lawrence published more verse. A similar hiatus had occurred between the composition of *Look!* and *Birds, Beasts and Flowers.* (I exclude *New Poems* and *Bay* because, as I have discussed earlier, most of the poems in these books were revisions of poems composed much earler.) Lawrence, of course, continued to write. Out of this period came memorable prose: the three versions of *Lady Chatterley's Lover,* which expand upon some of the ideas on sexuality introduced in *The Plumed Serpent* (e.g., "the greater sex, that could fill all the world with lustre," shared by Cipriano and Kate; *The Escaped Cock,* Lawrence's parable of resurrection; and "The Woman Who Rode Away" and other short stories published in the collection of that title. During this period, Lawrence also painted.

In the last two years of his life, Lawrence returned to poetry. It is not unlikely that the experience of revising for *Collected Poems* rekindled his versifying. He started writing *pensées,* as he first called these new poems, around the time that he finished *Collected Poems,* copying them into two extant notebooks. The first of these contains drafts of numerous poems later published in *Pansies* (Ferrier calls this notebook manuscript 79); the second includes early versions of several poems from *Pansies,* most of the verse published in revised form in *Nettles,* and the previously unpublished poems that Richard Aldington collected in "More Pansies" (Aldington calls this notebook manuscript B). Probably during the last year of his life, Lawrence copied yet more poetry into a third notebook that Aldington has named manuscript A, even though it almost certainly contains later work than does manuscript B. These poems became *Last Poems.*

It is instructive, and even necessary, I believe, to examine Lawrence's late poetry from the perspective of *Collected Poems,* keeping in mind what his revisions for this collection reveal about the development of his thought and art. Undeniably, the verse written immediately after *Collected Poems* evinces little of the lyrical quality that characterizes the best in *Collected Poems,* although Lawrence eventually returned to the lyrical mode in the poems in manuscript A. But as we shall see, the poems in *Pansies* and *Nettles,* as well as those poems in manuscripts A and B, share overriding themes with the poems in *Collected Poems.* They also further, each in its own way, Lawrence's mythic plan for *Collected Poems:* they continue to allow the demon to "say his say" through his "body of mere man," which Lawrence has given him in *Collected Poems.* In other words, Lawrence carried out in the late poetry what he defined in *Collected Poems* as his demonic task: to reveal to others the way past death to new life.

In considering Lawrence's revision of the later verse in the light of his changes for *Collected Poems,* one perceives the same creative process underway: Lawrence revised primarily for image and idea, and he continued to rewrite problematic material so thoroughly that the result was often a new poem. Analysis of representative manuscript versions of Lawrence's late poetry also supports the conclusion reached after analysis of drafts of the earlier poetry: Lawrence was a careful artist. And, finally, study of his revisions of the later poetry reveals what Lawrence's burning of the rough drafts of the poems in *Look!* and *Birds, Beasts and Flowers* denied us: a glimpse of the mature poet at work.

As in the case of *Collected Poems,* Lawrence wrote two prefaces to *Pansies,* a short foreword for the expurgated Secker edition of July 1929 and a longer introduction for the privately printed definitive edition issued in August 1929 (but dated June of that year). In the latter preface, Lawrence tells his readers that his title derives from words meaning "to think" and "to dress or soothe a wound." Using language congruent with his ideas on blood knowledge, Lawrence speaks of each poem as "a thought, not a bare idea or an opinion or a didactic statement, but a true thought, which comes as much from the heart and genitals as from the head." These poems, then, in Lawrence's view, issue from the whole person, not just the self-conscious mind.

Lawrence expresses his ideas on thought more fully in "Introduction to Pictures," written around March 1929 but unpublished in his lifetime. In this essay, which E. W. Tedlock suggests is probably an abandoned introduction to the reproductions of Lawrence's paintings,[8] Lawrence condemns the "self-aware-of-itself" unless it is "controlled by the divine, or demonish sanity which is greater than itself."[9] He goes on in this essay to explain in detail how true consciousness arises and of what it consists. Here, once again, Lawrence expands upon the idea of blood knowledge, relating it specifically to the demon, who bestows "vital sanity" (called "demonish sanity" as well) upon the individual.[10]

Does Lawrence conciously intend for us to read *Pansies* as the work of the demon? That conclusion seems inescapable considering the many poems in the collection that have sanity as their subject or imparting a sane point of view as their object. A sane point of view implies a divine perspective. Lawrence declares as much in "God": "Where sanity is, there God is." In other words, sanity is the state conducive to the divine, or demonic, and subsequent to it. I would suggest that the pervasive theme in *Pansies* is how the individual can achieve sanity in a world where a "mutilated social consciousness" renders everything insane. Near the end of the book, his message delivered, Lawrence enjoins the reader (of the definitive edition, at any rate) to "Be a Demon!" Because he is the only savior left us, Lawrence implies, it would be mad not to!

As he had in the preface to *Collected Poems*, Lawrence tells us in the introduction to *Pansies* to view this collection as a whole, although not as a collection of poems, per se. He writes, "[The pansies] are thoughts which run through the modern mind and body, each having its own separate existence, yet each of them combining with all the others to make up a complete state of mind." In these poems, Lawrence suggests, we will hear the demonic voice speaking through the verse, assessing human life from a divine perspective in order to heal "the mental and emotional wounds we suffer from." But these are hellish flowers as well as healing ones, he hastens to add in both the introduction and the foreword. Like the flowers of *Birds, Beasts and Flowers,* these have their roots in "earth and manure"; their faces wear a look "maybe Mephistophelian." Is it accidental that the name of the goat god, Pan, forerunner of Satan, as Lawrence has called him,[11] lies hidden in his title? Moreover, Lawrence must have relished the sexual ambiguity that the word connotes. "Live and let live, and each pansy will tip you its separate wink," says Lawrence slyly in the introduction. Lawrence of the satyric face winks, too.

Besides its demonic voice, *Pansies* shares another important similarity with *Collected Poems.* In the foreword to *Pansies,* Lawrence makes a claim similar to that made for certain of the poems in *Collected Poems.* In fact, he echoes his caveat of "Poetry of the Present" by warning his readers not to expect perfection. Instead, he promises, the pansies will make up in vitality what they lack in elegance. "I don't want everlasting flowers," he writes in the foreword. These poems breathe instead "the breath of the moment." Yet, as with *Collected Poems,* one would be mistaken to assume that these poems are either spontaneously composed or arbitrarily ordered.

From the extant manuscripts and typescripts that contain drafts of the poems from *Pansies,* we can form some idea of how extensively and frequently Lawrence rewrote "this little bunch of fragments," as he slightingly calls them in his introduction. Tedlock describes at length the holograph notebook in which Lawrence copied out drafts of the poems (i.e., manuscript 79).[12] These poems often differ markedly from their printed texts. Yet, judging from a group of *Pansies* also preserved at the beginning of manuscript B, Lawrence had already revised the verse, sometimes extensively, before he made fair copies of it in manuscript 79. "I am Well-off" in manuscript B, which Lawrence retitled "Wealth" in manuscript 79 (see App. O), suggests how thoroughly Lawrence rewrote the poems in *Pansies* before he copied them into manuscript 79.[13]

As his letters of this period indicate, Lawrence took advantage of every opportunity to revise *Pansies*. When several versions of one poem exist, they differ conspicuously more often than not. The manuscript B revision of "I am Well-off" is unusual in that Lawrence remained content with it long enough to copy it almost verbatim into manuscript 79, changing only its title. By its final publication in *Pansies,* however, he had changed the poem again, rewriting it according to a pattern that is typical of many extant revisions for this book. The most important consequence of his final revision is that he had developed a unifying image for the poem. Clearly, Lawrence's propensity in the early verse to proliferate images continued. Nevertheless, by the final version of this poem, he had settled on a metaphor that brings together the disparate images of earlier drafts. The image of the tree, rooted in the unknown and leafed in the beyond, allows him to explore coherently, but in a new way, his idea that well-being comes from the unconscious connection of the self with the other in its various manifestations. He also rephrased his idea that peace emanates from a center both within and without the individual to correspond with his apparently new enthusiasm for modern atomic theory, reflected in many of the *Pansies* poems (e.g., "Relativity" and "Sun in Me"). As he was wont to do in rewriting, Lawrence lengthened the poem, but only by two lines.

One perceives that same pattern of revision in the three extant versions of "Fidelity," a far longer poem (see app. P). Like many of the other poems in *Pansies,* "Fidelity" is a polemical poem that attempts to redefine for our age an abstraction whose meaning has become distorted and, consequently, life-denying. In this poem, as in the book as a whole, Lawrence attempts to purify language, purging it of unwholesome associations by aligning it with reality as he conceives it. As his introduction indicates, Lawrence saw such a task as essential to thinking and living well. The published version of "Fidelity" implicitly dismisses conventional notions of fidelity as willed by the conscious mind, prompted by duty, loyalty, or religious considerations. The poem explicitly denies that love necessarily involves fidelity, although it asserts that the latter presumes the former. Like love, fidelity forms beyond consciousness, the result of passionate feeling that, despite its transitory nature, can provoke the long struggle that paradoxically results in fidelity. Lawrence amplified similar ideas on love in "A Propos of *Lady Chatterley's Lover*," composed during the last half of 1929.[14]

The three versions of "Fidelity," written perforce within a relatively short space of time, demonstrate Lawrence's increasingly effective attempts to communicate through images his ideas on love and fidelity. In manuscript 79 and the revised typescript designated by Ferrier as transcript 80, the poem makes fundamental distinctions between love and fidelity but fails to develop their connections as does the final version of the poem: specifically, their mutual origin in the unconscious; their shared flux; their causality. In both manuscript 79 and transcript 80, Lawrence depends upon the likeness in shape of his metaphors for love and fidelity, the flower and the loving cup, respectively, to suggest the similarities of these abstractions.

Lawrence revises the poem extensively in transcript 80. Although he keeps the same basic metaphors, he replaces his former emphasis on knowledge as the source of permanence in human relationships with an assertion that the human heart itself outlasts fleeting emotions, generating over time the peace of fidelity. Almost doubling the length of the poem in transcript 80, Lawrence dwells upon the similarity of the heart to an ancient rock and of fidelity to a crystal.

By the final version of the poem, Lawrence is ready to dispense with the now superfluous metaphor of fidelity as a loving cup. He replaces it with the image of the gem, formed by terrific pressures beneath the earth's surface. Expanding the poem once again, he now develops his original metaphor of love as a flower, establishing its bright, momentary nature. He then contrasts with the "coloured gesture" of love the "slow flowing of the sapphire," which approximates permanence. In the last two stanzas of the poem, Lawrence uses imagery to clarify his view of human nature, first introduced into the poem in its transcript 80 version. Man and woman are like the earth, with soil above and rock beneath. As flowers spring from the upper earth, gems form beneath, produced by natural processes that Lawrence personifies as "wild orgasms of chaos." Thus, Lawrence prepares us through metaphor to accept the image of love's orgasms producing the "hard jewel of trust, the sapphire of fidelity" in the "ancient, once-more molten rocks / of two human hearts."

As in the case of most of the revisions for *Pansies,* Lawrence has gradually worked his way through the drafts of "Fidelity" to coherent, unified images that reflect his view that human and physical nature correspond to each other. In the proper recognition and expression of this connectedness, Lawrence implies, abstraction becomes tangible and language revitalized.

In manuscript 79, "Fidelity" forms part of a cluster of poems focused loosely on love relationships. In this notebook, as in his earlier ones, we notice Lawrence's tendency to group related poems together.[15] In *Pansies,* Lawrence places "Fidelity" close to poems that are near it in the manuscript, e.g., "The Mess of Love" and "All That I Ask," introducing into the sequence other poems that do not appear in manuscript form, such as "Ego-Bound Women" (printed only in the definitive edition). He continually repeats themes and images in related poems, so that a poem such as "Fidelity" is best understood in the context of the poems that surround it. The subject of possessiveness in love is prepared for in the poems preceding "Fidelity" in *Pansies:* "Jealousy" and "Ego-Bound Women," while "The Mess of Love" introduces the metaphor of love as a flower. "Know Thyself, Know Thyself More Deeply," the poem that follows "Fidelity" in the collection, elaborates on the comparatively permanent aspects of human nature, expanding the rock and gem metaphors. Thus, the poems in *Pansies* combine inobtrusively to form the "complete state of mind" that Lawrence promises us in his introduction.

What is this complete state of mind that Lawrence arranges *Pansies* to reveal? As one would expect, it lacks any overall chronological orientation, although every now and then Lawrence inserts a series of poems with a biographical slant. On the other hand, when one reads through *Pansies* from beginning to end, one notices a certain thematic coherence, not only within clusters of poems, but in the collection as a whole. Employing his own sort of dialectic, Lawrence juxtaposes poems and groups of poems to play off against each other in subject and mood even while they advance certain broad themes in the collection and contribute to its characteristic tone. Consider, for example, the first nineteen poems in the book. These poems range in subject from death by drowning in the first two to

circus elephants in the next four, with subsequent poems cover-
ing topics as diverse as the time of day, eating utensils, the end
of the world, and the affectations of the bourgeoisie. In mood,
the plaintiveness of the first thirteen poems turns to spleen in
the next six. Yet each poem refers to and furthers the apocalyp-
tic theme introduced in the first, "Our Day Is Over." Each
considers the question, Are we rushing to extinction like the
ancient species of which the elephant serves as sole reminder?
The poems on the bourgeoisie add another consideration: Do
we deserve extinction?

In this manner, which applies to the rest of *Pansies*, Law-
rence approximates the opposition inherent in human experi-
ence. He celebrates a scheme of things where—to borrow an
allusion he himself supplies in the introduction—the exquisite
Celia, truly sublime, shits real shit. Are we surprised, then, to
find prayerful and visionary poems such as "Give Us Gods,"
"To Let Go or to Hold On—?", and "Spiral Flame" coexisting
with the scurrilous "Demon Justice" or "The Jeune Fille"? As in
the other writings of this period, Lawrence is alert to the evils of
modern life, which he depicts in "Nemesis" as "social insanity /
which in the end is always homocidal." He is also aware of the
moments of transcendence that set us "reeling with connection"
as well as "the unconscious inclination we call religion / to-
wards the sun of suns." As Lawrence tells us in "Underneath,"
wholeness of consciousness is our way to change, as it is in
Birds, Beasts and Flowers, Lady Chatterley's Lover, and *The
Escaped Cock*.

A sexual motif sounds through *Pansies* as it does through
Collected Poems. Whether Lawrence writes about touch be-
tween lovers in "Touch Comes" or "What the old people call
immediate contact with God" in "The Primal Passions," he
expresses his belief that sexuality opens the way to individual
and societal wholeness. The final three poems of the definitive
Pansies, "Demon Justice," "Be a Demon!," and "The Jeune
Fille," prompt us variously to "remember / not quite to ignore /
the jolly little member." In these obstreperous poems, Lawrence
sums up the message of *Pansies*, not dissimilar to that of *Lady
Chatterley's Lover*. In "A Propos," Lawrence writes of the
novel in words that apply equally well to *Pansies*, "And this is
the real point of this book. I want men and women to be able to

think sex, fully, completely, honestly, and cleanly."[16] His emphasis on thought in this unlikely context refers us to the introduction to *Pansies,* where Lawrence instructs us that thought comes from the heart and genitals as well as from the head. Lawrence pursues this connection in the essay just quoted: "Ours is the day of realization rather than action. There has been so much action in the past, especially sexual action, a wearying repetition over and over, without a corresponding thought, a corresponding realization. Now our business is to realize sex. Today the full conscious realization of sex is even more important than the act itself."[17]

The union of sexual thought and deed is, I believe, the "complete state of mind" to which Lawrence refers in the introduction. It is as well the condition of vital sanity in man and society. One of the "sins of omission" cited in "Demon Justice" is our forgetfulness "that the face is not only / the mind's index, / but also the comely / shy flower of sex—." The poem reminds us that a complete state of mind is one prompted and made possible by the demon, at large in the world.

In *Nettles,* the last book that Lawrence published before he died,[18] the poet takes to task an emasculated England. As he had declared in "A Propos," he believed that only the phallus, "the great old symbol of godly vitality in a man, and of immediate contact,"[19] could regenerate England. As others have pointed out, the particular occasion of Lawrence's barbs was the suppression in England of his paintings and of his books, most recently *Pansies.* Lawrence interpreted this squeamishness as indicative of the physical and moral impotence of his countrymen.

Lawrence distinguishes *Nettles* from his earlier "pansies" because they sting. In a voice reminiscent of a schoolboy's taunting his fellows, these poems needle particular people, institutions, and organizations. By comparison, the satire of *Pansies* is broader, attacking general attitudes and types. In the first few *Nettles,* Lawrence assails the British public, aiming at a particular nationality his earlier criticisms of the bourgeoisie. He conveys metaphorically the infantilism of this group, still in the care of various "aunties." He suggests that changes in government merely change the guardians (all women, so powerless are the males) of a public that has not reached manhood. Indeed, most Englishmen will never be men, Lawrence asserts, because Auntie has "fixed" them. In "Cry of the Masses," "What Have They Done to You," and "Factory Cities," Lawrence mocks his countrymen, alienated from their bodies, unaware that "[their] manhood is utterly lost." Yet his tone changes in the last two poems in the collection, "Leaves of Grass, Flowers of Grass" and "Magnificent Democracy," a single poem in manuscript B, which contains early versions of all but a few of the poems in *Nettles*. In these two poems, Lawrence looks again to nature for an emblem of human wholeness. Going Whitman one better, he sings the praises of the grass in flower, almost ready to seed. It epitomizes "midsummer maleness" and potent natural superiority. This image counters that of the disembodied men of England evoked in the earlier poems. Thus, *Nettles* concludes with a positive image of sexuality uniting man with nature and making him whole. The message of this little book, however, smacks of "Demon Justice." Lawrence might appropriately have prefaced *Nettles* with these stanzas from that poem:

> Now bend you down
> to demon justice,
> and take sixty slashes
> across your rusties.
>
> Then with a sore
> arse perhaps you'll remember
> not quite to ignore
> the jolly little member.

In these poems, we experience the demon that puts salt instead of honey on our lips, to which Lawrence refers in "Kissing and Horrid Strife," one of *Last Poems*.

Versions of most of the poems in *Nettles* exist in manuscript B. They show how thoroughly Lawrence reworked the poems before he printed them. For example, Lawrence eliminates material from the manuscript B draft of "Leaves of Grass, Flowers of Grass," dividing it into two poems sometime before publication. He expands the final version of "The Factory Cities," and extensively rewrites sections of "Songs I Learnt at School: II. My Native Land," not only in manuscript B but again before publication. In several instances, he changes the title of a poem before publishing it. Yet the revisions for *Nettles* are not nearly so sweeping as those for *Pansies,* where Lawrence frequently alters meaning and adopts new images before he has finished with a poem. Rather, they are of the sort one finds in "Give Me a Sponge," on the level of phrasing instead of meaning. To all appearances, *Nettles* cost Lawrence less effort to write than did the more serious *Pansies.* Replete with unsophisticated rhyme and meter that often mimics nursery rhymes, *Nettles* is, in fact, Lawrence's "real doggerel," not *Pansies.*

Lawrence seems to have had no lofty purpose in mind for *Nettles.* These are the poems that he hoped would "sting the arses of all the Meads [sic] and Persians of shiny London."[20] Yet Lawrence's epic allusion gives us pause. Does one venture too far in supposing that it betrays Lawrence's assumption that the "stinging nettles" are the demon's weapons and, as such, are significant and worthy of respect?

Unanswerable questions plague the reader of the notebooks from which Richard Aldington printed *Last Poems,* including "More Pansies," i.e., manuscripts A and B, respectively. Why did Lawrence include so few of the poems in manuscript B in *Nettles,* considering the many others on similar themes written in a comparable style? Did he have a specific purpose in mind for the unpublished poems remaining in the two notebooks? The Brewsters, returned from Ceylon and living near the Lawrences in Italy, recall that when he selected poems for *Nettles,* Lawrence proposed another volume to be called *Dead Nettles,* presumably because the tone of the poems would be milder. At the same time, he mentioned that he had written some poems about death,[21] a statement that indicates that he perceived and intended a thematic connection among certain of the poems. Tedlock hypothesizes that these were the poems that Aldington collected in *Last Poems.*[22] Knowing Lawrence's practice of grouping his poems narratively, as in *Amores, Look!, Birds, Beasts and Flowers,* and the *Collected Poems*—or thematically—as in *Bay, Pansies,* and *Nettles,* one can speculate with some confidence that Lawrence intended to follow his own precedent when the time came to arrange these poems for publication in one or more volumes. Strengthening this speculation are the familiar clusters of poems on similar themes or subjects in both manuscripts A and B, suggesting that Lawrence had already initiated the process of arrangement as he copied poems into the notebooks. Most interesting in connection with this particular study are the numerous groups of poems that focus on the transcendent in human life. By whichever of his names Lawrence calls him, and Lawrence uses many in these manuscripts, we recognize the telltales of the demon. He may masquerade as the gods, singly or collectively, the fallen archangels, or the Holy Ghost. Whatever his aspect, however, he continues to personify individual wholeness and vital connection with all that is other than the self.

Judging from his last books and essays, Lawrence came to believe that the purpose of art is to reestablish in human life "the great relationships," by which he means participation in the cosmic cycle of birth, death and fruition. Lawrence identifies as man's greatest need "the renewal forever of the complete rhythm of life and death, the rhythm of the sun's year, the body's year of a lifetime, and the greater year of the stars, the soul's year of immortality. . . . It is a need of the mind and soul, body, spirit and sex: all."[23] He maintains that the soul, our "greater consciousness," thrives only in such relation, fostered by religion and poetry.[24]

In "More Pansies," as well as *Last Poems,* religion and poetry often merge. A surprisingly large number of poems in "More Pansies" have religious subjects. Some of these poems criticize contemporary forms of belief, as does "The Protestant Churches." Others posit the bases of a new religious system in the manner of "Future Religion." Frequently, they reformulate traditional religious and philosophic concepts or else redefine terms, as do, for example, "What Are the Gods?," "Belief," "Fatality," and "The Cross," which treats a complex of issues such as suffering and sacrifice from a Lawrencean point of view. As in *Pansies,* Lawrence is concerned with language itself, making every effort to infuse it and what it stands for with new vitality. Consequently, the poems in "More Pansies" often tend to the speculative.

Whatever approach to their subject the individual religious poems may take, we know from the first poem in "More Pansies" that we are in the company of the demon. "Image-

Making Love" is about the "anti-self"—i.e., the true self, or the demon. The speaker of the poem cherishes and yet rues his aloneness, the result of others mistaking his true identity:

> Always
> in the eyes of those who loved me
> I have seen at last the image of him they loved
> and took for me
> mistook for me.
>
> And always
> it was a simulacrum, something
> like me, and like a gibe at me.

The sequence of poems that follows explores the denial of the true self; other people prefer their own "simulacrum" as well as that of the speaker of the poems. Because of such denial, real love and genuine friendship are impossible. Under such conditions, the anti-self prefers isolation to human contact.

These first poems are sardonic, similar in tone to many of those in *Pansies*. Lawrence carries on in "More Pansies" his "series of scoldings," as Aldington has described these poems in the introduction to *Last Poems*. Yet this mood is not the only one nor is it the pervasive one in "More Pansies." A large number of poems witness to the demon's transforming and palpable presence in nature and in human life, often in a meditative tone like that of *Birds, Beasts and Flowers*. For example, in "Andraitx—Pomegranate Flowers," an early poem in manuscript B, Lawrence describes impersonally, through images reverberating with mythic overtones, the demonic force that asserts itself in nature through the flowering pomegranates. Lawrence describes the flowers as "short gasps of flame in the green of night . . . small sharp red fires in the night of leaves." The equivalent force in humans responds, and we realize for a brief moment our connection with nature:

> And noon is suddenly dark, is lustrous, is silent and dark
> men are unseen, beneath the shading hats;
> only from out the foliage of the secret loins
> red flamelets here and there reveal
> a man, a woman there.

Celebratory poems such as this one, or "The Heart of Man,"
"God Is Born," "Bells," or any of the score of other poems that
recount specific epiphanies in human life, share both content
and style with *Last Poems*. It is tempting to conjecture that had
he lived to publish them, Lawrence would have grouped all such
poems together as his religious testament, the story of his cove-
nant with the demon.

Although in "More Pansies" Lawrence expresses his reluc-
tance to name or describe the gods—his concern being to strip
away misapprehensions caused by traditional religious thinking
rather than add to them—he realizes that "the simple ask for
images!" In "Name the Gods," the very poem in which he
resolves that the simple must do without such images for the
time being, he promptly supplies both a description and a name
in the poem's last stanza:

> But all the time I see the gods:
> the man who is mowing the tall white corn,
> suddenly, as it curves, as it yields, the white wheat
> and sinks down with a swift rustle, and a strange, falling
>   flatness,
> ah! the gods, the swaying body of god!
> ah the fallen stillness of god, autumnus, and it is only July
> the pale-gold flesh of Priapus dropping asleep.

His capitulation in this poem signals a turn from the speculative
religious verse he has been writing to the mythic, even mystical
verse characteristic of *Last Poems*. The splendid "There Are No
Gods," which I join Sandra Gilbert in appreciating,[25] immedi-
ately follows, and not long after come "All Sorts of Gods,"
"For a Moment," which supplies a litany of divine names, and,
in manuscript B itself, early drafts of "Bavarian Gentians" and
"The Ship of Death."

As he writes in "A Propos" around this time, the regenera-
tion of human society requires a return to ancient forms.[26] He
follows this assertion with the crucial question, "How are we to
get back Apollo, and Attis, Demeter, Persephone, and the halls
of Dis?"[27] Phrased less mythically, Lawrence's question is how
can we return to the consciousness of our connection with a
living universe that these forms presume and that our pagan
forebears possessed? Lawrence has given his symbolic answer to

this question in *Birds, Beasts and Flowers* and *Collected Poems*. In them, we learn how Lawrence himself rediscovers the gods through a series of deaths and rebirths that parallel the initiation rites of primitive religions.[28] His initiation into the cosmic mysteries unites him with the divine in its many manifestations. Consequently, Lawrence can see "in two worlds."[29] This second sight of the initiate determines the dual perspective of *Last Poems,* where the luminous vision of a world alive with heroes and gods—and demons—is superimposed on a view—and a characteristically dim one, at that—of mundane reality.

Writing "More Pansies," *Apocalypse,* and numerous short essays such as "A Propos" helped Lawrence to formulate the religious insights fundamental to *Birds, Beasts and Flowers* and *Collected Poems* as a whole. By *Last Poems,* Lawrence was ready to embody them anew in image and symbol and animate them through myth. Now, however, instead of limiting himself to his own personal myth, he creates one for all of us.

By means of his last poems, Lawrence hopes to restore to us the "old flaming love of life and the strange shudder of the presence of the invisible dead," of which he speaks in *Apocalypse.*[30] And who of us does not shiver with excitement when the poet announces straightway in *Last Poems,* "The Greeks Are Coming!" and describes their ships to us as "a flash and a furl . . . coming, out of the morning end of the sea"? "Wait, wait," the poet cries in "The Argonauts," "don't bring me the coffee yet, nor the 'pain grille.' / The dawn is not off the sea, and Odysseus' ships / have not yet passed the islands, I must watch them still." In the presence of the invisible dead, Lawrence implies, we must put off what he has called our "mealtime" selves, even though, paradoxically, the gods themselves must become incarnate. As "Demiurge" explains, "Religion knows that Jesus was never Jesus / till he was born from a womb, and ate soup and bread." *Last Poems* invokes the demiurge (Lawrence's usual name in these poems, along wth "God" or "the gods," for the daimon or demon) in his multifarious incarnations. He appears as Odysseus; as the heros, "their faces scarlet, like the dolphin's blood"; as Dionysos, Helen, Hermes, and Aphrodite; and even as a red geranium and mating whales.

Through this poetry, we can participate in the "sense-awareness" and "sense-knowledge" that Lawrence describes in

Apocalypse. It triggers our instinct and intuition and imparts "a knowledge based not on words but on images . . . [that is] not logical but emotional."[31] By putting us in touch with the "great old symbols," the poems revive in us an "older, half-forgotten way of consciousness,"[32] which is life-giving and therefore truly religious. They give the lie to what "Stoic" calls "the greatest of all illusions . . . this illusion of the death of the undying."

Lawrence the initiate can say, "But all the time I see the gods"; Lawrence the poet can make us see them, too. His vision of the living gods, however, does not obscure his view of the world in which our mealtime selves have to live. *Last Poems,* like earlier collections of Lawrence's poetry, has its share of social criticism, delivered in the snide voice we recognize immediately from *Pansies*. In the first of the poems, the vision of the Aegean ships fades to reveal "an ocean liner, going east, like a small beetle walking the edge." It leaves behind it "a long thread of dark smoke / like a bad smell," Lawrence's wry voice informs us. In other poems, Lawrence finds several opportunities to point out unpleasant sides of modern life. For example, he derides modern cities: "There is even no more any weather / the weather in town is always benzine, or else petrol fumes / lubricating oil, exhaust gas"; eating habits: "The only way to eat an apple is to hog it down like a pig"; and popular entertainment: "Jazz and film and wireless / are all evil abstractions from life."

Not only does Lawrence take modern society to task in a number of *Last Poems* but he also continues to theorize on religious and philosophic ideas, indicating that he has not altogether abandoned the speculative mode of "More Pansies." The most obvious example of his theorizing is the long sequence of poems on the problem of evil. It begins with "Kissing and Horrid Strife," in which the poet witnesses to his own experiences of evil: "I have been defeated and dragged down by pain / and worsted by the evil world-soul of today." The second poem, "When Satan Fell," exonerates the archdemon of any responsibility for evil. He fell "only to keep a balance" because "the Lord Almighty rose a bit too high." "Doors" insists that "no, not the ithyphallic demons / not even the double Phallus of the devil himself / with his key to the two dark doors / is evil." Nor does evil dwell in the "halls of the great dark below," for, as the next poem tells us, "Evil Is Homeless." "What Then Is Evil?" asks the following poem, which promptly supplies an answer:

> Oh, in the world of the flesh of man
> iron gives the deadly wound
> and the wheel starts the principle of all evil.
> . . . .
> But in the world of the soul of man
> there, and there alone lies the pivot of pure evil
> only in the soul of man, when it pivots upon the ego.

Lawrence considers in the next eight poems particular examples of evil, often distinguishing conventional ideas of evil from true evil, as in "Death Is Not Evil, Evil Is Mechanical." So, we see that not all of *Last Poems* incarnates the gods, however committed it may be to religious concerns.

Undeniably, it is the mythic poems in this collection that stay with the reader. We reread and remember the ones that revive the "great old symbols," whether of Aphrodite "pouring sea-water over herself"; Hermes at the gate, "with his cloak over his arm, waiting to be asked in"; or the naked Moon, "more wonderful than anything we can stroke." Again and again, we reach the poet his gentian so that we can follow him, on a way made familiar in *Birds, Beasts and Flowers*, "down darker and darker stairs, where blue is darkened on blueness, / . . . to the sightless realm where darkness is awake upon the dark / and Persephone herself is but a voice." For the most part, though, we stay in the upper regions, near the sea; there we build our ship of death and prepare for "the longest journey" to the "flood-dawn" where the body, "like a worn sea-shell / emerges strange and lovely."

In the notebooks, Lawrence has left us a visible record of the energy he spent returning to the "ancient forms." Manuscripts A and B show us how hard Lawrence had to work to transform his religious insights into their mythic form, using image and symbol to do so. The poems in "More Pansies" and *Last Poems* must be considered incomplete, yet their manuscript drafts sometimes show more revisions than poems Lawrence prepared for publication. Also fascinating to anyone interested in the poetic process is the way an image or idea develops not only from one version of a poem to the next but also from one poem to another. In manuscript, Lawrence's poetry gives the impression of unfolding, both because one poem immediately follows another with no space between and also because an image or idea used in one poem often appears in subsequent ones.

"The Ship of Death" and "Bavarian Gentians" serve as apt examples of Lawrence's mature revisionary style in manuscripts A and B. Both of these poems have drafts in manuscript B that antedate those in manuscript A; they also share protopoems in manuscript B of the sort mentioned above, i.e., poems that contain ideas or images that form the basis for later poems. A survey of the evolution of "The Ship of Death" and "Bavarian Gentians" from these prototypes makes plain the way that Lawrence's poetry often interconnects, as well as the way that material in these particular notebooks displays frequent, marked similarities. The various drafts of these two poems (there are four of "Bavarian Gentians") are also representative of the profound differences that often exist between the first and final versions of a Lawrence poem. In general, they and their prototypes illustrate plainly Lawrence's "modus operandi"in revising the poems in manuscripts A and B. They also show the creative mind exercising its power to shape inchoate material and nurture the germ of an idea or an image until it matures.

Towards the end of manuscript B, three consecutive poems stand out as sharing a common subject with "Ship of Death," the third from last poem in that manuscript. In the order in which they appear, these are "Two Ways of Living and Dying," "So let me live," and "Gladness of Death" (see apps. Q, R, and S). The first of these appears to have little in common with "The Ship of Death" (see app. T) and even less with "Bavarian Gentians" (see app. U) until one reaches the last stanza. Up to that point, Lawrence has developed the poem through two basic metaphors prevalent in his writing: the first, organic activity, such as streams flowing, which represents vital existence; the other, mechanical energy, such as gears grinding, which refers to self-centered being. The images themselves suggest the conclusion of the poem. Just as the broken machine is discarded as useless, so when the self-willed die, their death is final; but as nature goes on renewing itself at its source, even so the vital continue. In reaching this conclusion, however, Lawrence tries out two general images to which he returns in various ways in subsequent poems.

In the first draft of the poem, Lawrence chooses to convey what death is like for the vital soul through the image of a flower. In his choice of the delphinium and in the images he uses to describe it, Lawrence anticipates "Bavarian Gentians." By giving the flower its Greek name instead of the more English "larkspur," which he briefly used then discarded in the first stanza, Lawrence subtly associates it with the gods and myth. His depiction of its seed pods as "pale dead sceptres" reinforces this connection; he will use this particular image again later, in "Bavarian Gentians," in a similar connection. The usual dark blue color of he flower also looks forward to both the dark pansy of "Gladness of Death" and the dark-blue gentians of "Bavarian Gentians." Finally, the image of the flower that in death scatters life-giving seeds parallels that of the mythic gentians in its intrinsic connection with fertility.

The other recurring image is one that Lawrence introduces in the final draft of the poem. Striking out the comparison of the godlike (because deathless) dead to the delphinium, he now describes them as "beyond us, now beyond, departing," repeating the metaphor several times in the course of the last stanza. The incipient image of death as a journey preoccupies Lawrence, judging from the number of times he returns to it, until he fully develops it in "The Ship of Death."

Indeed, Lawrence rewrites the next poem in the notebook, "So let me live," in order to include the incipient journey image. He depicts death as a "passing over" from life, introducing in this poem the related idea of the adventure of death. Obviously, the metaphor occurred to him as he was copying out the poem: he substitutes "adventure" for "mystery" in the third line. This change allows him to use a related simile in the last two lines of the poem in place of generalizations on what death may hold.

The first draft of "Gladness of Death," the third poem in this sequence, compares death with birth. It may be that death is painful, like childbirth, says the poem, but gladness will follow. Lawrence apparently thought better of using this hackneyed comparison, replacing it with two others in the final draft of the poem. In the manuscript B version of "The Ship of Death," Lawrence does return, if only briefly, to the womb image implicit in the earlier metaphor; he describes the goal of the journey as "the core / of sheer oblivion and of utter peace, / the womb of silence in the living night."

The two metaphors for the state of the soul after death that Lawrence settles on in "Gladness of Death" are, once again, those of the flower and the journey. In the flower metaphor, Lawrence compares himself with a dark pansy and death with a dark sun that brings the flower into blossom. Here is Lawrence's delphinium in a new manifestation. He adds in this poem the paradoxical idea of darkness as productive of light, speaking of the "dark sunrays" and "dark sunshine" of death in a way that recalls earlier poems, such as "Blueness" in *Collected Poems*. The manuscript A versions of "Bavarian Gentians" identify the flower itself as the source of illuminating darkness in a final synthesis of images introduced many poems earlier. The journey image, as well, reappears in "Gladness of Death," a companion to the flower image. The revised poem assures us of "the great adventure of death, where Thomas Cook cannot guide us." Lawrence gives us in this poem no detailed information about the adventure, nor does the penultimate line of the poem describe the "great spaces of death" to which it refers. However, in the next poem on death in manuscript B, "Ship of Death," Lawrence sets off to explore imaginatively and in detail that adventure and those spaces.

In charting the great "adventure" of death in the two extant versions of "The Ship of Death,"[33] Lawrence depends upon myth to help him explore the unknown, about which he admits knowing nothing—and everything—in "Gladness of Death." In "The Ship of Death," he employs several of the "great old symbols": most obviously, those of the journey and the sea. He also gives the poem a seasonal orientation, expanding his description of autumn in the second version to suggest an emblematic correspondence between human and physical nature, a device he used often in *Birds, Beasts and Flowers*. Thus, what we know of the falling fruit likewise applies to the "bruised Body." The "grim frost" that reaps the apples also ensures our continuing participation in the cycle of birth, death, and fruition. Faced with the necessity of death, the soul shrinks, contemplating even the "ego-bound" solution of suicide. Peace and ultimate union come, the poem tells us, from acceptance of and active participation in the natural cycle. We must "build our ship of death" in order to prepare for change, specifically "the long and painful death / that lies between the old self and the new." In words that echo the note to *Collected Poems,* Lawrence prepares us for the symbolic meaning of the poem.

The images in the poem also remind us of *Collected Poems,* which certainly was fresh in Lawrence's memory at the time he was composing his last poems. Years before, in the earliest notebooks, Lawrence had used similar images to describe a search for the self and the related confrontation with death. In the second manuscript 1 version of "Dreams: Old," Lawrence had described the soul as an explorer sailing in search of peace:

> among memories is a loving
> my soul {is a backward{ explorer.
>
>   hushèd
> All the bye-gone, {dream-tossed{ years
> Streaming
> {That stream{ back where the mist {of oblivion{ distils
> Into forgetfulness: soft-sailing waters, where fears
> No longer shake: where the silk sail fills
> With the unfelt breeze that ebbs over the seas when the
>   storm
> of living has passed, drifting on and on
> Through the coloured iridescence that swims in the warm
> Wave of the tumult spent and gone.

Typical of the old self, this vessel moves backwards, into past life, in search of peace, fleeing change. Lawrence inverts the direction of the journey in "The Ship of Death," yet his descriptions of both voyages resemble each other. In manuscript 5, Lawrence once more used the image of the ship and the sea. In "Blue," an early version of "The Shadow of Death," a poem about his emotional state after the death of his mother, the ship refers to the earth, moving in the poem from darkness to morning; the significance of the sea is unclear, although it appears to have some connection with death and darkness. The soul of the speaker stands at the prow of the ship, still "dripping with darkness like a drowned man brought again to tread the deck /

of life." As the ship carries him into "the morning sunlight jostle" of life, his soul longs for darkness, knowing itself "undawning." Although the ship in this poem moves forward instead of backward, the old self still pulls toward the past.

In contrast, the soul in the manuscript A "The Ship of Death" consents to the necessity of change, having recognized the "death-flood rising within us" and the consequent danger of drowning, escaped so narrowly and unwillingly by the speaker of "Blue." The soul must prepare itself not just to meet change but also to initiate it. As the poems in *Pansies* had done through invective, this poem instructs us through symbols to strip ourselves of all except necessities and to expect no certain course as we journey toward our elusive goal. If we endure total darkness and self-denial, the poem promises us that we will experience transformation and the new life it brings. "The initiate," says *Apocalypse*, "is twice-born."[34] His mystical journey into death and beyond, to new life, occurs in "The Ship of Death," not through the ritual of religion, but through the symbolism of poetry. If his poetry is Lawrence's ship of death, what, the poem compels each of us to ask, is ours?

Neither of the two versions of "The Ship of Death" betrays extensive revision in the notebooks; nevertheless, Lawrence has done prodigious rewriting sometime between the manuscript B and manuscript A drafts of the poem. Even a cursory comparison of these drafts discloses that Lawrence tightened organization by dividing the poem into related sections and by shortening it considerably. He eliminates from the revised poem a lengthy section (some 36 lines) that describes the pitiful state of the souls who have neglected to build their ships. Lawrence did not discard this material, however. As he so often did in earlier notebooks, he salvages whatever he can of it and other deleted bits, using the cast-off lines as the basis of new poems. Thus, the manuscript B "Ship of Death" becomes in its turn a protopoem for a cluster of related poems in manuscript A: "Difficult Death," "All Soul's Day," "The Houseless Dead," "Beware the Unhappy Dead!" and "After All Saints' Day," poems that immediately follow "The Ship of Death" in manuscript A. In fact, Lawrence uses an image from "Ship of Death" to rewrite "Song of Death," another poem that appears in both notebooks.

Such mining of old material is so typical of Lawrence's

revisionary method that it is worth pausing over. For example, Lawrence struck the following lines from "Ship of Death":

> And launching there his little ship
> wrapped in the dark-red mantle of the body's memories,
> the little, slender soul sits swiftly down, and takes the
>   oars
> and draws away, away, away, towards the dark depths,
> fathomless deep ahead, far, far from the grey shores that
>   fringe with shadow all this world's existence.

These lines reappear in manuscript A with only minor changes and additions as "After All Saints' Day," originally titled "The Happy Soul":

> Wrapped in the dark-red mantle of warm memories
> the little, slender soul sits swiftly down, and takes the oars
> and draws away, away towards dark depths
>   wafting with
> ⟨feeling the⟩ warm love from still-living hearts
>   breaking on
> ⟨filling⟩ his small frail sail, and helping him on
> to the fathomless deeps ahead, far, far from the grey shores
>   of marginal existence.

Now relegated to a separate poem, these lines nevertheless continue to relate to the themes, images, and language of the other poems grouped nearby in manuscript A. Even the poems that do not borrow directly from "Ship of Death" pick up on one or another of the above elements, so that every poem in manuscript A after "The Ship of Death," seventeen poems in all, relates to it or its earlier version somehow. This relatedness prompted Aldington to speculate in his introduction to *Last Poems* that had Lawrence possessed energy enough he would have combined all these poems into one great masterpiece. Aldington either ignored or overlooked the fact that most of these poems came into being as Lawrence pared down his first draft of the poem. As is apparent in the earlier notebooks as well as in this one, Lawrence consistently divided long poems (such as "Dreams Old and Nascent") into discrete parts, or into one or more different poems, or both. I see no sign of a desire to reverse his usual practice in the revision of "Ship of Death."

Lawrence not only eliminates large sections of "Ship of Death" in rewriting it, but he also condenses other sections, rendering them more evocative and enhancing the mythic quality of the entire poem as he involves the reader in the search for meaning. One of his most effective revisions of this sort is his revision of the journey itself. First, he makes the account more immediate by changing the mood of the sentence structure from indicative to imperative. He then eliminates the metaphors that make the voyage a parable of virtue: in its final version, the soul no longer eats the "brave bread of a wholesome knowledge" nor does the ship navigate "the strange whirlpools of remembered greed." Instead, the soul has "its store of food and little cooking pans"; the ship sails "the flood's black waste . . . the waters of the end." Later in the poem, Lawrence also simplifies his account of the soul's dissolution in death, increasing its drama. Instead of cataloguing the soul's lost gear, as he does in manuscript B, Lawrence describes the end in manuscript A with one stark sentence: "And everything is gone, the body is gone / completely under, gone, entirely gone." He then evokes annihilation with a potent metaphor: "The upper darkness is heavy on the lower, / between them the little ship / is gone / she is gone."

Brevity is not his chief aim, however. When he needs to, Lawrence takes the space to expand the poem. For instance, in part 2, he writes three more stanzas about autumn in order to establish the correspondence between inner and outer reality that proves crucial to the poem's effectiveness. He also adds parts 5 and 6, an apocalyptic message that increases the urgency of the poet's warning that we must prepare for coming destruction. Finally, Lawrence rewrites and expands the last section of the poem, which before had emphasized the delights of oblivion while only hinting at the possibility of the soul's rebirth. Lawrence adds a lengthy description of the dawn in part 9 and an account of the soul's reunion with her transformed body in part 10. The poem now ends with images suggestive of rebirth. They communicate the poem's final, mythic message.

Of all the poems in manuscripts A and B, "Bavarian Gentians" reveals Lawrence's revisionary style most completely. Four drafts of the poem remain, all characterized by considerable revision. They graphically represent the creative process; we observe as Lawrence's changes, instigated by his insights and associations, shape the poem before our eyes. Indeed, in the way it gradually discloses the mythic significance of human life, the evolving poem can serve as an emblem of Lawrence's revision of *Collected Poems;* thus, its consideration serves as a fitting conclusion to this study of Lawrence's poetry. Through both, though in different degrees, we see firsthand the power of myth to rescue the transitory event or object from oblivion, to inform the individual life with universal meaning, and by moving our "deep emotional centres," to involve us in the mystery of human existence.

From the first, Lawrence liked to write about flowers. He composed "To Guelder-Roses" and "To Campions," his first poems, one springtime morning in his twentieth year.[35] In the autumn of his forty-fifth year he wrote one of his last poems, on the same subject. Even in his two earliest poems, Lawrence connected flowers with love and death. In *Birds, Beasts and Flowers,* Lawrence went as far as to call flowers "hell's creatures," recounting in "Purple Anemones" their origin as "hellhounds on Persephone's heels." Lawrence followed Pluto's example when he created his own "hell-hounds" in *Pansies* and *Nettles,* inspired by a perverse love for his fellow man.

It cannot surprise us, then, that in "Bavarian Gentians" Lawrence identifies a flower as the gateway and beacon to hell. By means of the flower, the poet enters the heart of darkness, participating in the hellish rituals of death and love. The myth of Persephone and Pluto prepares us to grasp the paradoxes that follow: light and dark marry, youth and age merge, and life and death are made one. Each becomes its opposite in a dark epithalamium. For the eternal moment of the ceremony, the puzzle of life, its duality, is resolved. We understand that destruction is no more than creation. Like "The Ship of Death," this poem is about rebirth. Our way lit by dark lamps, it takes us to the source of life's renewal so that we can share in the mysterious process of beginning anew. In its subject and in its mythic mode of presentation, this poem reflects the content and method of both *Collected Poems* and *Last Poems*. In *Last Poems,* as illustrated by "Bavarian Gentians," myth becomes explicit as it never quite does in *Collected Poems*. Here, the demon speaks to us directly, in his own tongue.

Lawrence apparently did not recognize the mythic dimen-
sion of his material when he first wrote "Bavarian Gentians."
The first draft of the poem in manuscript B follows along the
lines of many others in that notebook. Lawrence first called the
poem "The State of Grace," evidently intending it to redefine a
traditional religious concept. The original poem starts with a
description of the gentians, introducing a tension between their
gloom and the sunniness of the room. The speaker of the poem
praises their "noble" darkness. Emblematically, they reveal the
"glory" of his soul, his state of grace, arrived at presumably
through blood-knowledge. He pleases a dark godhead through
his delight in and experience of the darkness. In this draft, the
poem ironically speaks in conventional terms (e.g., "grace,"
"baptism," and "godhead") about decidedly unconventional at-
titudes and experiences, to which Lawrence refers only vaguely.

Without recopying this draft, Lawrence emends it to elimi-
nate all explicitly religious terms. He changes the title of the
poem to "Glory of Darkness"; however, the phrase "the glory
of the [speaker's] soul," a combination suggestive of grace, be-
comes "blue joy." The "dark-blue godhead" of the flowers is
changed to "dark-blue fringes." The speaker's "baptism" in the
blue gloom becomes his "journey." We see the poem changing
from a speculative to a narrative piece.

His last substitution, i.e., of "journey" for "baptism," may
have touched off a connection with the Persephone myth for
Lawrence. In the right-hand margin of the first poem, not stop-
ping to recopy the first five lines of the poem, which he proba-
bly intended to keep as revised, he wrote in pencil in a large,
rapid hand, a new version of the poem, starting with line six.
The flower now becomes the doorway to hell, through which
Persephone has just passed, on her way to her wedding, where
all the "great dark ones" are gathering. Along with the new title
of the poem, this last image, of the elect who will attend the
ceremony, contains the only remaining suggestion of the poem's
first subject, grace. In this version, Lawrence redefines the sig-
nificance of the flower and the point of view of the speaker. No
longer a sign of the speaker's personal responsiveness to and
exploration of the divine, the gentian becomes an immediate
way to union with the dark gods, standing open to anyone. We
share the speaker's moment of discovery as he realizes the perti-

nence of myth to his own experience. "Oh, I know—" he exclaims, "Persephone has just gone back / down the thickening thickening gloom." This revision of the poem stresses the speaker's new insight, rather than his participation in the glory of the flowers. The essence of his knowledge comes to him and to us through myth, which embodies the faceless abstractions of the first poem. This version grips our emotions, chilling us with its intimations of death and dark desire. Nevertheless, the poem does not resolve the emotional tension roused by an uncommitted speaker. Will he enter the open doorway, like his mythical counterpart? We, too, stand hesitant on the edge of the stair, our mythic expectations unfulfilled.

Lawrence's third draft of the poem, in manuscript A, comes close to satisfying us. This is the version Aldington preferred of the two in manuscript A, although it is plainly an earlier draft than the one it immediately precedes.[36] Between the first and second notebooks, Lawrence has imaginatively assimilated the mythic dimension of his experience, which in turn infuses the ancient story with new vigor. In this poem, the speaker commits himself to follow Persephone into the underworld, thereby asserting the link between myth and life. Their experiences merge, so that her journey provides the clue to his, just as his imminent descent reaffirms the relevance of her cyclic return to darkness. The poem implies that the speaker will participate in one of the great cosmic mysteries of the sort described in *Apocalypse*.

Lawrence prepares for the central mythic revelation of the poem in its early lines, leading up to it with related images and apt allusions. Lawrence begins by telling us: "Not every man. has gentians in his house." Thus, he hints that not everyone is equipped for a journey such as his will be. In the reference to the speaker as one of the elect, we find a vestige of the earlier versions of the poem. Lawrence now sets the poem specifically in autumn, referring in a lengthened line to "Soft September, at slow, sad Michaelmas," the season of Persephone's return to hell. The poet also refines the image of the gentians as a source of gloom. From his deletions, we can tell that Lawrence considered comparing the tall flowers with the sheaves of grain characteristic of Persephone. Thinking better of the change, however, he connects them symbolically with Pluto: Lawrence tells us that the flowers are like torches that smoke with the "blueness of Pluto's gloom." He elaborates on the likeness through simile. The petals are like flame; they flatten on the ends in the day like flame-points in the wind. By the end of the second stanza, they have become through metaphor "black lamps from the halls of Dis," and we are on our way to hell.

The paradoxical image of darkness as illuminating recurs in Lawrence's poetry with regularity. He built several of the early poems around it: "Blue," "The Mystic Blue," and "Shades," for example. When he rewrote "Virgin Youth" for the *Collected Poems,* he represented the erect phallus as a lighthouse whose "dark light rolls / Into darkness, and darkly returns." As I mentioned earlier, the idea of the flower as a product of hell—specifically of hellish love—also intrigued him. Perhaps aided by the connotation of light in the term "glory," used often in the early drafts of the poem, Lawrence unites these two images in "Bavarian Gentians" in the figure of the flower as torch, which becomes by the end of the poem a symbol of demonic illumination. In its intense darkness, the larger darkness of existence takes shape. Its secret rites reveal themselves in "the splendour of torches of darkness, shedding darkness on the lost bride and her groom."

With these words, Lawrence ends the third draft of the poem. The ending apparently gave him trouble, however; two variants can be distinguished through his deletions. Lawrence seems to have first ended the poem with an ambiguous reference to a "pitch-dark room" where the torches burn. Is this hell, one wonders, reminded of Lawrence's early poems on the subject, "Late at Night" and "Next Morning"? Or are we back in the speaker's house, in the room with the gentians? Indeed, have we ever left his room? Lawrence slashes through this ending, next finishing with a reference to the nuptials themselves. This line, too, he eliminates, replacing it with the allusion to "the lost bride and her groom" quoted above. The longer line has a solemnity that its earlier versions lack. Yet, what does Lawrence mean by the "lost" bride? The adjective in the context of this poem connotes a damned soul. The description unsettles us, leaving us to ponder the benefits of such a journey for the speaker. Will he, too, be "lost"? This ending undermines the meaning of the myth and the poem, both of which center on the enigma of new life, which springs from the old.

In his final extant version of "Bavarian Gentians," Lawrence corrects this fundamental problem. He leaves much of the first part of the poem as it is, in general rewriting only to clarify images. He sharpens his description of the shape of the flowers: their petals are now depicted as "blown flat into points, by the white draught of day" instead of as "down flattening into points under the sweep of white day." He also refines the image of "Demeter's pale lamps [which] give off light," speaking instead of her "yellow-pale day." At the end of the third stanza, he does introduce a significant change. Here, he asks an unnamed emissary from the other world, "Whom have you come for, here in the white cast day?" This revision reinforces the idea of the speaker as chosen. Wary as he is, he starts willingly on the journey, embarking on what seems to be a familiar path. He guides himself, using only the gentian supplied by the ghostly presence. After expanding his description of the hellish passion that is initiating the trip, emphasizing its legitimacy—Lawrence specifies in the final version that darkness is "married" to dark; that Persephone is a "bride"; that the torches reveal "nuptials"—Lawrence is ready to deal with the problematic ending. He does so by adding another stanza of three lines to rectify two important omissions in the earlier manuscript A poem. He repeats the speaker's willingness to descend into the darkness once we are aware that he knows what awaits him, and Lawrence stresses the celebratory nature of the descent. The speaker goes to witness and rejoice at "the marriage of the living dark." As a wedding guest, he will take part in the ritual that is the clue to human life:[37] the ceremonial enacting of life's renewal through union with the other. As Lawrence writes in "A Propos," from this oneness "all things human spring, children and beauty and well-made things; all the true creations of humanity. And all we know of the will of God is that He wishes this, this oneness, to take place, fulfilled over a lifetime."[38]

In both *Collected Poems* and *Last Poems,* Lawrence celebrates the renewal of life through change. *Collected Poems* demonstrates that in any human life, ideas, emotions, and habits fall away imperceptibly, to be replaced by others. Some events, however, either inner or outer, alter one suddenly, acting as a catalyst for self-renewal and self-discovery. The quest to realize one's essential self may take all or most of one's life. Yet, as *Collected Poems* asserts, one can bring the new self to birth before death finally resolves the individual into union with the elemental cosmos. In *Last Poems,* Lawrence seeks to affirm the meaning of individual life as the manifestation of a transcendent force that challenges human understanding but can be grasped by it through myth, the language of the demon. In these poems, Lawrence continues his exploration of transformation through change, this time by imaginatively participating in the mystery of physical death and disintegration.

The last poem in the manuscript from which Aldington collected *Last Poems* is entitled "Phoenix." The subject of this poem is, of course, the mythic bird that Lawrence chose as his personal emblem. It sums up as well as any symbol the themes of Lawrence's work. It is the bird of paradoxes, signifying as it does both earth and fire, darkness and light, and recurring death and life. How better can I end this study of Lawrence's poetry than by quoting Lawrence's last poem in full?

> Are you willing to be sponged out, erased, cancelled,
> made nothing?
> Are you willing to be made nothing?
> dipped into oblivion?
>
> If not, you will never really change.
>
> The phoenix renews her youth
> only when she is burnt, burnt alive, burnt down
> to hot and flocculent ash.
> Then the small stirring of a new small bub in the nest
> with strands of down like floating ash
> Shows that she is renewing her youth like the eagle
> Immortal bird.

Appendixes
Notes
Bibliography
Index

Appendix A

Manuscript and Typescript Collections of Lawrence's Verse

Item	Description	Listing and Location
MS 1	A Nottingham University College Notebook that contains, in Lawrence's hand, Latin notes and 77 drafts of early poems dating from 1906.	*Roberts,* E317; *Ferrier,* MS 1. University of Nottingham Library (MS LaL2, formerly MS 1479).
MS 5	A Nottingham University College Notebook that contains, for the most part in Lawrence's hand, botany notes and 83 drafts of early poems, probably dating from early 1909.	*Ferrier,* MS 5. Private collection of L. D. Clarke.
MS 9	A holograph manuscript of four poems published in *The English Review,* with few changes, in November 1909.	*Roberts,* E34, E95a, and E104; *Ferrier,* MS 9 (10); *Tedlock,* pp. 77–79. University of Texas Library.
MS 14	Nineteen poems that appeared in *Love Poems,* all except one in Lawrence's hand; the exception is a printed poem. Four of these poems are designated LaL4 in the University of Nottingham Library; the rest are at the University of Texas Library.	*Roberts,* E32, E67 E114a, E423; *Ferrier,* MS 14 (14a). University of Nottingham Library and University of Texas Library.
MS 19	Forty-four drafts of poems in Lawrence's hand sent to Edward Garnett, some in late 1911.	*Ferrier,* MS 19. New York Public Library.

Item	Description	Listing and Location
MS 20	Poems sent to Edward Marsh, editor of *Georgian Poetry,* some in typescript, some in Lawrence's hand.	*Roberts,* E7, E9b, E37, E99, E152c, E168a and c, E173, E183, E264, E327, E371, E379, E434b; *Ferrier,* MS 20. New York Public Library.
MS 26	A notebook containing "Accounts at Porthcothan" plus 84 drafts of poems published, for the most part, in *Amores* and *New Poems.*	*Ferrier,* MS 26 (27). Private collection of L. D. Clarke.
MS 31	A draft of "The Blind" (called "Elysium" in *Look!*) in Lawrence's hand on the cover of one of the notebooks containing a draft of *Women in Love.*	*Ferrier,* MS 31. University of Texas Library.
MS 79	A notebook that contains, in Lawrence's hand, three prose texts, various fragments, and 165 early versions of poems, most of which appeared in revised form in *Pansies.*	*Roberts,* E302a; *Ferrier,* MS 79; *Tedlock,* pp. 104–12. University of Texas Library.
TS 80	A typescript of *Pansies* with corrections by Lawrence.	*Ferrier,* TS 80 Private collection of George Lazarus.
MSS A and B	Two notebooks from which Aldington took the poems published posthumously in *Last Poems.* The earlier notebook, MS B, contains 19 poems titled "Pensées," most of which appeared in revised form in *Pansies,* followed by poems published as "More Poems" interspersed with drafts of poems published in *Nettles.* MS A contains the poems published as *Last Poems.*	*Roberts,* E192; *Ferrier,* MS 98. University of Texas Library.

Appendix B

Order in *Collected Poems* of Poems from *Love Poems, Amores, New Poems,* and *Bay*

(Titles Lawrence changed for *Collected Poems* are followed by earlier form in parentheses.)

Order in Col-lected Poems	Love Poems	Amores	New Poems	Bay
1		"The Wild Common"		
2	"Dog Tired"			
3			"From a College Window"	
4		"Discord in Childhood"		
5	"Cherry Robbers"			
6	"Dream-Confused"			
7	"Renascence"			
8		"Virgin Youth"		
9		"Study"		
10			"Twilight" ("Palimpsest of Twilight")	
11	"Love on the Farm"			
12			"Gipsy"	
13	"The Collier's Wife"			
14			"Flapper"	
15			"Thief in the Night"	
16		"Monologue of a Mother"		
17				"The Little Town at Evening"
18		"In a Boat"		
19				"Last Hours"

157

Order in *Collected Poems*	*Love Poems*	*Amores*	*New Poems*	*Bay*
20			"Flat Suburbs . . ."	
21	"The Best of School"			
22		"Dreams: Old"		
23			"Suburbs on a Hazy Day"	
24		"Weeknight Service"		
25			"A Man Who Died" ("Bitterness of Death")	
26			"Letter from Town: Grey Morning"	
27			"Letter from Town: Almond Tree"	
28	"Wedding Morn"			
29	"Violets"			
30	"Lightning"			
31	"End of Another Home Holiday"			
32		"Baby Running Barefoot"		
33			"Sigh No More"	
34				"Guards!"
35	"Aware"			
36	"A Pang of Reminiscence"			
37	"A White Blossom"			
38	"Corot"			
39	"Michael Angelo"			
40			"Hyde Park at Night"	
41			"Picadilly Circus at Night"	
42				"After the Opera"
43	"Morning Work"			
44	"Transformations"			

Order in *Collected Poems*	Love Poems	Amores	New Poems	Bay
45		"A Baby Asleep after Pain"		
46	"Last Lesson of the Afternoon"			
47			"School on the Outskirts"	
48	"A Snowy Day in School"			
49	"Whether or Not"			
50		"A Winter's Tale"		
51	"Return"			
52	"The Appeal"			
53	"Lilies in the Fire"			
54	"Red Moon-Rise"			
55		"Scent of Irises"		
56		"Forecast" ("Epilogue")		
57		"Prophet"		
58		"Discipline"		
59		"The Punisher"		
60		"Tease"		
61		"Mystery"		
62	"Repulsed"			
63	"Coldness in Love"			
64		"Suspense" ("Patience")		
65		"Endless Anxiety" ("Anxiety")		
66		"The End"		
67		"The Bride"		
68		"The Virgin Mother"		
69		"At the Window"		
70	"Reminder"			
71		"Drunk"		
72		"Sorrow"		
73		"Dolour of Autumn"		

Order in *Collected Poems*	*Love Poems*	*Amores*	*New Poems*	*Bay*
74		"The Inheritance"		
75		"Silence"		
76		"Listening"		
77		"Brooding Grief"		
78		"Last Words to Miriam"		
79		"Malade"		
80		"Lotus and Frost" ("Lotus Hurt by the Cold")		
81		"The Yew-Tree on the Downs" ("Liason")		
82		"Troth with the Dead"		
83		"At a Loose End" ("Dissolute")		
84		"Submergence"		
85		"The Enkindled Spring"		
86		"Excursion Train" ("Excursion")		
87		"Release" ("Reproach")		
88		"These Clever Women" ("A Spiritual Woman")		
89		"Ballad of Another Ophelia"		
90	"Kisses in the Train"			
91		"Turned Down" ("Perfidy")		
92		"After Many Days"		
93		"Snap-Dragon"		
94		"Come Spring, Come Sorrow" ("Mating")		

Order in *Collected Poems*	Love Poems	Amores	New Poems	Bay
95		"The Hands of the Betrothed"		
96		"A Love Song"		
97			"Twofold" ("Two-Fold")	
98			"Tarantella"	
99			"Under the Oak"	
100		"Brother and Sister"		
101		"The Shadow of Death" ("Blue")		
102			"Birdcage Walk"	
103		"In Trouble and Shame"		
104		"Call into Death" ("Elegy")		
105		"Grey Evening"		
106		"Firelight and Nightfall"		
107		"Blueness" ("The Mystic Blue")		
108		"A Passing Bell"		
109	"The Drained Cup"			
110			"Late at Night" ("Phantasmagoria")	
111			"Next Morning"	
112			"Winter in the Blvd."	
113			"Parliament Hill"	
114			"Embankment: Charity"	
115			"Embankment: Outcasts"	
116			"Sickness"	
117			"In Church"	
118			"Piano"	
119			"The North Country"	

Order in *Col-lected Poems*	Love Poems	Amores	New Poems	Bay
120			"Love Storm"	
121			"Passing Visit to Helen" ("Intime")	
122			"Twenty Years Ago"	
123			"Reading a Letter"	
124			"Seven Seals"	
125			"Two Wives"	
126			"Noise of Battle" ("Apprehension")	
127			"At the Front" ("Heimweh")	
128			"Reality of Peace, 1916" ("Débâcle")	
129			"Narcissus"	
130				"Tommies in the Train"
131				"On the March"
132				"Ruination"
133				"The Attack"
134				"Winter-Lull"
135				"Bombardment"
136				"Rondeau . . ."
137				"Obsequial Ode"
138				"Going Back"
139				"Shades"
140				"Town in 1917"
141				"Bread on the Waters"
142				"War-Baby"
143				"Nostalgia"
144		"Dreams: Nascent"		
145			"On That Day"	
146			"Autumn Sunshine"	

Appendix C
Manuscript 1 Version of "The Songless"

1. ⟨Today⟩ Tonight

We have shut the doors behind us, and the velvet flowers of night
Lean about us scattering sprinkling their pollen dust of golden light.

Now at last we lift our faces, and our faces come aflower
To the hush'd, grey-winged ministrants the bats of night devour

Now at last the closèd calyx opens from our tired eyes
And out of the chambered weariness wanders a perfume abroad on its
    enterprise.

   out of
If ⟨from out⟩ the ⟨golden⟩ dreary halls of Dis Persephone had risen
To find the golden grainèd night aflower across the sky
Would she have caught the last trail of her garment away from her prison
And run and tossed and swung in ecstasy
Over the meadows?—She would have stood on the threshold
With her face to the stars, and spread
{T, H} er arms upon the night the fresh, cold
Night, and at last have uttered
Her long low passion of escape
           at last
And muffled her face, Δ in the nights black woollen crape.

Appendix D

"The Wild Common"

⟨No Title⟩

Into a deep pond, an old sheep dip,
Dark, overgrown with willows, cool, with the brook ebbing through so slow.
Naked on the steep {sweet, soft} lip
Of the bank I stand watching my own white shadow quivering to and fro.

Restless it makes as if it would leave me,
Then quick slips back to my feet, as my fond and fluctuant soul
After pretending 'twere good to bereave me
And wander spirit free, cleaves to my flesh as shaken wine clings in its bowl.

When gorse flowers shrivel their gold is lost
And without the pulsing waters where were the marigolds and the songs of the
    brook?
If my veins and my breasts with love embossed

                                    as
Withered, my insolent soul would be lost {with} the flower-gold which the hot
    wind took.

So my soul like a passionate woman turns
Filled with remorseful terror, to the man she scorned, and her love
For myself in my eye's laughter burns
Ecstatic over the pliant folds rippling down to my belly from the breast-lights
    above.

Over my sunlit skin the warm clinging air
Rich with songs of seven larks singing at once goes kissing me glad.
And the soul of the wind and my blood compare
Their wandering happiness, and the wind, wasted in liberty, drifts on and is
    sad.

Oh but the water loves me and folds me
Plays with me, sways me, lifts me and sinks me as though it were living blood
            heaving woman   who holds me
Blood of a {woman who is herself} {would mould me}
Owning my supple body a rare glad thing, supremely good.

2. *Amores* Version

The quick sparks on the gorse bushes are leaping
Little jets of sunlight-texture imitating flame;
Above them, exultant, the peewits are sweeping:
They are lords of the desolate wastes of sadness their screamings proclaim.

Rabbits, handfuls of brown earth, lie
Low-rounded on the mournful grass they have bitten down to the quick.
Are they asleep?—are they alive?—Now see, when I
Move my arms the hill bursts and heaves under their spurting kick.

The common flaunts bravely; but below, from the rushes
Crowds of glittering king-cups surge to challenge the blossoming bushes;
There the lazy streamlet pushes
Its curious course mildly; here it wakes again, leaps, laughs, and gushes.

Into a deep pond, an old sheep-dip,
Dark, overgrown with willows, cool, with the brook ebbing through so slow;
Naked on the steep, soft lip
Of the bank I stand watching my own white shadow quivering to and fro.

What if the gorse flowers shrivelled, and kissing were lost?
Without the pulsing waters, where were the marigolds and the songs of the
    brook?
If my veins and my breasts with love embossed
Withered, my insolent soul would be gone like flowers that the hot wind took.

So my soul like a passionate woman turns,
Filled with remorseful terror to the man she scorned, and her love
For myself in my own eyes' laughter burns,
Runs ecstatic over the pliant folds rippling down to my belly from the
    breast-lights above.

Over my sunlit skin the warm, clinging air
Rich with the songs of seven larks singing at once, goes kissing me glad.
And with the soul of the wind and my blood compare
Their wandering happiness, and the wind, wasted in liberty, drifts on and is
    sad.

Oh but the water loves me and folds me,
Plays with me, sways me, lifts me and sinks me as though it were living blood,
Blood of a heaving woman who holds me,
Owning my supple body a rare glad thing, supremely good.

3. *Collected Poems* Version

The quick sparks on the gorse-bushes are leaping
Little jets of sunlight texture imitating flame;
Above them, exultant, the peewits are sweeping:
They have triumphed again o'er the ages, their screamings proclaim.

Rabbits, handfuls of brown earth, lie
Low-rounded on the mournful turf they have bitten down to the quick.
Are they asleep?—are they living?—Now see, when I
Lift my arms, the hill bursts and heaves under their spurting kick!

The common flaunts bravely; but below, from the rushes
Crowds of glittering king-cups surge to challenge the blossoming bushes;
There the lazy streamlet pushes
His bent course mildly; here wakes again, leaps, laughs, and gushes

Into a deep pond, an old sheep-dip,
Dark, overgrown with willows, cool, with the brook ebbing through so slow;
Naked on the steep, soft lip
Of the turf I stand watching my own white shadow quivering to and fro.

What if the gorse-flowers shrivelled, and I were gone?
What if the waters ceased, where were the marigolds then, and the gudgeon?
What is this thing that I look down upon?
White on the water wimples my shadow, strains like a dog on a string, to run
    on.

How it looks back, like a white dog to its master!
I on the bank all substance, my shadow all shadow looking up to me, looking
    back!
And the water runs, and runs faster, runs faster,
And the white dog dances and quivers, I am holding his cord quite slack.

But how splendid it is to be substance, here!
My shadow is neither here nor there; but I, I am royally here!
I am here! I am here! screams the peewit; the may-blobs burst out in a laugh
    as they hear!
Here! flick the rabbits. Here! pants the gorse. Here! say the insects far and
    near.

Over my skin in the sunshine, the warm, clinging air
Flushed with the songs of seven larks singing at once, goes kissing me glad.
You are here! You are here! We have found you! Everywhere
We sought you substantial, you touchstone of caresses, you naked lad!

Oh but the water loves me and folds me,
Plays with me, sways me, lifts me and sinks me, murmurs: Oh marvellous
    stuff!
No longer shadow!—and it holds me
Close, and it rolls me, enfolds me, touches me, as if never it could touch me
    enough.

Sun, but in substance, yellow water-blobs!
Wings and feathers on the crying, mysterious ages, peewits wheeling!
All that is right, all that is good; all that is God takes substance! a rabbit lobs
In confirmation, I hear sevenfold lark-songs pealing.

Appendix E

"Dreams: Old" and "Dreams: Nascent"

1. Manuscript 1 Versions

Version A. A Still Afternoon in School

I have opened the window to warm my hands on the sill
Where the sunshine soaks in the stone. The afternoon
Is full of dreams, my Love, the boys are adream, all still
In a wishful dream of Lorna Doone.

The clink of the shunting engines is sharp and fine
Like ⟨saf⟩ savage music striking far-off.
On the great, uplifted blue Palace, light-pools stir and shine

  In   distance
⟨Among⟩ the blue grass, domed and Δ soft.

There lies the world, my darling, full of wonder and wistfulness and strange
Recognitions and greetings of unknown things:
The frail blue palace, which my {change, wonderful} , working years cannot
    change—*

                              forgotten ⟨the old⟩ music
Far-off, hollow pleasure-domes, where Δ ⟨no merriment⟩ sings*

Dream of a great blue place uplifted, and a nearer dream
{o, O} f Dora {D, C} opperfield and Norwood Hill
Wandering down the long dream tossed years where the hill and the gleam
Of glass open the doors of the years that now lie still

I can see no hill aright, for the snows of yesteryear
Still cover the slopes with memories and soft
Warm reflections from the sunsets of glowing souls that were here
Once, and are here forever.

There they lie, they are visible like a picture, But the men who move
Along the railway, the active figures of men
They have a secret, that flows in their limbs as they move
⟨Far⟩ In the distance, and they command my drea {d, m} ful world.

Here in the subtle, rounded flesh, and eternal eyes
Lies the great desired, the beloved

Waving line drawn by Lawrence through this line.

167

                                                labours
Here in the rounded flesh [is throned] the power, the hope, the God
The eternal creator—these are creators—the rest are dreams, the finished, the
    created

Oh my boys, bending your heads over your books
It is in you that life is trembling and fusing and creating
The new pattern of a dream—dream of a generation
I watch you to see the creators, the power that patterns the dreams

Dreams are beautiful, fixed and finite,
But Oh My Love, the dream-stuff is molten and moving mysteriously
Fascinating my eyes, for I, am I not also dream stuff
Am I not quickening diffusing myself in the pattern, shaping and shapen

Here in my class is the answer for the {g, G} reat {y, Y} earning
Eyes where {one, I} can watch the swim of dreams reflected on the molten
    metal of dreams
Watch the stir which is rhythmic, and moves them all like a heart-beat moves
    the blood
Here, in the swelling flesh the great activity working
Visible there in the change of eyes and the face

Oh the great mystery and fascination of the unseen shaper, [Life]
Oh the power of the melting, fusing force
Heat, light, colour, everything great and mysterious in One swelling and
    shaping the dreams in the flesh
Oh the terrible ecstasy of the consciousness {of, that} I am life
Oh the unconscious rapture that moves unthought *(illeg.)* with Life
Oh the miracle of the whole, the widespread labouring concentration of life
Swelling mankind like one bud to bring forth the fruit of a dream*
That makes the whole of mankind at once one bud to bring forth the fruit of a
    dream,
Oh the terror of lifting the innermost I out of the sweep of the impulse of Life
And watching the Great thing labouring through the whole round flesh of the
    world
And striving to catch a glimpse of the shape of the coming dream
And the scent and colour of the coming dream
Then to fall back exhausted into the molten unconscious life.

                        Version B. A Still Afternoon in School
                        Dreams Old and [Unborn] Nascent

I have opened the window to warm my hands on the sill
Where the sunshine soaks in the stone. The afternoon
Is full of dreams, my Love: the boys are [reading,] all still
In a wishful dream of Lorna Doone.

───────────────

Lawrence wrote this line above the original ones, apparently uncertain which to use.

The clink of the shunting engines is sharp and fine
Like savage music striking far off,
And far-off, on the great, uplifted blue Palace light-pools shine
And stir, where the blue grass is domèd soft.
        among the†

> There lies the world, my darling, full of wonder and wistfulness, and
>   strange
> Recognitions and greetings of half-acquaint things
> The cloud of blue Palace aloft there is one of {my, the} dreams which
>   range
> Beyond
> ⟨Along⟩ the horizon of my experience—my mother sings

There lies the world, my darling, full of wonder and wistfulness and strange
Recognitions and greetings of half-acquaint things as I greet the cloud
Of blue Palace aloft there, among the misty indefinite dreams that range
At the back of the horizon of my experience, where dreams from the past life
   crowd:
Nearer to me is Norwood Hill, but the sunrays that beam
And the {y, re} crowds nearer over Norwood Hill, ⟨a cherished dream⟩
 Warmly upon it are the rays of the bygone years of Dora
⟨Of the child wife Dora⟩
And Gypp; and a little laughter of old love, and a few tears gleam
                    among memories is a loving
Over Norwood Hill; my soul ⟨is a backward⟩ explorer.

          hushèd
All the bye-gone, ⟨dream-tossed⟩ years
 Streaming
⟨That stream⟩ back where the mist ⟨of oblivion⟩ distils
Into forgetfulness: soft-sailing waters, where fears*
Have left me the savour of their laughter and tears;
No longer shake: where the silk sail fills*
And the sweet live dream of the old-time fills
With the unfelt breeze that ebbs over the seas when the storm*
With colour, the sketch of my own world's form.
Of living has passed, drifting on and on*
⟨And⟩ {m, M} y world is a painted fresco of the past
Through the coloured iridescence that swims in the warm*
Where the old lives linger blurred and warm
Wave of the tumult spent and gone.*
                         the
Hiding the substance of this year with the shadow of Δ last.
⟨Observing my own grey world's substance to the last.⟩

---

†*Lawrence drew a line under "where the," writing these two words directly under it.*
**Lawrence has squeezed the lines marked by an asterisk in tiny handwriting between the lines of larger writing. This interlining apparently represents alternative verse forms.*

My world is a painted fresco, where coloured shapes
of old, ineffectual lives linger blurred and warm
a woven endless tapestry the past life drapes
Over the living whose pictures are gathering form.*

The surface of dreams is broken.
The picture of the past is shaken and scattered.
Fluent, active figures of men pass along the railway and I am woken
From the dreams that distance flattered.

Fluent, active figures of men pass along the railway.
They have a secret that flows in their limbs as they move
                                                    Nearer
[Nearer[{o, O} ut of the distance—Δ here in the subtle, rounded flesh
Lives the active ecstasy, and in the sudden lifting of the eyes it is clearer:
The fascination of the quick, rest-less {c, C} reator moving through the mesh
Of men, vibrating in ecstasy through the rounded flesh.

Oh my boys bending over your books
In you is trembling and fusing the creation
Of a new-patterned dream, dream of a generation

Old dreams are beloved, beautiful, fixed and sure
But the dream stuff is molten and moving mysteriously
Fascinating me—And me, am I not also pure
Molten dream-stuff, diffusing myself in the pattern, flowing into place
    seriously?

Herein shall I find an answer for my life-heavy yearning:
                                                    dreams
Eyes where I can watch the [reflection[swim of old [years[reflected on the
    molten metal of dreams.
 Watch   which   [stirring[and shoves them
[Flesh where[the stir, Δ is rhythmic, [moving them all[all like a heart beat
    moves the blood;
Through the swelling flesh, the great Activity working,
Impelling, shaping, visible there in the change of the eyes and the features.

Oh the great mystery and fascination of the unseen shaper
The power of the melting, fusing force—Heat, Light everything in One
Everything great and mysterious in One, swelling and shaping the dreams in
    the flesh
As it swells and shapes into blossom a bud

Oh the terrible ecstasy that acknowledges that I am life
Oh the unconscious rapture, that moves unthoughtful with life.

This stanza added in the upper margin of the page.

Here is the miracle: the whole, wide-spread, labouring concentration of life
Swelling the gigantic flesh of the world
Into one bud, rounded and swelling with the fruit of a dream.

Oh the terror of lifting the innermost "I" out of the sweep of the impulse of
  Life
Watching the Great Thing labouring through the whole round flesh of the
  world
Striving to catch a glimpse of the shape of the coming dream
And the scent and the colour of the coming dream
Then to fall back—exhausted into the molten unconscious life

2. Manuscripts 5 and 9 and *The English Review* Versions

A Still Afternoon/Dreams Old and Nascent/I. Old

⟨MS 9 has no title; the first 10 lines of the poem in this version have been
lost.⟩

I ⟨MS 5: 1⟩

I have opened the window to warm my hands on the sill
Where the sunlight soaks in the stone: the afternoon
Is full of dreams, my love; the boys are all still
In a wishful dream of Lorna Doone.

The clink of the shunting engines is sharp and fine
Like savage music striking far off; and away
On the uplifted blue Palace, light pools stir and shine
Where the glass is domed up the blue, soft day. ⟨MS 5: blue soft⟩

II ⟨MS 5: 2⟩

There lies the world, my Darling, full of wonder, and wistfulness, and strange
  ⟨MS 5: wonder and⟩
Recognitions and greetings of half-acquaint things, as I greet the cloud
Of blue Palace aloft there, among the misty indefinite dreams that range ⟨MS
  9 begins with this line⟩
At the back of my life's horizon, where the dreams from the past lives crowd.
  ⟨MSS 5 and 9: crowd:⟩

Over the nearness of Norwood Hill, through the mellow veil ⟨MS 5: Hill
  through⟩
Of the afternoon, glows only the old romance of David and Dora,
With the old, sweet, soothing tears, and laughter that shakes the sail
Of the ship of the soul over seas where dreamed dreams lure the unoceaned
  explorer.

III

Over the bygone, hushèd years ⟨MS 5: bye-gone hushèd; MS 9: by-gone,
  hushèd⟩
Streaming back where the mist distils
Into forgetfulness: soft sailing waters, where fears ⟨MS 5: soft-sailing⟩

No longer shake: where the silk sail fills
With the unfelt breeze that ebbs over the seas, when the storm
Of living has passed, on and on
Through the coloured iridescence that swims in the warm
Wake of the hushèd tumult now spent and gone
Drifts my boat, wistfully lapsing after
The mists of receding tears, and the echo of laughter. ⟨MS 5: {f, t} ears⟩

IV ⟨MSS 5 and 9: 3⟩

My world is a painted fresco, where coloured shapes
Of old ineffectual lives linger blurred and warm:
An endless tapestry the past has woven, drapes ⟨MSS 5 and 9: —An; MS 5:
    woven drapes⟩
The halls of my life, and compels my soul to conform.

II. Nascent

V ⟨MSS 5 and 9: 4⟩

Through the wakened afternoon, riding down my dreams
Fluent active figures of men pass along the railway.
There is something stirs in me from the flow of their limbs as they move ⟨MS
    5: Something; MS 9: There is {s, S} omething⟩
Out of the distance, nearer. ⟨MS 5: {o, O} ut⟩
Here in the subtle, rounded flesh
Beats the active ecstasy, suddenly lifting my eyes
Into quick response.
The fascination of the restless Creator, through the mesh of men
Moving, vibrating endlessly in the rounded flesh
Challenges me, and is answered.

VI ⟨MSS 5 and 9: 5⟩

Oh my boys, bending over your books
In you is trembling and fusing
The creation of a new-patterned dream, dream of a generation.

VII ⟨MSS 5 and 9: 6⟩

The old dreams are beloved, beautiful, soft-toned, and sure ⟨MS 5: soft
    toned⟩
But the dream-stuff is molten and moving mysteriously. ⟨MS 5: dream stuff⟩
This is no wistful allure
For am I not also dream-stuff, diffusing myself in the pattern ⟨MS 9: al {l,
    so}⟩
Flowing I know not how, yet seriously
Going into my place.

VIII ⟨MS 9: |6|⁷⟩

Here have I found an answer for my hollow yearning:
Eyes where I can watch the swim of old dreams reflected on the molten metal
    of dreams,

Watch the stir whose rhythm is secret, whose secret is sure and safe: ⟨MS 9:
⟨safe⟩ sure and {sur, safe}⟩
The great activity swelling, through the round flesh pulsing, ⟨MS 5: swelling
through⟩
Impelling, shaping the coming dream;
Visible under the changing eyes,
Under the mobile features.

$$\text{IX} \left[\text{MS 9: } \frac{8}{\lfloor 7 \rfloor} \right]$$

The flush of the great mystery, ⟨MSS 5 and 9: mystery⟩
The radiance of the Unseen Shaper,
Is in me a trembling gladness,
As the subtle heat
Quickens the hastening, white-hot metal, ·
The power of the melting, fusing force, ⟨MS 5: force⟩
The great, mysterious One, is swelling and shaping the dreams in the flesh,
⟨MSS 5 and 9: flesh⟩
Is swelling and shaping a bud into blossom, ⟨MS 5: blossom.⟩
The whole teeming flesh of mankind.
The gigantic flesh of the world*
Is swelling with widespread, labouring concentration* ⟨MSS 5 and 9:
wide-spread⟩
Into one bud on the stalk of eternity,
Rounded and swelling towards the fruit of a dream.

3. Manuscript 19 Versions

A Still Afternoon in School/1. The Old Dream

1.

I have opened the window to warm my hands on the sill
Where the sunlight soaks in the stone: the afternoon
Is full of dreams; my love; the boys are all still
In a wistful dream of "Lorna Doone."

The clink of the shunting engines is sharp and fine
Like savage music striking far off; and away
On the blue
⟨Uplifted on⟩ uplifted Palace, lights stir and shine
In the glass domed up ⟨the⟩ among the blue, soft day.

2.

There lies the world, my darling, full of wonder and wistfulness and strange
Recognitions and greetings of half-acquaint things, as I greet the cloud
Of blue Palace aloft there, among the misty, indefinite things that range
At the back of my life's horizon, among the dead lives' vast dream-crowd.

These two lines comprise one line in MS 5.

Over the nearness of Norwood Hill, through the mellow veil
Of the afternoon, glows only the old romance of David and Dora,
With the old, sweet, soothing tears, and laughter that shakes the sail
Of the ship of the soul over seas where dreamed dreams lure the unoceaned
    explorer.

 Over the by-gone, hushèd years
Reaching back where the mist distils
In forgetfulness: soft-sailing waters where fears
No longer ⟨sail⟩ shake; where the silk sail fills
With (illeg.) the drift of a dream that goes ebbing over
The seas where the storm of living has passed;

                on
On and on, ⟨with⟩ still wings the rover
Floats through the iridescence that last
Year's ship leaves swimming in her wake;

                                        in the warm
Through the iridescence that ⟨sp⟩ swims ⟨in the wake⟩
Wake of the tumult now spent and gone
Drifts my boat but half awake;

            on
Safe, ⟨sa⟩ the deep of a dream, from storm
Of living and loving every one,
My boat drifts, wistfully lapsing after
The mists of vanishing tears, and the echo of laughter.

My world is a painted fresco, where coloured shapes
                    lives
Of old ineffectual ⟨shapes⟩ linger blurred and warm,
The endless tapestry of past years drapes
My halls and bids my soul conform.*

                    2. Nascent
Through the wakened afternoon, riding down my dreams
Fluent active figures of men pass along the railway.
There is something stirs in me from the flow of their limbs as they move
Out of the distance nearer.
Here in the subtle, rounded flesh
Beats the active ecstasy, suddenly
Lifting my eyes into quick response.
The fascination of the restless Creator, through the mesh of men
Moving, vibrating endlessly in the moulded flesh
Challenges me and is answered.

---

*This stanza heavily deleted by Lawrence.

Ah, in you, my boys bending over your books
Sudden I see in you is trembling

    new pattern
The ʃcreationʃ of a dream, the dream of a generation.

3.
       soft-toned
The old dreams are beloved, beautiful, ʃfixedʃ and sure:
But the dream stuff is molten and moving mysteriously.
This is no wistful allure,
For am I not also dream-stuff, diffusing myself in the pattern
Flowing I know not how, yet seriously
Going into my place!
Here have I found an answer for hollow yearning:
Eyes where I can watch the swim of old dreams reflected {On, on} the molten
    metal of dreams,
Watch the stir whose rhythm is secret, whose secret is sure and safe:
The great activity swelling, through the round flesh pulsing
Impelling, shaping the coming dream,
Visible under the changing eyes
Under the mobile features.
The flush of the mystery,
The radiance of the Shaper,
Is in me a trembling gladness.
⌈ ʃAs the subtle heat,ʃ   ⌉
| ʃQuickensʃ |
⌊ ʃQuickens the hastening, white-hot metal,ʃ ⌋
Oh the terrible ecstasy that acknowledges I am life,
ʃOhʃ {t, T} he unconscious rapture, that moves unthoughtful with life.
Here is the miracle: the whole, wide-spread, labouring concentration of life
Swelling the gigantic flesh of the world
Into one bud, rounded and swelling with the fruit of a dream,
Everything great and mysterious in one, swelling and shaping the dreams in
    the flesh,
As it swells and shapes into blossom a bud,
Into one bud on the stalk of eternity.

And ah! the terror of lifting the innermost "I" out of the sweep of the impulse
    of life,
  Watching the great thing labouring through the whole round flesh of the
    world,

          a
Striving to catch ʃtheʃ glimpse of the shape of the coming dream,
And the scent and the colour of the ʃdreamʃ coming dream,
          exhausted
Then to fall back ʃunconsciousʃ into the molten unconscious life.

4. *Amores* and Manuscript 26 Versions

Dreams Old and Nascent/Old

I have opened the window to warm my hands on the sill
Where the sunlight soaks in the stone: the afternoon
Is full of dreams, my love, the boys are all still
In a wistful dream of Lorna Doone.

The clink of the shunting engines is sharp and fine, ⟨MS 26: fine⟩
Like savage music striking far off, and there
On the great, uplifted blue palace, lights stir and shine
Where the glass is domed in the blue, soft air.

There lies the world, my darling, full of wonder and wistfulness and strange
Recognition and greetings of half-acquaint things, as I greet the cloud ⟨MS
     26: Recognitions⟩
Of blue palace aloft there, among misty indefinite dreams that range ⟨MS 26:
     Palace⟩
At the back of my life's horizon, where the dreamings of past lives crowd.

Over the nearness of Norwood Hill, through the mellow veil
Of the afternoon glows to me the old romance of David and Dora,

⟨ MS 26: ⟨only⟩   to me ⟩

With the old, sweet, soothing tears, and laughter that shakes the sail
Of the ship of the soul over seas where dreamed dreams lure the

⟨ MS 26: dreams Δ the unoceaned explorer.   lure ⟩

All the bygone, hushèd years
Streaming back where the mist distils
Into forgetfulness: soft-sailing waters where fears
No longer shake, where the silk sail fills
With an unfelt breeze that ebbs over the seas, where the storm
Of living has passed, ebbing on
Through the coloured iridescence that swims in the warm
Wake of the tumult now spent and gone,
Drifts my boat, wistfully lapsing after
The mists of vanishing tears, and the echo of laughter.

Dreams Old and Nascent/Nascent

My world is a painted fresco, where coloured shapes ⟨MS 26: colored⟩
Of old, ineffectual lives linger blurred and warm;
An endless tapestry the past has woven drapes
The halls of my life, compelling my soul to conform.

The surface of dreams is broken,
The picture of the past is shaken and scattered. ⟨MS 26: scattered⟩
Fluent, active figures of men pass along the railway, and I am woken
From the dreams that the distance flattered.

Along the railway, active figures of men.
$\Big\langle$ Along the railway, the active figures of men! $\Big\rangle$
   MS 26: ⟨Fluent active figures of men pass along⟩
They have a secret that stirs in their limbs as they move
Out of the distance, nearer, commanding my dreamy world.
$\Big\langle$ nearer $\Big\rangle$
   MS 26: distance, Δ commanding

Here in the subtle, rounded flesh
Beats the active ecstasy. ⟨MS 26: ecstasy⟩
In the sudden lifting my eyes, it is clearer, ⟨MS 26: ⟨And⟩ {i, I} n⟩
The fascination of the quick, restless Creator moving through the mesh
Of men, vibrating in ecstasy through the rounded flesh.

Oh my boys, bending over your books,
In you is trembling and fusing
The creation of a new-patterned dream, dream of a generation:
And I watch to see the Creator, the power that patterns the dream.

The old dreams are beautiful, beloved, soft-toned and sure, ⟨MS 26: sure⟩
But the dream-stuff is molten and moving mysteriously, ⟨MS 26:
    mysteriously⟩
Alluring my eyes; for I, am I not also dream-stuff,
Am I not quickening, diffusing myself in the pattern, shaping and shapen?

Here in my class is the answer for the great yearning:
Eyes where I can watch the swim of old dreams reflected on the molten metal
    of dreams,
Watch the stir which is rhythmic and moves them all as a heart-beat moves
    the blood,
$\Big\langle$ and mov {es, ing} them all as a $\Big\rangle$
   MS 26: rhythmic, ⟨whose heart-beat moves⟩ heart-beat moves the
   blood,
Here in the swelling flesh the great activity working,
Visible there in the change of eyes and the mobile features.

Oh the great mystery and fascination of the unseen Shaper,
The power of the melting, fusing Force—heat, light, all in one, ⟨MS 26:
    force⟩,⟨—heat⟩
Everything great and mysterious in one, swelling and shaping the dream in the
    flesh,
As it swells and shapes a bud into blossom.
$\Big\langle$ As it swells and shapes a bud into blossom. $\Big\rangle$
   MS 26: ⟨Impelling, changing seen in the change of eyes and the features⟩

Oh the terrible ecstasy of the consciousness that I am life!
Oh the miracle of the whole, the widespread, labouring concentration
Swelling mankind like one bud to bring forth the fruit of a dream,
Oh the terror of lifting the innermost I out of the sweep of the impulse of life,

⟨
    Oh the terror of lifting the innermost I
    ⟨Oh the terror of lifting the innermost⟩
    ⟨Swelling the gigantic flesh of the world⟩
MS 26: ⟨Into one bud, rounded and swelling with the fruit of a dream⟩
⟩

And watching the great Thing labouring through the whole round flesh of the
    world;
And striving to catch a glimpse of the shape of the coming dream,
As it quickens within the labouring, white-hot metal,

⟨
      As it
MS 26: ⟨That⟩ quickens
⟩

Catch the scent and the colour of the coming dream, ⟨MS 26: {And, Catch}⟩
Then to fall back exhausted into the unconscious, molten life!

5. *Collected Poems* Versions

Old

I have opened the windows to warm my hands on the sill
Where the sunlight soaks in the stone: the afternoon
Is full of dreams, my love; the boys are all still
In a wistful dream of Lorna Doone.

The clink of the shunting engines is sharp and fine
Like savage music striking far off; and there
On the great blue palace at Sydenham, lights stir and shine
Where the glass is domed on the silent air.

There lies the world, my darling, full of wonder and wistfulness, and strange
Recognitions and greetings of half-acquaint things, as I greet the cloud
Of glass palace aloft there, among misty, indefinite things that range
At the back of my life's experience, where dreams from the old lives crowd.

Over the nearness of Norwood Hill, through the mellow veil
Of the afternoon glows still the old romance of David and Dora,
With the old, sweet, soothing tears, and laughter that shakes the sail
Of the ship of the soul over seas where dreamed dreams lure the unoceaned
    explorer.

All the bygone, hushèd years
Streaming back where the mists distil
To forgetfulness: soft-sailing waters where fears
No longer hurt where the silk sails fill

With that unfelt breeze that ebbs over the seas where the storm
Of living has passed, ebbing on
Through the stirred iridescence that swims in the warm
Wake of a tumult now spent and gone,
Drifts my boat, wistfully lapsing after
The silence of vanishing tears, and the echoes of laughter.

Nascent

The world is a painted memory, where coloured shapes
Of old, spent lives linger blurred and warm;
An endless tapestry the past has woven, drapes
The halls of my mind, compelling my life to conform.

I have lived delighted in the halls of the past
Where dead men's lives glow gently, and iron hurts
No more, and money stinks not, and death at last
Is only sad men taking off their shirts.

But now I think I have seen it all, and now
I feel thick walls of stone behind the arras.
I am shut in, a prisoner, I know not how.
And past lives hamper me, clog and embarrass.

They have no hands, they have no bodies, all
These shapes that now are dreams and once were men.
And so my heart begins to cry and call
But to get out from this dim, dreadful den.

       •   •   •   •   •   •

The surface of dreams is broken, the arras is torn,
There's a breach in the walls of the past, lets the daylight through.
Fluent figures of men go down the upborne
Track of the railway, alive, and with something to do.

Along the railway, active figures of men!
Each with a secret which stirs in his limbs, as they move
Out of the distance nearer, coming to prove
With a touch the dead and the living, while time counts ten.

In the subtle lift of the thighs as they come unmarching
Beats the new fresh air of life. They come for strife,
For the ripping of arras, and smashing of walls, and the fight for life;
With axe in hand, and the hammer, and the pick-axe over-arching.

Oh come, and break this prison, this house of yesterday!
The arras is all illusion, oh come and tear it away!
The walls are thick, and the inner rooms are such, they dismay
The heart, all crowded with slaves, most working, some few at play.

       •   •   •   •   •   •

The old dreams are beautiful, beloved, soft-toned and sure,
But worn out, they hide no more the walls they stand before.
Walled in, walled in, the whole world is a vast impure
Interior, a house of dreams where the dreamers writhe and snore.

Oh come, and wake us up from the ghastly dream of to-day.
We asphyxiate in a sleep of dreams, rebreathing the impure air.
For the house is shut and sealed, and the breath of the hosts is grey
As they dream corrupted dreams, all poisoned with care.

The ghastly dream of labour, and the stench of steel and of oil.
The writhing of myriads of workmen, all dreaming they are going to be rich
And giving off dreadful effluvia in a ghastly effort of toil
Unfinished for ever, but gasping for money, as they dream and they itch.

The ghastly dream of riches, of masses of money to spend,
Of walking over the faces of men, like cobble-stones!
Of riding, and being envied, such envy as has no end!
Of making a triumph of envy, the rich and successful ones.

·   ·   ·   ·   ·   ·

The whole wide world is interior now, and we're all shut up.
The air is all close and poisonous, it has drugged our souls, so we sleep
A sleep that is writhing stupor, weighed down, so we can't wake up.
The rich and the poor alike dreaming and writhing, all in one heap.

Oh come, oh, men along the railway! Oh come as men
And break the walls of possession of all the wide world!
Give us air, we cry. Oh, let us but breathe again!
Let us breathe fresh air and wake from foul dreams in which we are furled.

To feel fresh air in our throats, to have fresh breath in our breasts,
To make new words with our lips, to escape the foul dream
Of having and getting and owning, the struggle which wrests
Money from out of the earth or the beast or the man, as they labour in steam.

·   ·   ·   ·   ·   ·

Oh, men with the axe and the pick-axe, break the walls of the filthy dream
And release us, poor ones and rich ones, let us breathe and touch
One another in wonder of wakening, let us wake to the gleam
Of real daylight upon us, released from the foul dream's hutch.

For the proper dream-stuff is molten, and moving mysteriously,
And the bodies of men and women are molten matter of dreams
That stirs with a stir which is cosmic, as ever, invisibly
The heart of the live world pulses, and the blood of the live world teems.

And what is life, but the swelling and shaping the dream in the flesh!
And our bodies molten drops of dream-blood that swirl and swell
In a tissue, as all the molten cells in the living mesh
Of a rose-tree move to roses and thorns and a delicate smell.

Appendix F.

"Virgin Youth"

1. Manuscript 1 Version

Movements/ . . . 3. The Body Awake

Now and again
All my body springs alive
And the life that is polarised in my eyes
That quivers in smiles and thoughts between my eyes and my mouth
Flies like a wild thing escaped along my body
Leaving my eyes half empty and clamourous,
Filling my still breasts with a flush and a flame,
Gathering the soft ripples below my breasts
Into urgent, passionate waves,
And my soft, slumbering belly,
Quivering awake with one impulse of desire,
Gathers itself fiercely together;
And my docile, fluent arms
Knotting themselves with wild strength
To clasp—what they have never clasped.
Then I tremble, and go trembling
Under the wild, sweet tyranny of my body
Till it has spent itself
And the relentless nodality of my eyes reasserts itself
Till the bursten flood of life ebbs back to my eyes
Back from my beautiful, lonely body
Tired and unsatisfied.

2. *Amores* Version

Now and again
All my body springs alive,
And the life that is polarised in my eyes,
That quivers between my eyes and mouth,
Flies like a wild thing across my body,
Leaving my eyes half empty, and clamorous,
Filling my still breasts with a flush and a flame,
Gathering the soft ripples below my breasts
Into urgent, passionate waves,

And my soft, slumbering belly
Quivering awake with one impulse of desire,
Gathers itself fiercely together;
And my docile, fluent arms
Knotting themselves with wild strength
To clasp—what they have never clasped.
Then I tremble, and go trembling
Under the wild, strange tyranny of my body,
Till it has spent itself,
And the relentless nodality of my eyes reasserts itself,
Till the bursten flood of life ebbs back to my eyes,
Back from my beautiful, lonely body
Tired and unsatisfied.

3. *Collected Poems* Version

Now and again
The life that looks through my eyes
And quivers in words through my mouth,
And behaves like the rest of men,
Slips away, so I gasp in surprise.

And then
My unknown breasts begin
To wake, and down the thin
Ripples below the breast an urgent
Rhythm starts, and my silent and slumberous belly
In one moment rouses insurgent.

My soft, slumbering belly,
Quivering awake with one impulse and one will,
Then willy nilly
A lower me gets up and greets me;
Homunculus stirs from his roots, and strives until,
Risen up, he beats me.

He stands, and I tremble before him.
—Who then art thou?—
He is wordless, but sultry and vast.
And I can't deplore him.
—Who art thou? What hast
Thou to do with me, thou lustrous one, iconoclast?—

How beautiful he is! without sound,
Without eyes, without hands;
Yet, flame of the living ground
He stands, the column of fire by night.
And he knows from the depths; he quite
Alone understands.

Quite alone, he alone
Understands and knows.
Lustrously sure, unknown
Out of nowhere he rose.

I tremble in his shadow, as he burns
For the dark goal.
He stands like a lighthouse, night churns
Round his base, his dark light rolls
Into darkness, and darkly returns.

Is he calling, the lone one? Is his deep
Silence full of summons?
Is he moving invisibly? Does his steep
Curve sweep towards a woman's?

Traveller, column of fire,
It is vain.
The glow of thy full desire
Becomes pain.

Dark, ruddy pillar, forgive me! I
Am helplessly bound
To the rock of virginity. Thy
Strange voice has no sound.

We cry in the wilderness. Forgive me, I
Would so gladly lie
In the womanly valley, and ply
Thy twofold dance.

Thou dark one, thou proud, curved beauty! I
Would worship thee, letting my buttocks prance.
But the hosts of men with one voice deny
Me the chance.

They have taken the gates from the hinges
And built up the way. I salute thee
But to deflower thee. Thy tower impinges
On nothingness. Pardon me!

Appendix G
"Discipline"

1. Manuscript 1 Version

It is stormy, and rain drops cling like silver bees to the pane,
The thin sycamore in the garden is swinging with flattened leaves
The heads of my boys move dimly through the yellow gloom that stains
The class: over them all the darkness of my discipline weaves.

It is no good, my dear, ⟨gentleness and forebearance⟩ I endured too long.
                                                  in
I have pushed my hands ⟨under⟩ the dark soil under the flowers of my soul,
Under the caress of leaves, and felt where the roots were strong
Fixed and grappling in the darkness for the deep-soil's little control.

It is no good, my darling, Life does not lead us with a daisy chain
We are schooled by pain, and only in suffering are we brothers
So I've torn some roots from my soul, twisted them, good or bane
Into thongs of discipline: from my anguished submission weaving another's.

And, quivering with the contest, I have bound and beaten my fifty boys.
The fight was so cruel, my love; I have torn the deep strings from my soul
And fought with the blood in my eyes, and established the equipose
Of law and obedience—my class is a cosmos, a whole.

⎡ Greatest of all is Jehovah, the Father, the Law-Giver, the Stern   ⎤
⎢ Punisher: Forgiveness is only a flower from the almighty trees.   ⎥
⎢ I am a son of Jehovah—out of suffering I must learn   ⎥
⎢ To judge and punish like a God, though I yearn to put forth mercy, and   ⎥
⎣   ease.   ⎦

2. *The English Review* Version

It is stormy, and rain-drops cling like silver bees to the pane,
The thin sycamore in the playground is swinging with flattened leaves;
The heads of my boys move dimly through the yellow gloom that stains
The class: over them all the dark net of my discipline weaves.

It is no good, dear, meekness and forbearance—I endured too long.
I have pushed my hands in the dark loam under the flowers of my soul,
Under the caressing leaves, and felt where the roots were strong
Fixed in the darkness, grappling for the deep soil's little control.

Far and wide run the easy roots that bear the leaves of pity.
I'd have torn them up had they borne away the patient bulbs of my hopes:
Oh I tore them up, though the wistful leaves were fragrant, and soft, and
    pretty,
And I twisted them over the broken leaves into unbreakable ropes.

Ah, my Darling, when over the purple horizon shall loom
The shrouded Mother of a new idea, men hide their faces,
Cry out, and fend her off, as she seeks her procreant groom,
Wounding themselves against her, denying her great embraces.

And do I not seek to mate my grown, desirous soul
With the lusty souls of my boys?—yet they hide their faces,
And strike with a blindness of fury against me; can I cajole
The hate of terror?—or deny the fecund soul her embraces?

The flower of forgiveness is plucked from off the offender's plot
To wither on the bosom of the merciful:—so many seeds the less,
So much more room for riot! The great God spareth not,
He waters our face with tears, our young fruits fills with bitterness.

3. *Amores* Version

It is stormy, and raindrops cling like silver bees to the pane,
The thin sycamores in the playground are swinging with flattened leaves;
The heads of the boys move dimly through a yellow gloom that stains
The class; over them all the dark net of my discipline weaves.

It is no good, dear, gentleness and forbearance, I endured too long.
I have pushed my hands in the dark soil, under the flower of my soul
And the gentle leaves, and have felt where the roots are strong
Fixed in the darkness, grappling for the deep soil's little control.

And there is the dark, my darling, where the roots are entangled and fight
Each one for its hold on the oblivious darkness, I know that there
In the night where we first have being, before we rise on the light,
We are not brothers, my darling, we fight and we do not spare.

And in the original dark the roots cannot keep, cannot know
Any communion whatever, but they bind themselves on to the dark,
And drawing the darkness together, crush from it a twilight, a slow
Burning that breaks at last into leaves and a flower's bright spark.

I came to the boys with love, my dear, but they turned on me;
I came with gentleness, with my heart 'twixt my hands like a bowl,
Like a loving-cup, like a grail, but they spilt it triumphantly
And tried to break the vessel, and to violate my soul.

But what have I to do with the boys, deep down in my soul, my love?
I throw from out of the darkness my self like a flower into sight,
Like a flower from out of the night-time, I lift my face, and those
Who will warm their hands at me, comfort this night.

But whosoever would pluck apart my flowering shall burn their hands,
So flowers are tender folk, and roots can only hide,
Yet my flowerings of love are a fire, and the scarlet brands
Of my love are roses to look at, but flames to chide.

But comfort me, my love, now the fires are low,
Now I am broken to earth like a winter destroyed, and all
Myself but a knowledge of roots, of roots in the dark that throw
A net on the undersoil, which lies passive beneath their thrall.

But comfort me, for henceforth my love is yours alone,
To you alone will I offer the bowl, to you will I give
My essence only; but love me, and I will atone
To you for my general loving, atone as long as I live.

4. *Collected Poems* Version

It is stormy, and raindrops cling like silver bees to the panes,
The thin sycamore in the playground is swinging with flattened leaves;
The heads of the boys move dimly through a yellow gloom that stains
The class; over them all the dark net of my discipline weaves.

It is no good, dear, gentleness and forbearance; I endured too long.
I have pushed my hands in the dark soil, under the flower of my soul
And the gentle leaves, and have felt where the roots are strong
Fixed in the darkness, grappling for the deep soil's crowded control.

And there in the dark, my darling, where the roots are entangled and fight
Each one for its hold on the concrete darkness, I know that there
In the night where we first have being, before we rise on the light,
We are not lovers, my darling, we fight and we do not spare.

And in the original dark the roots cannot keep, cannot know
Any communion whatever, but they bind themselves on to the dark,
And drawing the darkness together, crush from it a twilight, a slow
Dim self that rises slowly to leaves and the flower's gay spark.

I came to the boys with love, dear, and only they turned on me;
With gentleness came I, with my heart 'twixt my hands like a bowl,
Like a loving-cup, like a grail, but they spilt it triumphantly
And tried to break the vessel, and violate my soul.

And perhaps they were right, for the young are busy deep down at the roots,
And love would only weaken their under-earth grip, make shallow
Their hold on reality, enfeeble their rising shoots
With too much tincture of me, instead of the dark's deep fallow.

I thought that love would do all things, but now I know I am wrong.
There are depths below depths, my darling, where love does not belong.
Where the fight that is fight for being is fought throughout the long
Young years, and the old must not win, not even if they love and are strong.

I must not win their souls, no never, I only must win
The brief material control of the hour, leave them free of me.
Learn they must to obey, for all harmony is discipline,
And only in harmony with others the single soul can be free.

Let them live, the boys, and learn not to trespass; I had to learn
Not to trespass on them with love, they must learn not to trespass in the
    young
Cruel self; the fight is not for existence, the fight is to burn
At last into blossom of being, each one his own flower outflung.

They are here to learn but one lesson, that they shall not thwart each other
Nor be thwarted, in life's slow struggle to unfold the flower of the self.
They draw their sap from the Godhead, not from me, but they must not
    smother
The sun from their neighbour either, nor be smothered in turn by pelf.

I will teach them the beginning of the lesson at the roots, and then no more.
I throw from out of the darkness myself like a flower into sight
Of the day, but it's nothing to do with the boys, so let them ignore
What's beyond them, and fight with me in discipline's little fight.

But whoever would pluck apart my flowering will burn their hands,
For flowers are tender folk, and roots can only hide.
But sometimes the opening petals are fire, and the scarlet brands
Of the blossom are roses to look at, but flames when they're tried.

But now I am trodden to earth, and my fires are low;
Now I am broken down like a plant in winter, and all
Myself but a knowledge of roots, of roots in the dark, that throw
A net on the undersoil, that lies passive, and quickened with gall.

Yet wait awhile, for henceforth I will love when a blossom calls
To my blossom in perfume and seed-dust, and only then; I will give
My love where it is wanted. Yet wait awhile! My fall
Is complete for the moment, yet wait, and you'll see that my flower will live.

Appendix H
"Blue" and "Blueness"

1. *Amores* Version of "Blue"

The earth again like a ship steams out of the dark sea over
The edge of the blue, and the sun stands up to see us glide
Slowly into another day; slowly the rover
Vessel of darkness takes the rising tide.

I, on the deck, am startled by this dawn confronting
Me who am issued amazed from the darkness, stripped
And quailing here in the sunshine, betrayed from haunting
The soundless night whereon our days are shipped.

Feeling myself undawning, the day's light playing upon me,
I who am substance of shadow, I all compact
Of the stuff of the night, finding myself all wrongly
Among the crowds of things in the sunshine jostled and racked.

I with the night on my lips, I sigh with the silence of death;
And what do I care though the very stones should cry me unreal, though the
    clouds
Shine in conceit of substance upon me, who am less than the rain.
Do I not know the darkness within them? What are they but shrouds?

The clouds go down the sky with a wealthy ease
Casting a shadow of scorn upon me for my share in death; but I
Hold my own in the midst of them, darkling, defy
The whole of the day to extinguish the shadow I lift on the breeze.

Yea, though the very clouds have vantage over me,
Enjoying their glancing flight, though love is dead,
I still am not homeless here, I've a tent by day
Of darkness where she sleeps on her perfect bed.

And I know the Host, the minute sparkling of darkness
Which vibrates untouched and perfect through the grandeur of night,
But which, when dawn crows challenge, assaulting the vivid motes
Of living darkness, bursts fretfully, and is bright:

  Runs like a fretted arc-lamp into light,
  Stirred by conflict to shining, which else
  Were dark and whole with the night.

188

Runs to a fret of speed like a racing wheel,
Which else were aslumber along with the whole
Of the dark, swinging rhythmic instead of a-reel.

Is chafed to anger, bursts into rage like thunder;
Which else were a silent grasp that held the heavens
Arrested, beating thick with wonder.

Leaps like a fountain of blue sparks leaping
In a jet from out of obscurity,
Which erst was darkness sleeping.

Runs into streams of bright blue drops,
Water and stones and stars, and myriads
Of twin-blue eyes, and crops

Of floury grain, and all the hosts of day,
All lovely hosts of ripples caused by fretting
The Darkness into play.

2. *Collected Poems* Version of "Blueness"

Out of the darkness, fretted sometimes in its sleeping,
Jets of sparks in fountains of blue come leaping
To sight, revealing a secret, numberless secrets keeping.

Sometimes the darkness trapped within a wheel
Runs into speed like a dream, the blue of the steel
Showing the rocking darkness now a-reel.

And out of the invisible, streams of bright blue drops
Rain from the showery heavens, and bright blue crops
Of flowers surge from below to their ladder-tops.

And all the manifold blue, amazing eyes,
The rainbow arching over in the skies,
New sparks of wonder opening in surprise:

All these pure things come foam and spray of the sea
Of Darkness abundant, which shaken mysteriously
Breaks into dazzle of living, as dolphins leap from the sea
Of midnight and shake it to fire, till the flame of the shadow we see.

Appendix I
"Troth with the Dead"

The moon is broken in twain, and half a moon
Before me lies on the floor of a still pale sky;
The other half, the broken coin of troth,
I have in my pocket, I press against my thigh.

I buried her half in the grave when I buried her,
I pushed it in among the thick of her hair
Where it gathered towards the plait, over her ear,
Like a moon in the dark I hid it secretly there.

And it has risen again, to recall to me
The troth with her is ever, is ever to keep—
No need, ah Moon-in twain- to remind me this,
                    like the ⟨still⟩ dark of
Memory lies in my heart ⟨still, strange as⟩ sleep.

Still in my heart inviolate sleep lies shut
      leaden
In a ⟨drowsy⟩ -lidded dream which trespasses o'er
$$\left[\begin{array}{l} \qquad\qquad\qquad\qquad\text{soul} \\ \qquad\qquad\qquad\qquad\text{⟨eyes⟩} \\ \text{The wonder-faint world of my wakeful ⟨thought⟩ , so I} \end{array}\right]$$
      mid the things
Am lost ⟨in a world⟩ I knew so well before.

       as it   s
This spring ⟨that has⟩ come Δ bursts up in bonfires green
                        and bushes
O {n, f} wild, of puffing emerald trees ⟨like fires⟩ ;
             clouds
Pear-blossom lifts in ⟨wreaths⟩ of smoke between,
$$\left[\begin{array}{l} \text{Where} \\ \text{⟨And⟩ fire of musical birds out quivers and gushes.} \\ \text{⟨And pointed flames lick out from the⟩} \end{array}\right]$$

I am amazed at this spring, this conflagration
Green inflaming the soil of {the, this} earth, this blaze
    these
 Of blossom, ʲandʲ puffing ʲofʲ sparks in wild gyration,
       ing
ʲAs theʲ {f, F} aces of people flash Δ across my gaze.

   where am I myself?
And ʲI myself am changed,ʲ ah I have lost
My old acquaintance with the throng of things;
        ʲahʲ
Tossed in the leaping combustion of spring, Δ tossed
    flame that leaps
Like a ʲleaping flameʲ for the dark, my spirit swings;

Ah love, I leap to the dark to overtake
        blur
You who have leapt before me into the ʲdarkʲ;
Ah broken moon, till the years at last shall break
   flame
My ʲspiritʲ from off this candle, I am true to her.

Many years have I still to burn, detained
Like a candle flame on this body, but I enshrine
    where her is
A dark within me, ʲyourʲ troth ʲI keepʲ unstained
   her
By life, ʲyourʲ spirit dreams in the core of mine.

      from
And though for long I blaze ʲonʲ the fuel of life
      on
What matter the stuff I lick ʲuponʲ my living flame,
⎡   an empty   ⎤
    ʲtheʲ ʲaʲ
⎣ Since I keep ʲin myʲ heart-core free from strife ⎦
   she
Wherein ʲyouʲ dreams my dream for me, ever the same.

2. *Amores* Version

The moon is broken in twain, and half a moon
Before me lies on the still, pale floor of the sky;
The other half of the broken coin of troth
Is buried away in the dark, where the dead all lie.

They buried her half in the grave when they laid her away;
Pushed away gently into the thick of her hair
Where it gathered towards the plait, on that very last day;
And like a moon in secret it is shining there.

Here half lies on the sky, for a general sign
Of the troth with the dead that I am pledged to keep;
Turning its broken edge to the dark, it lies
Like a broken lover who turns to the dark of sleep.

Against my heart the inviolate sleep breaks still
In darkened waves whose drift beats more and more
Through the world of my wakeful day, till I am lost
In the midst of the places I knew so well before.

3. *Collected Poems* Version

The moon is broken in twain, and half a moon
Beyond me lies on the low, still floor of the sky;
The other half of the broken coin of troth
Is buried away in the dark, where the dead all lie.

They buried her half in the grave when they laid her away;
Pushed gently away and hidden in the thick of her hair
Where it gathered towards the plait, on that very last day;
And like a moon unshowing it must still shine there.

So half lies on the sky, for a general sign
Of the troth with the dead that we are pledged to keep;
Turning its broken edge to the dark, its shine
Ends like a broken love, that turns to the dark of sleep.

And half lies there in the dark where the dead all lie
Lost and yet still connected; and between the two
Strange beams must travel still, for I feel that I
Am lit beneath my heart with a half-moon, weird and blue.

Appendix J
"Two Wives"

1. Manuscript 19 Version

White

Into the shadow-white chamber silts the white
Flux of another dawn: the wind that all night
Long has waited breathless, suddenly wafts
A storm like snow from the plum-trees and the pear
And the cherry trees between the window shafts
Till ⟨the⟩ petals are strewed in a withering snowdrift there.

A nurse in white at the dawning, foam-flowered pane
Lets down the blinds whose shadows scarcely stain
The ermine rugs on the floor, nor the lofty bed
Which rears like a still white berg in the silent room,
A pyre of snow with the austere line of the dead
            carved simply
Ridging its crest ⟨and carved from⟩ out of the gloom.

Less than a year the four white feet have pressed
Proudly the white-furred floor: and now at rest
For ever the feet of the bridegroom are closed and folded:
Only three days ago in his fine white breast
            as he laughingly
His heart swung happily ⟨and his red mouth⟩ scolded
     loving   ever   ever
His wife for ⟨giving⟩ him ⟨always⟩ , ⟨always⟩ the best.

And only a little while ago the red
Burst blood has been wiped from his lips, that in sickness have said
⟨Alas⟩ {o, O} ver much. She sat in her splendour there,
Erect in her splendid pallor beside the bed,
$$\left[\begin{array}{c} \text{closed over} \\ \text{⟨was closed⟩ and sank} \\ \text{And slowly her heart ⟨did flood and sink⟩ in despair} \end{array}\right]$$
Under the snow of sorrow his sick soul shed.
  She heard him plead his
⟨He pleaded against his⟩ fault of having wed
       she heard him promise
In pride, ⟨and promised piteously⟩ when dead

193

To register in heaven his soul as her's
        paid   for it   pain
Who had Δ the price ⌊of it⌋ in love and ⌊truth⌋
              ⌊plaintive⌋ an uneasy
When young: and like ⌊a little⌋ wind that autumn stirs
              old
Came his repentance, and his Δ love like rain.

And she who waited in silence, watched and saw
         dawn ⌊into⌋ consciousness, then flaw
His eyes ⌊grow dark and conscious, and take a flaw⌋
 With a darkness of shame in their
⌊Of shame within their⌋ depths at meeting her eyes.
She saw his spent soul flinch from her and draw
Away, she saw the sigh of the vanquished rise ·
And sink again out of his breast, like a blaze out of straw.

Then they took her away, they laid her to sleep, and she slept
The numb, grey swoon of despair, that did not break
When he died, nor knew that their sullied-white chamber was swept
Of his sickness clean, nor did her soul once shake
As cold and hard he set against her at last
The bitter barriers that let not even love past.

Tall she was, with her silk ⌊,⌋ white gown aflow
As she strode her naked limbs amongst it: but ⌊ere⌋ before
She opened the door, her heart did suddenly know
That he was gone, and she feared to open the door. . . .
She saw him raised in outline as on a pyre
       only   hastening arms of the
Awaiting Δ the ⌊swift-sped chariot of⌋ fire

Upraised and folded his feet were, erect as the prow
Of a ship of death, and his head lay back like the stern,
But the ship was froze in ⌊the⌋ seas of shadowy snow.
She drooped her head to her breast like a folded fern,
She sank to the ground, as a rich white peony slips
Its silk to the ground when summer the flower-thread clips.

Still she lay as a shed flower spent, nor heard
The heavy door sweep open to his love,
The small, the dark-eyed woman who had dared
At last to come and claim him, he above
Her in his wilful wealth, her who had bowed
 Her Too ⌊all⌋   for   who was all too
⌊Herself too⌋ willingly ⌊, to⌋ him, ⌊for his heart was⌋ proud.

Short her hair was shorn as a lad's dark poll,
And ivory smooth her face: her grey eyes would assail
With silence whomever she looked upon; the whole

Great silence of suffering, the wounds of the shameful nail
                     for
And spear showed deep in her eyes: ⟨and⟩ she had died
Too willingly for him, and for his pride.

But now she stepped past the silken flower shed
 In
⟨Her⟩ white on the ermine floor, nor ever turned
Her head aside, but straight towards the bed
Moved with still feet, and her eyes flame steady burned.
She looked at him as he lay with banded cheek,
And at last, as if he could hear, began to speak . . .

"I knew it would come to this," she said. "I knew,
Ah soon it would come to this, so I did not fight,
I let you go, I let you go and strew
Your wealth of life away upon the white
Proud marble of your choice: and now you lie
Sleeping alone again as I have slept
These years since you have left me: nor did I
Die any less than you, you love adept."

       whose fingers
Twas I ⟨whose⟩ ⟨did⟩ did draw up the young
            till
Fine lily of your body ⟨un til it⟩ did tower
         all
Away above me ⟨till⟩ its blossoms, spring
Beyond my grasp, a wondrous wealth of flower
           ⟨Bearing⟩
 Borne up ⟨It bore⟩
⟨You were⟩ aloft: and it was I who taught
Your eyes to take the ⟨softn⟩ glamour of the moon:
And it was I who, when your young mouth sought
Blindly the sacraments of love, the boon
Of swift initiation, the extreme
          in God's
Joy of partaking ⟨in the⟩ Mystery,
Twas I who gave the Cup, which still, I deem,
      the Blood   you did drink from me:
Contains ⟨God's blood⟩—and ⟨you partook of me⟩
And I did place the toga of manhood on
Your youthful smoothness, ⟨and⟩ I did clothe your limbs
     fervent
With ⟨golden⟩ manhood that in fine fleece shone,
And filled your eyes with fire to their brims.
I set your heart to its strong beat, I threw
Strength and great pride upon you like a cloak

                                    very
Of scarlet shining ⟨ever⟩ brave and new:
And then my servile love became a yoke
You could not brook, and I must watch you go
Across the Rubicon of innocence,
Eager to let your blazoned banner blow
Above the fawning hosts of dependence:
And you have conquered strange magnificence,
And you have lived awhile delightedly,

                                    bright
And you have had your own ⟨vain⟩ recompense
Blossoming all your splendid vanity:
And you have sunk to death most wastefully,
Oh many a song you should have sung for me
Unuttered on your perished lips I see;
And I am full of woe, ah misery

                                    that
That I have been too weak, Δ—I could not be

                            to
Great enough to defeat you, Δ enslave you to me . . ."

"But you are given back once more to me,
Who keep intact for you your virginity;
Who for the rest of life walk down the road
Watching the great clouds fold and unfold their roses,
Watching the crimson cloak of ⟨the⟩ eve bestowed
Upon the waters and the seaward closes,
Watching the ⟨s⟩ moon her silvery freight unload
Over the hill where the tarnished flock reposes;
And so we are together, you and I,

            are
You ⟨still⟩ restored to your beautiful games, and I
Still watch and wonder . . .
                            Ah, and I do dream
God bows his head and grants me this supreme
Pure look of your last dead face—has taken away
The swift elusion, and the wilful play

                            features
Of passions from off your ⟨face⟩,—to show me again
The wondrous you who gazed around in amaze,
Seeing God in every bush and blossom ablaze
  When you were mine—
⟨As you used to do,⟩ in token to me that when
I seek you I shall find you as I used

  Touching at   of speech, and song
⟨Upon the⟩ beauty with lips ⟨and son⟩
With eyes of revelation—Ah, I refused
Eve {n, r} at the worst that you had done her wrong . . .

The wife rose up in fear, and slowly nearing
The bed, she saw the dead rejected her.
"Oh bitter friend," she said, "I have been hearing
    which has driven
Your triumph, ⟨and it drove⟩ me with its spur
       away.
Back into life, or I might have swooned to ⟨death.⟩
And you have come to triumph over me,
You have come to exult in your own old awful way:
You arch your neck serene in pride, I see
You are glad to think that he has gone away,
Ah you rejoice to see me standing here
Discarded, a flower broke off at the stem, a mere
Useless beautiful thing, a camellia flower
Without a stem, beauty, and no one to wear it.
But ah, I tell you, even from this hour
I cherish the seed of his life within me, I bear it
As an offering unto God—Grant it, God!
God, I will wear my grief like a priest's ephod,
God, I will be an altar, I will bear
His seed of sacrifice for Thee; and I
Will be a briar with {a, one} flower on my bare
Thorned stalk, ah God, my grafting try,
Ah lift me up his flower on my strong stem
   that
Of life, ⟨so⟩ when {th, folk} look I show to them
A rose fledged with his wonder, his rosy gem . . ."

And looking still at the dead did the other say:
  would
"I ⟨should⟩ have borne his children: I did pray
My soul into prayer like iris scent to God
{G, S} o grant it so—yet He did never nod.
—Still I am planted with the dream of him,
Still I will dream his dreams, and I will limn
Thee beautiful dreams, O God, for fruit of him:
     his dreams
Will lay ⟨them⟩ at Thine altar Δ , in the eyes
Of all folk lay the dreams that blossoming rise
From the seed of his sowing in my soul: and never
Let it be said that he is dead . . .

2. *New Poems* Version

I

Into the shadow-white chamber silts the white
Flux of another dawn. The wind that all night
Long has waited restless, suddenly wafts

A whirl like snow from the plum-trees and the pear,
Till petals heaped between the window-shafts
          In a drift die there.

A nurse in white, at the dawning, flower-foamed pane
Draws down the blinds, whose shadows scarcely stain
The white rugs on the floor, nor the silent bed
That rides the room like a frozen berg, its crest
Finally ridged with the austere line of the dead
          Stretched out at rest.

Less than a year the fourfold feet had pressed
The peaceful floor, when fell the sword on their rest.
Yet soon, too soon, she had him home again
With wounds between them, and suffering like a guest
That will not go. Now suddenly going, the pain
          Leaves an empty breast.

                              II
A tall woman, with her long white gown aflow
As she strode her limbs amongst it, once more
She hastened towards the room. Did she know
As she listened in silence outside the silent door?
Entering, she saw him in outline, raised on a pyre
          Awaiting the fire.
Upraised on the bed, with feet erect as a bow,
Like the prow of a boat, his head laid back like the stern
Of a ship that stands in a shadowy sea of snow
With frozen rigging, she saw him; she drooped like a fern
Refolding, she slipped to the floor as a ghost-white peony slips
          When the thread clips.

Soft she lay as a shed flower fallen, nor heard
The ominous entry, nor saw the other love,
The dark, the grave-eyed mistress who thus dared
At such an hour to lay her claim, above
A stricken wife, so sunk in oblivion, bowed
          With misery, no more proud.

                              III
The stranger's hair was shorn like a lad's dark poll
And pale her ivory face: her eyes would fail
In silence when she looked: for all the whole
Darkness of failure was in them, without avail.
Dark in indomitable failure, she who had lost
          Now claimed the host,

She softly passed the sorrowful flower shed
In blonde and white on the floor, nor even turned
Her head aside, but straight towards the bed

Moved with slow feet, and her eyes' flame steadily burned.
She looked at him as he lay with banded cheek,
    And she started to speak

Softly: "I knew it would come to this," she said,
"I knew that some day, soon, I should find you thus.
So I did not fight you. You went your way instead
Of coming mine—and of the two of us
I died the first, I, in the after-life
    Am now your wife."

IV

" 'Twas I whose fingers did draw up the young
Plant of your body: to me you looked e'er sprung
The secret of the moon within your eyes!
My mouth you met before your fine red mouth
Was set to song—and never your song denies
    My love, till you went south."

" 'Twas I who placed the bloom of manhood on
Your youthful smoothness: I fleeced where fleece was none
Your fervent limbs with flickers and tendrils of new
Knowledge; I set your heart to its stronger beat;
I put my strength upon you, and I threw
    My life at your feet."

"But I whom the years had reared to be your bride,
Who for years was sun for your shivering, shade for your sweat,
Who for one strange year was as a bride to you—you set me aside
With all the old, sweet things of our youth;—and never yet
Have I ceased to grieve that I was not great enough
    To defeat your baser stuff."

V

"But you are given back again to me
Who have kept intact for you your virginity.
Who for the rest of life walk out of care,
Indifferent here of myself, since I am gone
Where you are gone, and you and I out there
    Walk now as one."

"Your widow am I, and only I. I dream
God bows his head and grants me this supreme
Pure look of your last dead face, whence now is gone
The mobility, the panther's gambolling,
And all your being is given to me, so none
    Can mock my struggling."

"And now at last I kiss your perfect face,
Perfecting now our unfinished, first embrace.
Your young hushed look that then saw God ablaze

In every bush, is given you back, and we
Are met at length to finish our rest of days
      In a unity."

3. Stanzas Added to the *New Poems* Version for *Collected Poems*

VI

The other woman rose, and swiftly said:
"So! you have come to get him now he's dead!
Now you can triumph, now he is no more
Than a dream of yours! 'twas all you ever could
See in him, your self's dream in his sore
      Heart's blood."

"How did you love him, you who only roused
His mind until it burnt his heart away!
'Twas you who killed him, when you both caroused
In words and things well said. But the other way
He never loved you, never with desire
      Touched you to fire."

"Take what you've got, your memory of words
Between you, but his touch you never knew.
Caresses never flew to you like birds.
You never bore his children, never drew
His body down in weight to rest in you
      The night through."

VII

"Take then eternity, for what is that
But another word, conceit and vanity!
But do not touch this man who never yet
Took pleasure in touching you. Mortality
Is not for you, and he is mortal still
      Against his will."

"Even dead, he still is mortal, and his hair
Is soft though it is cold. Do not dare
To touch him while he still is lying there!
Stand a way off, and if you like commune
With his wan spirit somewhere in the air
      Like a lost tune."

"But do not touch him, for he hated you
To touch him, and he said so, and you knew.
Why are you here? What is his corpse to you?
Stand you far off and triumph like a Jew
That he is dead and you are not. But stand
      Back, you understand!"

Appendix K
"Last Words to Miriam"

1. Manuscript 1 Version

Last Words to Muriel

It is
Δ You have borne the shame and sorrow
  But the disgrace is mine;
Your love was innocent and thorough,
Mine was the love of the sun for the flower
⟨It⟩ {l, L} aved to life in sunshine.

⟨Yea, I was {if, d} iligent-fine⟩
         explore
  Yea, I was fine enough to ⟨form⟩ you
Blossom you stalk by stalk
Till {m, th} y full-fed fire of curiosity bore you
Shrivelling down in the final dour
  Flesh-anguish, then I suffered a balk.

I heard thy cries of pain, and they broke
  My fine, craftsman's nerve,
Flawed my delicate courage in its stroke,
        in my cowardice
And I failed ⟨from weakness⟩ to give thee the last
  Bright torture thou didst deserve.

Thou art shapely, thou art adorned
  But opaque and dull in the flesh,
Who ⟨m⟩ if but I had piercèd with the thorned
Fire-threshing anguish, had been fused and {c, pl} ast
  In a lovely illumined mesh.

Like a painted window: {f, t} hat last suffering
  Would have withered through thy flesh,
Undrossed it and blessed it with a quivering
Sweet wisdom of grace. Now who will free
  Thy body from it's ⟨sic⟩ terrors awkward leash.
  ⟨Thee from thy body's blind leash.⟩

And who will remove from me the disgrace
     live   sad
  Of a {liv, work} , a ⟨live⟩ work unfinished;

Oh
Δ A mute nearly beautiful thing is thy face
That fills with grief all those that see

 It truely, ⟨sic⟩ a God-thought diminished*
⟨Thee a God-joy diminished⟩

2. *Amores* Version

Yours is the shame and sorrow,
  But the disgrace is mine;
Your love was dark and thorough,
Mine was the love of the sun for a flower
  He creates with his shine.

I was diligent to explore you,
  Blossom you stalk by stalk,
Till my fire of creation bore you
Shrivelling down in the final dour
  Anguish—then I suffered a balk.

I knew your pain, and it broke
  My fine, craftsman's nerve;
Your body quailed at my stroke,
And my courage failed to give you the last
  Fine torture you did deserve.

You are shapely, you are adorned,
  But opaque and dull in the flesh,
Who, had I but pierced with the thorned
Fire-threshing anguish, were fused and cast
  In a lovely illumined mesh.

Like a painted window: the best
  Suffering burnt through your flesh,
Undrossed it and left it blest
With a quivering sweet wisdom of grace:
  but now
  Who shall take you afresh?

Now who will burn you free
  From your body's terrors and dross,
Since the fire has failed in me?
What man will stoop in your flesh to plough
  The shrieking cross?

A mute, nearly beautiful thing
  Is your face, that fills me with shame
As I see it hardening,
Warping the perfect image of God,
  And darkening my eternal fame.

---

*The last two stanzas of this poem are written sideways across the poem that follows it
in MS 1.*

3. *Collected Poems* Version

Yours is the sullen sorrow,
  The disgrace is also mine;
Your love was intense and thorough,
Mine was the love of a growing flower
  For the sunshine.

You had the power to explore me,
  Blossom me stalk by stalk;
You woke my spirit, you bore me
To consciousness, you gave me the dour
  Awareness—then I suffered a balk.

Body to body I could not
  Love you, although I would.
We kissed, we kissed though we should not.
You yielded, we threw the last cast,
  And it was no good.

You only endured, and it broke
  My craftsman's nerve.
No flesh responded to my stroke;
So I failed to give you the last
  Fine torture you did deserve.

You are shapely, you are adorned
  But opaque and null in the flesh;
Who, had I but pierced with the thorned
Full anguish, perhaps had been cast
  In a lovely illumined mesh

Like a painted window; the best
  Fire passed through your flesh,
Undrossed it, and left it blest
In clean new awareness. But now
  Who shall take you afresh?

Now who will burn you free
  From your body's deadness and dross?
Since the fire has failed in me,
What man will stoop in your flesh to plough
  The shieking cross?

A mute, nearly beautiful thing
  Is your face, that fills me with shame
As I see it hardening;
I should have been cruel enough to bring
  You through the flame.

Appendix L
Collected Poems Version of "Bei Hennef"

The little river twittering in the twilight,
The wan, wondering look of the pale sky,
  This is almost bliss.

And everything shut up and gone to sleep.
All the troubles and anxieties and pain
  Gone under the twilight.

Only the twilight now, and the soft "Sh!" of the river
  That will last for ever.

And at last I know my love for you is here;
I can see it all, it is whole like the twilight,
It is large, so large, I could not see it before,
Because of the little lights and flickers and interruptions,
  Troubles, anxieties and pains.

You are the call and I am the answer,
You are the wish, and I the fulfilment,
You are the night, and I the day.
  What else? it is perfect enough.
  It is perfectly complete,
  You and I,
  What more—?

Strange, how we suffer in spite of this!

Hennef am Rhein.

204

Appendix M

"The Street-Lamps"

1. Manuscript 5 Version

The great gold apples of night
  Hang from the street's long bough,
  Dripping the sweetness of their light
On the faces which drift below
  Carelessly, as dandelion-angels go
  $\{$o, O$\}$ ver
  ⎰Drifting across⎱ the grass in the wind's sough.

The plumèd seeds from the day-crown
         along
  Go roving ⎰down⎱ the street
  Like balls of ⎰thistle⎱ down,
  Gold, with an innermost speck
     brilliance
Of ⎰silver⎱ , rolling slowly without check
$\left[\begin{array}{l} \text{Beneath} \\ \text{⎰Against⎱} \quad \cdot \qquad \text{spread} \\ \text{⎰Below⎱ the night's ⎰low-hanging purple⎱ sheet} \end{array}\right]$

Large, luminous insects of night
  ⎰Go⎱ Going slowly towards their aim,
  With the golden blur of their flight
Dazing the purple distance
With gold-dust, clustering with strange insistence
At the end of the street, in a golden game.

The ripeness of these apples of night
  Distilling over me,
  Sets me longing for the white
Apples a ⎰s⎱-glisten on your breast
And my thoughts, like leaves, stretch out to arrest
You where you wander, and enthicket you for me.

These round day-seeds, in their flight
  Repeat each one the pull,
  Of the gold-strung tail of a kite
  Pursuing a steady desire:
My kite, with the wind at its breast, rising higher
Away from my past's old prudence-loggèd hull.

They have found you, the night's gold flies;
  They are hovering with luminous notes
  Down the purple-grey haze. —I arise
  And haste along the street . . .
I shall know you by the hovering of your eyes when we meet
By your lips where the luminous thistledown floats
By your pale cheek-apples, for me to eat.

2. Manuscript 19 Version

The great gold apples of night
Hang from the street's long bough
  Dripping their light
On the faces that drift below,
Drift as dandelion-angels go
Glistening in the wind's soft sough
  Of life tonight.

The round gold seeds from the crown
Of day rove down the street
  Like balls of down,
Gold, with an innermost ⸾brilliant⸾ speck
Rolling slowly without check,
A golden, floating, silent fleet
  That makes for the town.

Large, luminous insects of light
Wing slowly towards their aim
  At the end of the street,
Dazing the purple, perfumed night
                    winging on
With gold dust, ⸾flying insistent⸾ to meet
  In a determined
⸾Determined⸾ ⸾{o, i} n the⸾ golden game
  At the end of the street.

The glow of these apples of night
Distilling over me,
  Makes me long for the bright
Apples a-ripe on your breast:
                eager
And I lift my ⸾yearning⸾ lips to arrest
Your thoughts, and bring them home to me
  Like travelling globes of light.

These round rich seeds of light
Repeat each one the pull
  To   goal   all
  ⸾Towards⸾ the ⸾aim⸾ of ⸾their⸾ flight;

And I am drawn as well
Somewhere you-wards, and I tell
   still
The lamps to stand Δ when they find you, and full
 Pour upon you their light.
 ⟨Reveal you to my sight.⟩

They have found you, the night's golden flies
They are hovering with luminous notes
 Where the towers uprise.
I am hastening down the street,
And
Δ {M, m} y lips and my breasts and my hands and my feet
Till we meet and mingle like light that floats
 From two lamps in the skies.

3. *Collected Poems* Version of "People" and "Street Lamps"

People

The great gold apples of night
Hang from the street's long bough
 Dripping their light
On the faces that drift below,
On the faces that drift and blow
Down the night-time, out of sight
 In the wind's sad sough.

The ripeness of these apples of night
Distilling over me
 Makes sickening the white
Ghost-flux of faces that hie
Them endlessly, endlessly by
Without meaning or reason why
 They ever should be.

Street Lamps

Gold, with an innermost speck
Of silver, singing afloat
 Beneath the night,
Like balls of thistledown
Wandering up and down
Over the whispering town
 Seeking where to alight!

Slowly, above the street,
Above the ebb of feet
 Drifting in flight;

Still, in the purple distance
The gold of their strange persistence
  As they cross and part and meet
    And pass out of sight!

The seed-ball of the sun
Is broken at last, and done
  Is the orb of day.
Now to their separate ends
Seed after day-seed wends
  A separate way.

No sun will ever rise
Again on the wonted skies
  In the midst of the spheres.
The globe of the day, over-ripe,
Is shattered at last beneath the stripe
Of the wind, and its oneness veers
  Out myriad-wise.

Seed after seed after seed
Drifts over the town, in its need
  To sink and have done;
To settle at last in the dark,
To bury its weary spark
  Where the end is begun.

Darkness, and depth of sleep,
Nothing to know or to weep
  Where the seed sinks in
To the earth of the under-night
Where all is silent, quite
Still, and the darknesses steep
  Out all the sin.

Appendix N

"The Blind" and "Elysium"

1. Manuscript 31 Version of "The Blind"

I have found a place of lo {n, v} eliness
Lo {n, v} elier than Lyonesse
Lonelier than Paradise.

stillness

Full of a sweet ⟨cleanness⟩
Which no day can {dis, trans} gress

$$\left[\begin{array}{l} \text{noise} \\ \text{⟨lamp⟩ transgress} \\ \text{Never a ⟨word⟩ ⟨distress⟩} \end{array} \right]$$

sank

The moon ⟨rose⟩ in state.
I heard her stand and wait
For her watchers to shut the gate

Then I knew myself
⟨Heaving⟩ *(illeg.)* in a wonderland.

falling with

All of darkness ⟨reft *illeg.*)⟩ sand

hours

{Out, Of} ⟨of silence⟩ hard to understand
Till waiting on, again
⟨I waited still, and then⟩ I knew

presence

The ⟨silence⟩ of the flowers that grew
Noiseless, their wonder noiseless blew.

And flashing kingfishers that flew

transient

In ⟨soundless⟩ beauty—and the few
Shadows the passing wild beast threw.

Then

⟨And⟩ Eve discovered on the ground

strange

Soft- {*(illeg.)*, given}, ⟨given⟩ and never a sound
To break the Embrace that Eve had found.

The perfect Consummation
In knowledge, paradisal One
          since   world
Created ⟨now⟩ the ⟨night⟩ was gone.

The perfect Consummation
The finest, paradisal One
Recovered since the world was gone.

2. *Collected Poems* Version of "Elysium"

I have found a place of loneliness
Lonelier than Lyonesse,
Lovelier than Paradise;

Full of sweet stillness
That no noise can transgress,
Never a lamp distress.

The full moon sank in state.
I saw her stand and wait
For her watchers to shut the gate.

Then I found myself in a wonderland
All of shadow and of bland
Silence hard to understand.

I waited therefore; then I knew
The presence of the flowers that grew
Noiseless, their wonder noiseless blew.

And flashing kingfishers that flew
In sightless beauty, and the few
Shadows the passing wild-beast threw.

And Eve approaching over the ground
Unheard and subtle, never a sound
To let me know that I was found.

Invisible the hands of Eve
Upon me travelling to reeve
Me from the matrix, to relieve

Me from the rest! Ah, terribly*
Between the body of life and me
Her hands slid in and set me free.

Ah, with a fearful, strange detection
She found the source of my subjection
To the All, and severed the connection.

---

*The Look! version of this poem shows no comma after "Ah."

Delivered helpless and amazed
From the womb of the All, I am waiting, dazed
For memory to be erased.

Then I shall know the Elysium
That lies outside the monstrous womb
Of time from out of which I come.

Appendix O
"Wealth"

1. Manuscript B Version

I am Well-off

Peace I have from the sun, ⟨and from the sun of suns⟩

 and grace, if I don't lose it, from the sun of suns.*
⟨A certain grace to move in the world of winters and summers.⟩

 and the world of winter and summer, storming and being still.
⟨A little way off, a few workmen are working in peace⟩
and in the distance, a few workmen working in peace.
And a still woman. ⟨is with me.⟩

 and then silence, and a long aloneness,
⟨Then I have silence, and the soft aloneness,⟩ away from peaceless gritty
   people.

2. Manuscript 79 Version

Peace ⟨,⟩ I have from the sun.
And grace, if I don't lose it, from the sun of suns.
And the world of winter and summer, storming and being still.
And in the distance, a few workman ⟨sic⟩ working in peace.
And a still woman.
And then silence, and a long aloneness, away from peaceless gritty people.

3. *Pansies* Version

Peace I have from the core of the atom, from the core of space,
and grace, if I don't lose it, from the same place.
And I look shabby, yet my roots go beyond my knowing,
deep beyond the world of man.
And where my little leaves flutter highest
there are no people, nor ever will be.

Yet my roots are in a woman, too.
And my leaves are green with the breath of human experience.

---

*Although Lawrence did not capitalize any of the revised lines, he did use end punctua-
tion.*

Appendix P
"Fidelity"

1. Manuscript 79 Version

Fidelity and love are two different things, like a flower and a loving-cup.
The flower is a loving-cup too, but we have no power over it, it will die.
Whereas it is given us to say: I have loved you, we know each other well.

                through the years
We have established Δ a little peace between us, ⟩through the years,⟨
Crystalline
And the crystal chalice won't wither, and the water in it
Is bright, if it is not wine.*
Let us not break the loving-cup that has crystallized out of the years,
Nor break the little spring of trust that bubbles from our twin depths.*
Let us not make it a question of love
Let us make it a question of knowledge*
We know {each, one} another, in many, many senses including love.
Let us rest on that.
Whatever other person we may love, we shall never know that person as we
    know one another.
Let us take our stand on knowledge, since it is a knowledge that includes love
And many, many other things as well.

2. Typescript 80 Version

Fidelity and love are two different things, like a flower and a loving-cup.
The flower is a loving-cup too, but we have no power over it, it will die.
Whereas it is given us to say: I love you, I have loved you;
I will be true to you as a human being, as a creature, an entity.

I loved you, and loving you, established a little peace with you.
We established a peace with each other, we know each other well.

We know each other well, we have found each other good,
and a peace has formed between us, as a crystal forms, with time,
and something, some little substantial meeting-point, some grain of dust
infinitesimal, for a common ground in the spirit of you and me.

Lawrence indicates with a ")" that a space should occur between this line and the next.

213

A crystal has formed between us, like a crystalline loving-cup
out of which we can drink a little peace, each of us, a crystal cruse.
A little crystal cruse, in which a little spring
of trust, of mutual trust, rises perpetual, if intermittent.

Let us not make it a question of love; love is a flower.
And anyhow we have loved, the flower has flowered,
And human beings are older than flowers, older even than ferns,
older than forameniferae, older than plasm,
old as the rocks in which crystals form, old as the ancient rock
is the human being, and when the crystal forms, the sapphire,
the crystal of any sort, mere quartz or spar
it is peace in the old old rock of the human heart; let it be;
it is older and older than love, than life, protozoa, forameniferae.
Old old gem of a crystal, and a loving-cup between rocks, or spar,
the two ancient rocks of a man and a woman's heart;
it is peace, which is older than love, older than life, old as the oldest me
                                        come
and the oldest you, the rock which we are, ⟨crystallized⟩ out into peace
a sort of loving cup.

There are things older than love, old, older than love.
There is peace which is old as the rocks, older even than God above.
And if peace has formed like a crystal, full of limpidity
it is better to be true to peace than to love, for peace goes
                deeper
    deeper in me, ⟨and⟩ in thee.

3. *Pansies* Version

Fidelity and love are two different things, like a flower and a gem.
And love, like a flower, will fade, will change into something else
or it would not be flowery.

O flowers they fade because they are moving swiftly; a little torrent of life
leaps up to the summit of the stem, gleams, turns over round the bend
of the parabola of curved flight,
sinks, and is gone, like a comet curving into the invisible.

O flowers they are all the time travelling
like comets, and they come into our ken
for a day, for two days, and withdraw, slowly vanish again.

And we, we must take them on the wing, and let them go.
Embalmed flowers are not flowers, immortelles are not flowers;
flowers are just a motion, a swift motion, a coloured gesture;
that is their loveliness. And that is love.

But a gem is different. It lasts so much longer than we do
so much much much longer
that it seems to last forever.
Yet we know it is flowing away
as flowers are, and we are, only slower.
The wonderful slow flowing of the sapphire!

All flows, and every flow is related to every other flow.
Flowers and sapphires and us, diversely streaming.
In the old days, when sapphires were breathed upon and brought forth
during the wild orgasms of chaos
time was much slower, when the rocks came forth.
It took æons to make a sapphire, æons for it to pass away.

And a flower it takes a summer.

And man and woman are like the earth, that brings forth flowers
in summer, and love, but underneath is rock.
Older than flowers, older than ferns, older than foraminiferæ
older than plasm altogether is the soul of a man underneath.

And when, throughout all the wild orgasms of love
slowly a gem forms, in the ancient, once-more-molten rocks
of two human hearts, two ancient rocks, a man's heart and a woman's,
that is the crystal of peace, the slow hard jewel of trust,
the sapphire of fidelity.
The gem of mutual peace emerging from the wild chaos of love.

Appendix Q

Manuscript B Version of "Two ways of living and dying"

While people ∤truly∤ live the life
                restless skies
They are open to the ∤living world∤, and streams flow in and out
darkly from the fecund cosmos, from the angry red sun, from the moon
up from the bounding earth, strange pregnant streams, in and out
      the flesh
  of ∤a man∤,
and man is {a, an} ∤strange∤ iridescent fountain, rising up to flower
for a moment godly, like Baal or Krishna, or Adonis or Balder or Lucifer.
∤like larkspur or the wheated ears of lavender, or flapping, of* noxious
    poppies.∤

But when people are only self-conscious and self-willed
        cannot
They ∤truly∤ die, ∤though∤ their corpus still runs on,
 While
∤But∤
∤Then∤ nothing comes from the open heaven, from earth, from the sun and
    moon
To them, nothing, nothing;
only the mechanical power of self-directed energy
drives them on and on, like machines,
on and on, with the triumphant sense of power, like machines,
on and on, and their triumph in mere motion
full of friction, full of grinding, full of danger to the gentle passengers
of growing life,
but on and on, on and on, till the friction wears them out
and the machine begins to wobble
and with hideous shrieks of steely rage and frustration
the worn-out machine at last breaks down:
it is finished, its race is over.

So self-willed, self-centered, self-conscious people die
the death of nothingness, worn-out machines, kaput!

---

*Struck out before the rest of the line was deleted.

But when living people die in the ripeness of their time
terrible and strange the god lies on the bed, wistful, coldly wonderful
⟨it is like when delphiniums lift up their pale dead sceptres⟩
beyond us, now beyond, departing with that purity
⟨at the end, tall septres of pale, pouched pods⟩
that flickered forth in the best hours of life,
⟨that open at last like pitchers in the winy autumn sun⟩
so
when the man was himself, ⟨and⟩ a god in his singleness,
⟨and spill mysterious seeds, mysterious seeds on the receptive earth⟩
and the woman was herself, never to be duplicated, a goddess there
⟨with a strange, sad autumnal happiness⟩
gleaming her hour in life as she now gleams in death
⟨that* loveliness of accepted death⟩
and departing inviolate, nothing can lay hands on her,
⟨so full of peace and seeds.⟩
herself,
she who at her best hours was herself, warm, flickering, Δ

    therefore
    ⟨and⟩ a goddess,
and who now draws slowly away, cold, the wistful goddess receding.

Struck out before the rest of the line was deleted.

Appendix R

Manuscript B Version of "So let me live"

So let me live that I may die
  eagerly   entanglement
⌊in peace⌋, passing over from the ⌊mystery⌋ of life
        adventure   eagerness
to the ⌊mystery⌋ of death, in ⌊peace⌋
  turning   turn to beauty
⌊believing⌋ {in, to} death as I ⌊believe in life⌋
{(*illeg.*) to} the breath, that is, of new beauty, unfolding in death.
⌊that each has to do with me, more than I know.⌋

Appendix S

Manuscript B Version of "Gladness of Death"

Oh death
about you I know nothing, nothing—
  about the afterwards
⌞nothing of the afterwards⌝
as a matter of fact, we know nothing

  Yet oh death, oh death
⌞And of the transit I am afraid⌝
  also I know so much about you
⌞as a woman is afraid who has got to give birth to a child.⌝

  the knowledge is within me, without being a matter of fact.
⌞But afterwards she is glad.⌝

And so I know
                    painful experience of dying
after the painful, ⌞parturition into death⌝
there comes an after-gladness, a strange joy
⌞I shall be glad.⌝
in a great adventure

⎡   ⌞I am sure, with me⌝   ⎤
⎢   ⌞goes over with me⌝   ⎥
⎣ ⌞Gladness goes over, I am sure, into death.⌝ ⎦
Oh the great adventure of death, where Thomas Cook cannot guide us.
⎡ ⌞Because gladness is at oneness.⌝   ⎤
⎢ ⌞At oneness with death as with life; gladness of death⌝ ⎥
⎣ ⌞in the at-one-ment.⌝   ⎦

  I have always wanted to be as the flowers are
⌞And the gladness of death, I am convinced⌝

  so unhampered in their living and dying,
⌞will not be less than the gladness of life, ah no, but lustrous and different⌝

  and in death I believe I shall be as the flowers are.
⌞Since the at-oneness will not be less.⌝

  I shall blossom like a dark pansy, and be delighted
⌞Till now I have been, on the whole, at one with life and glad⌝
there among the dark sun-rays of death.

  I can feel myself unfolding in the dark sunshine of death
⌞And when my time comes, I shall look forward to being⌝

219

 to something flowery and fulfilled, and with a strange sweet perfume.
[glad and at one with death[

Men prevent one another from being men
but in the great spaces of death
the winds of the afterwards kiss us into blossom of manhood!*

This stanza added in bottom margin.

Appendix T
"The Ship of Death"

1. Manuscript B Version

Ship of Death

I sing of autumn and the falling fruit

  and the long
⎨the apples f⎨ journey towards oblivion

The apples falling like great drops of dew
to bruise themselves an exit from themselves.

Have you built your ship of death, oh, have you?
Build then your ship of death, for you will {*(illeg.)* n} eed it!

Can man his own quietus make
with a bare bodkin?

With daggers, bodkins, bullets, man can make
a bruise or break of ⟨*sic*⟩ exit for his life ⎨and soul⎨
but is that a quietus, oh tell me, is it quietus?

Quietus is the goal of the long journey
the longest journey towards oblivion.

             one
Slips out the soul, invisible ⎨goal⎨, wrapped still
in the white shirt of the mind's experiences

            unseen
and folded in the dark-red ⎨invisible⎨

         still mortal
mantle of the body's ⎨immortal⎨ memories.

Frightened and alone, the soul slips out of the house
or is pushed out
to find himself on the crowded, arid margins of existence.

The margins, the grey beaches of shadow
strewn with dim wreckage, and crowded with crying souls
the ⟨*sic*⟩ lie outside the silvery walls of our body's builded city.

Oh, it is not so easy, I tell you it is not so easy
to set softly forth on the longest journey, the longest journey.

It is easy to be pushed out of the silvery city of the body
through any breach in the wall,
thrust out onto the grey grey beaches of shadow
the long marginal stretches of existence crowded with lost souls
that intervene between our tower and the shaking sea of the beyond.

Oh build your ship of death, oh build it in time
and build it lovingly, and put it between the hands of your soul.

Once outside the gate of this walled silvery life of days
once outside, upon the grey marsh beaches, where lost souls moan
in millions, unable to depart,
having no boat to launch upon the shaken, soundless,
deepest and longest of seas,
once outside the gate,
what will you do, if you have no ship of the soul?

Oh pity the dead that are dead, but cannot take
the journey, still they moan and beat
against the silvery adamant walls of this our exclusive existence.
They moan and beat, they gnash, they rage
they fall upon the new outcoming souls with rage

        arrows
and they send {daggers} of anger, bullets and bombs of frustration
over the adamant walls of this, our by-no-means impregnable existence.

Pity, oh pity the poor dead that are only ousted from life
and crowd there on the grey mud beaches of the margins
gaunt and horrible
waiting, waiting till at last the ancient boatman with the common barge
shall take them aboard, towards the great goal of {pure} oblivion.

Pity the poor gaunt {angry} dead that cannot die
into the distance with receding oars
but must roam like outcast dogs on the margins of life,
and think of them, and with the soul's deep sigh
waft nearer to them the bark of delivery.

But for myself, but for my soul, dear soul,
let me build a little ship with oars and food
and little dishes, and all accoutrements
dainty and ready for the departing soul.

And put it between the hands of the trembling soul.
So that when the hour comes, and the last door closes behind him
he shall slip down the shores invisible
between the half-visible hordes
to where the furthest and the longest sea
touches the margins of our life's existence

        unwilling
with wincing {little} waves.

And launching there his little ship,
wrapped in the dark-red mantle of the body's memories,
the little, slender soul sits swiftly down, and takes the oars
and draws away, away, away, towards the dark depths
fathomless deep ahead, far, far from the grey shores
that fringe with shadow all this world's existence.

Over the sea, over the farthest sea,
on the longest journey
past the jutting rocks of shadow
past the lurking, octopus arms of agonised memory
past the strange whirlpools of remembered greed
through the dead weed of a life-time's falsity,
slow, slow my soul, in his little ship
on the most soundless of all seas
taking the longest journey.

Pulling the long oars of a life-time's courage
drinking the confident water from the little jug
and eating the brave bread of a wholesome knowledge
row, little soul, row on
on the longest journey, towards the greatest goal.

Neither straight nor crokked, neither here nor there
but shadows folded on deeper shadows
and deeper, to a core of sheer oblivion
like the convolutions of shadow-shell
or deeper, like the foldings and involvings of a womb.

Drift on, drift on, my soul, towards the most pure
most dark oblivion.

     at
And ⁅*(illeg.)*⁆ the penultimate porches, the dark red mantle
of the body's memories slips and is absorbed
into the shell-like, womb-like convoluted shadow.

               bend
And ⁅at that last⁆ round the great final ⁅turning⁆ of unbroken dark
        the
the shirt of Δ spirit's experience has melted away
the oars have gone from the boat, and the little dishes
gone, gone, and the boat dissolves like pearl

$$\left[\begin{array}{l} \qquad\qquad\quad \text{perfect} \\ \text{the}\qquad\quad \text{at last} \ \ ⁅\text{sperm-like}⁆ \\ \text{as }⁅\text{the last}⁆\text{ soul }\Delta\text{ slips }\Delta\text{ into the goal, the }⁅\text{perfect}⁆\text{ core} \end{array} \right]$$

  sheer   and
of ⁅final⁆ oblivion Δ of utter peace,
the womb of silence in the living night.
⁅the living silence in the living dark.⁆

Ah peace, ah lovely peace, most lovely lapsing
⸤Say, is it death, or is it a begetting⸥
of this my soul into the plasm of peace.
⸤or are they the same thing?⸥

 Oh lovely
⸤Is the⸥ last, last lapse of death, into pure oblivion
at the end of the longest journey
peace, complete peace—!
⸤is it procreation of new forthgoing souls⸥?
But can it be that also it is procreation?

Oh build your ship of death
Oh build it!
Oh, nothing matters but the longest journey.

2. Manuscript A Version

Now it is autumn and the falling fruit
and the long journey towards oblivion.

the apples falling like great drops of dew
to bruise themselves an exit from themselves.

And it is time to go, to bid farewell
to one's own self, and find an exit
from the fallen self.

II.

Have you built your ship of death, O have you?
O build your ship of death, for you will need it.

The grim frost is at hand, when the apples will fall
thick, almost thundrous, on the hardened earth.

And death is on the air like a smell of ashes!
Ah! can't you smell it?

         in   bruised   frightened
And ⸤out of⸥ the ⸤broken⸥ body, the ⸤homeless⸥ soul
             shrinking, wincing from the cold
finds itself ⸤driven down to the endless sea⸥
that blows upon it through the orifices.
⸤washing upon the shore.⸥

III.

And can a man his own quietus make
with a bare bodkin?

With daggers, bodkins, bullets, man can make
a bruise or break of exit for his life;
but is that a quietus, O tell me, is it quietus?

Surely not so! for how could murder, even self-murder

             a
{*(illeg.)*, ever} {his own} quietus make?

IV.

O let us talk of quiet that we know,
that we can know, the deep and lovely quiet
of a strong heart at peace!

How can we this, our own quietus, make?

V.

Build then the ship of death, for you must take
the longest journey, to oblivion.

And die the death, the long and painful death
that lies between the old self and the new.

Already our bodies are fallen, bruised, badly bruised,
already our souls are oozing through the exit
of the cruel bruise.

Already the dark and endless ocean of the end
is washing in through the breaches of our wounds,
already the flood is upon us.

Oh build your ship of death, your little ark
and furnish it with food, with little cakes, and wine
for the dark flight down oblivion.

VI.

Piecemeal the body dies, and the timid soul
has her footing washed away, as the dark flood rises.

We are dying, we are dying, we are all of us dying
and nothing will stay the death-flood rising within us
and soon it will rise on the world, on the outside world.

We are dying, we are dying, piecemeal our bodies are dying
and our strength leaves us,
and our soul cowers naked in the dark rain over the flood,
cowering in the last branches of the tree of our life.

VII.

We are dying, we are dying, so all we can do
is now to be willing to die, and to build the ship
of death to carry the soul on the longest journey.

A little ship, with oars and food
and little dishes, and all accoutrements
 fitting
{dainty} and ready for the departing soul.

Now
⟨And⟩ launch the small ship, now as the body dies
and life departs, launch out, the fragile soul
in the fragile ship of courage, the ark of faith
 its store of
with ⟨all its⟩ food and little cooking pans
and change of clothes,
upon the flood's black waste
upon the waters of the end
upon the sea of death, where still we sail
darkly, for we cannot steer, and have no port.

There is no port, there is nowhere to go
only the deepening black ⟨ness⟩ darkening still
blacker upon the soundless, ungurgling flood
darkness at one with darkness, up and down
and sideways utterly dark, so there is no direction any more.
And the little ship is there; yet she is gone.
She is not seen, for there is nothing to see her by.
She is gone! gone! and yet
somewhere she is there.
Nowhere!

VIII.

And everything is gone, the body is gone
completely under, gone, entirely gone.
The upper darkness is heavy on the lower,
between them the little ship
is gone
she is gone.

It is the end, it is oblivion.

IX.

And yet out of eternity a thread
separates itself on the blackness,
a horizontal thread
that fumes a little with pallor upon the dark.

Is it illusion? or does the pallor fume
A little higher?

Ah wait, wait, for there's the dawn,
the cruel dawn of coming back to life
out of oblivion.

Wait, wait, the little ship
drifting, beneath the deathly ashy grey
of a flood-dawn.

Wait, wait! even so, a flush of yellow
                          O
and strangely, ʃohʃ chilled wan soul, a flush of rose.

A flush of rose, and the whole thing starts again.

X.

The flood subsides, and the body, like a worn sea-shell
emerges strange and lovely.
And the little ship wings home, faltering and lapsing
on the pink flood,
and the frail soul steps out, into her house again
filling the heart with peace.

Swings the heart renewed with peace
even of oblivion.

Oh build your ship of death, oh build it!
for you will need it.
For the voyage of oblivion awaits you.

Appendix U

"Bavarian Gentians"

1. Manuscript B Versions (1 and 2)

Version 1: Glory of darkness

〖The State of Grace.〗

Blue and dark
Oh
Δ 〖the〗 Bavarian gentians, tall ones
 make
〖making〗 a 〖magnificent〗 dark-blue gloom
in the sunny room

〖Deepening〗
〖Depth of colour〗 They have added blueness to blueness 〖to blueness,〗 until
it   beauty
Δ is dark 〖ness;〗 Oh you, 〖glory of darkness〗
 blue joy
〖and the glory〗 of my soul
 Bavarian
〖is in you, dark〗 gentians
Your dark blue gloom is so noble!

How deep I have gone
dark gentians
 since I embarked on your dark blue fringes,
〖in your marvellous dark-blue godhead〗
how deep, how deep, how happy!

          journey
What a 〖baptism〗 for
〖How happy to sink〗 my soul
in the blue dark gloom
Of gentians here in the sunny room!

Version 2: Glory of darkness

Blue and dark
Oh Bavarian gentians, tall ones
Make a dark-blue gloom
in the sunny room

They have added blueness to blueness, until
⌊Oh,⌋ it is dark
and the door is open
to the depths

It is so blue, it is so dark
in the dark doorway
and the way is open
to Hades.

Oh, I know—
Persephone has just gone back
down the thickening thickening gloom
of {B, d} ark-blue gentians
to Pluto
to her bridegroom
in the dark

and all the dead
and all the dark great ones
of the underworld
down there, down there
down the blue depths of mountain gentian flowers
cold, cold
are gathering to a wedding in the winter dark
down the dark-blue path

What a dark-blue gloom
of gentians here in the sunny room!

2. Manuscript A Versions (1 and 2)

Version 1

Not every man has gentians in his house
in Soft September, at slow, sad Michaelmas.

Bavarian gentians, big and dark, only dark
darkening the day-time, torch
⌊torch⌋   with the
⌊and sheaf-like, sheaf⌋ -like ⌊in⌋ smoking blueness of Pluto's gloom,
             blaze
  ribbed and torch-like, with their ⌊flame⌋ of darkness spread blue
⌊many cups sharp-lipped, erect, oh very erect⌋
down flattening into

                    sweep
⌊and flaming in⌋ points, ⌊and⌋ flattened under the ⌊weight⌋ of ⌊day⌋ white day
⌊long and erect and fathomless, dark sharp cups of pure blue darkness,⌋
       the   daze
torch flower of Δ blue-smoking darkness, Pluto's dark-blue ⌊blaze⌋

|and burning with dark blue power,|
black lamps from the halls of Dis, burning dark blue,
giving off darkness, blue darkness, as Demeter's pale lamps give off light,
lead me then, lead the way.

Reach me a gentian, give me a torch!
let me guide myself with the blue, forked torch of this flower
down the darker and darker stairs, where blue is darkened on blueness
       even   from
|to| where Persephone goes, just now, |in| the frosted September
to the sightless realm where darkness is {awareness, awake} upon the dark
and Persephone herself is but a voice
or a darkness invisible unfolded in the deeper dark
of the arms Plutonic, and pierced with the passion of dense gloom,
    among
|in| the splendor of torches of darkness, shedding darkness

⎡   the lost bride her   ⎤
⎢ |nuptials| and |the| groom.   ⎥
⎣   {in, on} |the| |pitch-dark room.| ⎦

                    Version 2

Not every man has gentians in his {(illeg.) house}
in soft September, at slow, sad Michaelmas.

Bavarian gentians, tall and dark, but dark
  darkening the daytime torch-like   the
|till they darken the day-time torch-like| with |their| smoking |dark| blueness
    of Pluto's gloom,

                              with their blaze of darkness spread blue
ribbed hellish flowers |so| erect, |their dark-blue blaze of the underworld|
blown flat |and out| into points, by the heavy white draught of the day.

Torch flowers of the blue-smoking darkness, Pluto's dark-blue blaze
                    Dis,
black lamps from the halls of |the hell of the underworld,| smoking dark blue
giving off darkness, blue darkness, upon Demeter's yellow-pale day
  Whom have you come
|What are you waiting| for, here in the white-cast day?

Reach me a gentian, give me a |flower| torch!
let me guide myself with the blue, forked torch of

    a
|this| flower
down the darker and darker stairs, where blue is darkened on blueness
down the way Persephone goes, just now, in first-frosted September

to the sightless realm where darkness is married to dark
and Persephone herself is but a voice, as a bride
a gloom invisible enfolded in {a, the} deeper dark
of the arms of Pluto as he ravishes her once again
and pierces her once more with his passion of
   the utter dark
   ⟨dense darkness⟩
among the splendour of black-blue torches, shedding
   fathomless
   Δ darkness on the nuptials.

Give me a flower on a tall stem, and three dark {flowers, flames},
for I will go ⟨down⟩ to the wedding, and be wedding-guest
at the marriage of the living dark.

Notes

1. *Lawrence's Design for* Collected Poems

¹Lawrence, *CP*

²*CP*, pp. 5–7.

³Lawrence's actual words ("From first to last these poems cover all but twenty years") compel one to take the year of the publication of the *CP* as the end point of the poetic biography—not 1923, the date of the publication of *Birds, Beasts and Flowers,* as one might expect.

⁴Published in *Phoenix: The Posthumous Papers of D. H. Lawrence,* ed. Edward D. McDonald (1936. Reprint. [New York: Viking, 1968]), pp. 251–54, as well as in *The Complete Poems of D. H. Lawrence,* collected and ed. Vivian de Sola Pinto and Warren Roberts (1964. Reprint. [London: Heinemann; New York: Viking, 1971]), pp. 849–52. The holograph manuscript of the foreword, of which I used a microfilmed copy, forms part of the D. H. Lawrence collection at the Univ. of California at Los Angeles.

⁵Lawrence, *Etruscan Places* (1932. Reprint. [London: Penguin Books, in association with Heinemann, 1950]), p. 81.

⁶For example, Richard Aldington in the preface to *Last Poems;* Harry T. Moore in *The Priest of Love;* and Graham Hough in *The Dark Sun.*

⁷Lawrence uses the two names interchangeably in the foreword to *CP.*

⁸For example, V. de Sola Pinto takes the first point of view in the introduction to *Complete Poems;* R. P. Blackmur assumes the second in "D. H. Lawrence and Expressive Form" in *The Double Agent.*

⁹Aldous Huxley, "Introduction to the *Letters of D. H. Lawrence,*" (1932). Reprint in the app. to *The Collected Letters of D. H. Lawrence* (New York: Viking, 1962), 2:1252.

¹⁰For this connection, I am indebted to the remarks of Charles I. Patterson, Jr., of the Univ. of Georgia, who delivered a paper on "The Romantic Rediscovery of the Daimon" at the 93rd Annual Convention of the Modern Language Association in New York City, 27–30 Dec. 1978.

¹¹See Lawrence, *Letters,* 1:473–74, for a reference to this book, which Lawrence indicates he has already read; and Richard Aldington, *Portrait of a Genius, But . . .* (London: Heinemann, 1950) for Aldington's comments on the importance of Burnet's book to Lawrence's thought.

¹²Baruch Hochman, *Another Ego: The Changing View of the Self and Society in the Work of D. H. Lawrence* (Columbia: Univ. of South Carolina Pr., 1970), p. 188.

¹³See Lawrence, "Climbing Down Pisgah" in *Phoenix* (1936), pp. 740–44. In this essay, written during 1924, Lawrence speaks of the demon's dual desire, in man and in nature, "to give himself forth into creation and . . . to

take himself back, in death" (p. 743). He also equates the habits of "the vast demon of life" with the scientific laws of the universe. He maintains, however, the essential unpredicability of the demon.

[14]Lawrence does use the term "Holy Ghost" in a few of the poems published posthumously as "More Pansies." He may have decided in his last months that he no longer objected to the term, as was the case with the word "God" (see Earl Brewster's comments in Edward Nehls, *D. H. Lawrence: A Composite Biography* 3 [Madison: Univ. of Wisconsin Pr., 1959]):405. In any case, Lawrence continues to define the term unorthodoxly, as in "God and the Holy Ghost."

[15]Lawrence, "Him with the Tail in His Mouth" in *Reflections on the Death of a Porcupine* (1925, rpt. in *Phoenix II, Uncollected, Unpublished, and Other Prose Works by D. H. Lawrence,* collected and ed. by Warren Roberts and Harry T. Moore (New York: Viking 1968), pp. 434–35. Cited hereafter in the text as *Reflections*. Additional references to this title in the text (with page numbers in parentheses) are to this edition.

[16]Lawrence, *Letters* 1:369.

[17]Lawrence, *Reflections*, p. 481. In this same essay, Lawrence uses the term "clue" to signify "being." He says, "The clue to all existence is being. . . . Being is *not* ideal, as Plato would have it: nor spiritual. It is a transcendent form of existence, as much material as existence is" (p. 470). Lawrence expresses here, as elsewhere, his idea of the consubstantial nature of being.

[18]Lawrence, *Fantasia of the Unconscious* (1922. Reprint. [New York: Viking, 1976]), p.71.

[19]Lawrence, *Fantasia*, p. 165.

[20]Lawrence, "Edgar Allan Poe," *Studies in Classic American Literature* (1923. Reprint. [London: Martin Secker, 1933]), p. 84.

[21]Extract from a letter to Amy Lowell, 5 Apr. 1919, Houghton Library, Harvard Univ.

[22]Lawrence, *Complete Poems,* pp. 181–86.

[23]T. S. Eliot, "Ulysses, Order, and Myth," *The Dial* 75 (1923):480–83.

[24]Lawrence, *Apocalypse* (1931. Reprint. [New York: Viking, 1966]), p. 126.

[25]Lawrence, *Collected Letters* 2:1098.

[26]Also betraying Lawrence's attitude to *CP* as revelatory of the self are his words to his friend Koteliansky, to whom Lawrence wrote in 1928: "Meanwhile I'm collecting my poems together for my *Collected Poems.* I'll sort of feel I've got everything behind me, when they are done." George J. Zytaruk, ed., *The Quest for Rananim: D. H. Lawrence's Letters to S. S. Kotelinansky, 1914–1930* (Montreal and London: McGill-Queen's Univ. Pr., 1970). p. 336.

2. The Incorporation of Love Poems, Amores, New Poems, *and* Bay *into "Rhyming Poems"*

[1]This group contains "Today" ("Hyde Park at Night, Before the War: Clerks" in *Collected Poems*) and "Tomorrow" ("Piccadilly Circus at Night, Before the War: Street-Walkers" in *Collected Poems*).

²Here and hereafter, whenever useful, the number of each poem included in volume 1 of *Collected Poems,* both in its original collection and in *Collected Poems,* will follow the title in parentheses, along with different titles.

³Sandra Gilbert used this term in a paper delivered at the 93rd Annual Convention of the Modern Language Association in New York City, 27–30 Dec. 1978, which has since been published as "Hell on Earth: *Birds, Beasts and Flowers* as Subversive Narrative" in *The D. H. Lawrence Review* 12 (Fall 1979):256–73.

⁴For a description of de la Mare's role in shaping *LP,* see Lawrence's letter of 22 Aug. 1912 to Edward Garnett. De la Mare at the time was acting as a reader for the Heinemann publishing house.

⁵MS 14 contains the only manuscript versions of these poems; their order is that of *LP.*

⁶These sets of poems were paired for the first time in MS 14.

⁷The other poems in this sequence are "Evening" ("Parliament Hill in the Evening" [*NP* 17, *CP* 113]); "Morning" ("Flat Suburbs SW in the Morning" [*NP* 7, *CP* 20]); and "The Inanimate That Changes Not in Shape" ("Suburbs on a Hazy Day" [*NP* 10, *CP* 23]).

⁸These poems had been previously published in two issues of the *Saturday Westminister Gazette,* those of 18 May and 1 June 1912, as part of a six-poem sequence published in four consecutive issues. Of the other poems in this series, two others, "The Punisher" and "Evening," were collected, the first in *Am* (25), then in *CP* (59), the second as "Rondeau of a Conscientious Objector" in *Bay* (15) and *CP* (136).

⁹Lawrence proposed the first title in a letter dated 18 Apr. 1918 (*Letters,* 1:550); the second appears in an unpublished letter to Amy Lowell dated 18 June 1918 (housed at the Houghton Library of Harvard Univ.). Lawrence also told his agent, J. B. Pinker, in an unpublished letter of the same date (in the special collections at Stanford Univ.) that he had once split the manuscript into two books, one called *In London* and the other *Choir of Women.*

¹⁰Lawrence wrote to Pinker in Jan. 1917 in reference to the volume that later became *Look! We Have Come Through!,* "I am doing out a last book of poems: real poems: my chief poems, and best. This will be the last book of poems I shall have, for years to come" (*Letters,* 1:499). This letter implies that Lawrence had already been working on the collections that became *Bay* and *NP*‡. Almost one year earlier, Lawrence had written both Lady Ottoline Morrell and Lady Cynthia Asquith that he had finally gotten his manuscript books from Italy (see his letters of 24 Jan. 1916 and 7 Feb. 1916, *Letters,* 1:417 and 422, respectively). It seems that the arrival of the old notebooks spurred Lawrence to set to work not just on *Am* and on *Look! We Have Come Through!* but also on *Bay* and *NP.* Indeed, by Dec. 1916, the *Bay* manuscript was in good enough shape for Lawrence to send it to Lady Cynthia Asquith (*Letters,* 1:491). In Mar. 1918 he reminded her that he put the *Bay* poems together long before but held them back because they were "ironical and a bit wicked" (*Letters* 1:544). By Apr. of 1918, *Bay* was ready for the publisher and *New Poems* was about to be assembled in some final shape (*Letters,* 1:549).

[11]For example, in MS 5, "To My Dead Mother" ("The End" [*Am* 26, *CP* 66]); "The Dead Mother" ("The Bride" [*Am* 27, *CP* 67]); and "My Love, My Mother" ("The Virgin Mother" [*Am* 28, *CP* 68]) form a unit, as they do in MS 26.

[12]Lawrence, *Letters*, 1:419.

3. The Chronologic, Thematic, and Mythic Structure of "Rhyming Poems"

[1]In the foreword to *CP*, Lawrence says that he wrote "The Wild Common" when he was nineteen. This was sometime between one and two years before he matriculated at Nottingham Univ. College, the point at which he began systematically collecting his verse in the notebook designated as MS 1.

[2]Lawrence includes with this material "Bei Hennef," originally published in *LP*, and "Coming Awake" and "Everlasting Flowers," both from *NP*. He also inserted "Song of a Man Who Has Come Through," which the publisher wished left out of *Look!*

[3]According to Jessie Chambers, Lawrence gave her "The End," "The Bride," and "The Virgin Mother" the day before his mother's funeral (Jessie Chambers, *D. H. Lawrence: A Personal Record*, by E. T., 2d ed. [New York: Barnes, 1965], pp. 183–84).

[4]For a discussion of the difficulties involved in dating the poems in the notebooks, see Carole Ferrier and Egon Tiedje, "D. H. Lawrence's Pre-1920 Poetry: The Textual Approach: An Exchange." *The D. H. Lawrence Review* 5 (Summer 1972):149–57.

[5]The earlier titles of these poems and the manuscripts in which they appear are, respectively: "On the Road" in MS 1; "School—I. Morning/The Waste Lands" in MS 5; "Spring in the City" in MS 5; and "Coming Home from School/Rondeau Redouble" in MS 1.

[6]"Sentimentalism," according to Lawrence, "is the working off on yourself of feelings you haven't really got. We all *want* to have certain feelings: feelings of love, of passionate sex, of kindliness, or anything else that goes at all deep. So the mass just fake these feelings inside themselves. Faked feelings!" Lawrence, "John Galsworthy" in *Phoenix*, p. 545. In this connection, the early titles in MS 26 of the two "Letters from Town" are interesting. Lawrence calls them both "Sentimental Correspondence."

[7]Lawrence uses this phrase in "Poetry of the Present," the introduction to the American edition of *NP*, reprinted in the *Complete Poems*. See p. 185 in this connection.

[8]It seems likely that Lawrence considered using the image of the town as a wounded beast in a cave as an ending for "The Inheritance" but later used it as the core of a separate poem.

[9]See in particular the letters to Lady Cynthia Asquith dated 1 Sept. 1916 and 8 Mar. 1918, as well as a letter to Cecil Gray dated 18 Apr. 1918. Lawrence, *Letters*, 1:471, 544, and 549, respectively.

[10]In MS 26, this poem, similar to the version in *NP* in other respects, is

called "Spring Oath," amended to read "Spring Fire." None of the versions previous to that in *NP* is set in autumn; all celebrate spring in one way or another.

11"Love on the Farm" and "Dream Confused" use a similar technique to generate metaphoric relationship between physical and mythical realities. The metaphors suggest that the physical world thinly veils a metaphysical world. The question, then—a device Lawrence consistently uses to initiate metaphor—becomes central to the poem's development.

12The earlier versions of this poem in MSS 5 and 26 make the theme of judgment explicit. For example, the conclusion of the poem in MS 5 is as follows:

> Like to the dead arraigned to answer, by the great Mind
> brought
> Before the terrible court of Justice, what they have done
> To extend one word the wisdom of the ever increasing Law
> Which cold and implacable, establishes harmony
> Shall outlive the heat of discord, of misery and revelry.

13By inference, then, her son assumes Christ-like characteristics. In "Reminder," for example, he suffers through her agony his own "Gethsemane."

14For details of the worship of Cybele and Attis, see Sir James George Frazer, *The Golden Bough,* the abridged edition (1922. Reprint. [Toronto: Macmillan, 1969, pp. 403–13]). Lawrence was familiar with *The Golden Bough;* he writes Bertrand Russell in 1915 that he has been reading it (*Letters,* 1:393).

15In a letter to Edward Garnett written in 1911, Lawrence refers to the poem as "Nils Lyhne," suggesting its connection with the Danish writer Jens Peter Jacobsen's autobiographical novel *Nihls Lyhne,* which stresses as does Lawrence's poem that each soul exists alone. Lawrence, *Letters,* 1:84.

16In MS 26, Lawrence titles it "Sentimental Correspondence: 1. The Almond Tree."

17This project had long been on Lawrence's mind. Martin Secker first suggested such a volume to Lawrence as early as 1919 (see Lawrence, *Letters,* 1:591), though Lawrence himself seems to have felt such a collection premature. For whatever reason, he delayed it, although he was much in need of the money it would have brought him.

4. The Scope of the Revisions for "Rhyming Poems"

1Reference to these texts, hereafter referred to as *Psychoanalysis* and *Fantasia,* is to the 1976 reprint of the books by the Viking Pr. noted earlier.

2Besides fully exploring this idea in *Psychoanalysis* and *Fantasia,* Lawrence explains it in several letters, one dated as early as Jan. 1913 (*Letters,* 1:179–80), the other dated Dec. 1915 (*Letters,* 1:393–94). Obviously, these ideas were a long time in unfolding. Reading Burnet's *Early Greek Philosophy* in 1916 no doubt influenced Lawrence's ideas on blood-knowledge, a concept similar to one developed by Empedocles.

³For a description of the demon as demi-urge, see *Phoenix* "Climbing down Pisgah" (pp. 740–44), an essay written around 1924 according to E. W. Tedlock, *The Frieda Lawrence Collection of D. H. Lawrence Manuscripts: A Descriptive Bibliography* (Albuquerque: University of New Mexico Press, 1948), p. 161.

⁴*Letters,* 2:878. For a detailed account of Lawrence's life and thought during this period, see Paul Delany, *D. H. Lawrence's Nightmare: The Writer and His Circle During the Years of the Great War* (New York: Basic Books, 1978).

⁵*Letters,* 1:508.

⁶Based on Frieda Lawrence's recollection of when her husband first wrote this essay, Tedlock dates it from the Cornwall period (Tedlock, p. 133).

⁷Emile Delavenay discusses this book in *D. H. Lawrence, The Man and His Work: The Formative Years: 1885–1919* (Carbondale and Edwardsville: Southern Illinois Univ. Pr., 1972), p. 388.

⁸For example, *Study of Thomas Hardy* and "The Crown," the latter of which became the first essay in *Reflections,* were written in the fall of 1915, just before Lawrence went down to Cornwall. The six essays tht Lawrence titled *Psychoanalysis and the Unconscious* were finished early in Jan. 1920, as Lawrence wrote his publisher (*Letters,* 1:618). These followed naturally from his thought for *Studies in Classical American Literature,* which he described as the foundation of a new science of psychology (*Letters,* 1:595–96).

⁹In the note, Lawrence says that *Bay* "appeared in 1919, but the poems were written mostly in 1917 and 1918, after I left Cornwall perforce." Yet he sent Cynthia Asquith on 11 Dec. 1916 from Higher Tregerthen, Cornwall, a "MS of a tiny book of poems, to see if you like them." He promised to inscribe them to her once he found a publisher (*Letters,* 1:491). This manuscript is without doubt *Bay.* His letters indicate that Lawrence continued to work on these poems, on and off, for the next two years at the same time at which he prepared *Look!* and *NP,* both of which were published first, although most probably begun after *Bay.* In the note, Lawrence is interested in maintaining the illusion of chronology and perhaps conveniently forgot the actual period when *Bay* was first conceived.

¹⁰Carole Ferrier describes this privately owned, previously unlisted manuscript in her diss. "The Earlier Poetry of D. H. Lawrence: A Variorum Text, Comprising All Extant Incunabula and Published Poems up to and Including the Year 1919," The Univ. of Auckland, 1971), 1:8–9, 35–37. This notebook contains in part Lawrence's household accounts during his stay at Porthcothan, at the beginning of the Cornwall period.

¹¹In *D. H. Lawrence at Work: The Emergence of the "Prussian Officer" Stories* (Charlottesville, Univ. of Virginia Pr., 1978), Keith Cushman posits an earlier date, viz., 1914, for the maturation of Lawrence's thought. He makes this claim on the basis of his research on Lawrence's revisions for *The Prussian Officer* stories. A study of the revisions of the poetry as well as the prose that Lawrence wrote in this period supports a later date.

¹²On 1 Feb. 1916, Lawrence sent the manuscript of *Am* to Lady Ottoline Morrell, along with the notebooks "from which these poems were chiefly

collected" (*Letters,* 1:419). These notebooks arrived from Italy, where Lawrence had left them on his return to England in 1914, sometime between 5 and 24 Jan. 1916 (*Letters,* 1:408, 417). Lawrence began work on *Bay* and *NP* around the same time as *Am,* judging from his letters and from MS 26, which contains drafts of poems published in each of the three volumes.

¹³See p. 14 of this book.

¹⁴Warren Roberts gives this date for the completion of the novel in *A Bibliography of D. H. Lawrence* (London: Rupert Hart-Davis, 1963), p. 45. See also Delany for a detailed account of the impact of the war on Lawrence's final revision of this novel.

5. Revision of the Subjective Poems for "Rhyming Poems"

¹For a description of this lyric form, see M. H. Abrams, "Structure and Style in the Greater Romantic Lyric," in Fredrick W. Hilles and Harold Bloom, eds., *From Sensibility to Romanticism: Essays Presented to Frederick A. Pottle* (New York: Oxford Univ. Pr., 1965), pp. 527–60. The connection between the lyrics of the romantic poets and Lawrence's poetry in *Look!* and *Birds, Beasts and Flowers* was first suggested to me by Father John Gerber, C.S.C. He did not, however, extend the connection to the poems collected in "Rhyming Poems," as I have done.

²*Letters,* 1:179–81 and 393–94, respectively.

³*Psychoanalysis,* p. 15.

⁴*Fantasia,* p. 60.

⁵*Psychoanalysis,* p. 12.

⁶ Frazer. Pages 220 ff. refer to the shadow and reflection, pp. 792 ff. describe the animal as external soul, and pp. 519 ff. treat the dog as a manifestation of the corn spirit.

⁷This quotation and the two that follow are from *Psychoanalysis,* p. 15.

⁸Hereafter, I will designate these poems by the short titles "Dreams: Old" and "Dreams: Nascent," respectively.

⁹Tedlock suggests that the incomplete MS 9 is the one Jessie Chambers sent off to *The English Review* (Tedlock, p. 78).

¹⁰*Letters,* 1:465–69.

¹¹Ferrier describes MS 5 in "Earlier Poetry," p. 28; Tedlock describes MS 9 in the *Bibliography,* pp. 77–79.

¹²Sandra Gilbert, *Acts of Attention: The Poems of D. H. Lawrence* (Ithaca and New York: Cornell Univ. Pr., 1972), pp. 25–27.

¹³Ferrier suggests this date for MS 19 in "Earlier Poetry," p. 17.

¹⁴Phyllis Bartlett, "Lawrence's *Collected Poems:* The Demon Takes Over" (*PMLA* 66 [1951]:583–93), p. 586.

¹⁵*Letters,* 2:878.

¹⁶Ibid., 1:393.

¹⁷Lawrence, "A Propos of *Lady Chatterley's Lover,*" *Phoenix II,* p. 508.

¹⁸In this connection, see chap. 9, "The Birth of Sex," in *Fantasia.*

¹⁹See chap. 6, "Human Relations and the Unconscious," in *Psychoanalysis.*

[20]MS 1 preserves a version of the poem; MS 5 (which contains two drafts of it) and MS 9 parallel *The English Review* poem; and MS 26 parallels the *Am* version.

6. Inclusion of the Fictional, Dedicatory, and Descriptive Poems in "Rhyming Poems"

[1]Lawrence, "The Crown" in *Reflections,* reprinted in *Phoenix II,* pp. 377 ff.

[2]Lawrence, "The Reality of Peace" in *Phoenix* (1936), p. 693.

[3]Lawrence, "On Human Destiny" in *Assorted Articles,* reprinted in *Phoenix II,* p. 629.

[4]See pp. 398–516 of *Phoenix.*

[5]Lawrence, "The Crown," p. 395.

[6]Ibid., p. 399.

[7]Coleridge often addressed his lyrics to someone, as did Wordsworth in "Tintern Abbey." Lawrence sometimes addressed another person in the subjective poems, as he did in "Dreams: Old"; however, the poem does not attempt to explore their relationship as a dedicatory poem would.

[8]Lawrence, "The Crown," pp. 393–96. Lawrence implies in this poem that although sexual union was impossible, he and Miriam might have overcome their egos through frictional reduction of the sort described in "The Crown." His will failed them, however.

[9]Garnett makes this comment in Nehls' *Biography* 1:302.

[10]Lawrence, *Phoenix* (1936), pp. 444–45.

[11]He condemns "Flapper" in the foreword to the *CP* and admits his dislike of "Love on the Farm," then called "Cruelty in Love," in an undated letter to Edward Marsh (probably written around Sept. 1915), in the Houghton Library, Harvard Univ. Collection of Lawrence's unpublished letters.

[12]This collection is described by Roberts, pp. 85–86.

[13]Delavenay, p. 62.

[14]Harriet Monroe made these comments in an unsigned review of *CP* published in *Poetry: A Magazine of Verse* 35 (Feb. 1930):273–79.

[15]Lawrence, "Poetry of the Present" in *Complete Poems,* p. 184.

[16]Ibid., p. 182.

[17]Gilbert, *Acts,* pp. 29–30.

[18]Harry T. Moore, *The Intelligent Heart* (New York: Farrar, 1954), p. 65.

7. The New Self Emerges: The Assimilation of Look! We Have Come Through! into Collected Poems

[1]*Letters,* I:500.

[2]Ibid., p. 498.

[3]Referred to hereafter as *Look!*

[4]*Letters,* I, p. 500.

[5]Ibid., p. 526.

[6]*Study of Thomas Hardy* in *Phoenix*, p. 513.

[7]Ibid., p. 509.

[8]Ibid., p. 514.

[9]Ibid., p. 403.

[10]This is part of the foreword that originally prefaced *Look!* but that Lawrence eliminated from *CP,* most likely because the note invites readers to regard the entire *CP* as such a story, history, or confession.

[11]*Letters,* I, p. 521.

[12]Delavenay, p. 145.

[13]*Letters,* I, p. 117.

[14]Ibid., p. 196 ff.

[15]Ibid., p. 237. Here, Lawrence refers to the poem as "a woman trying various ideals—Aphrodite, Apostle John, etc."

[16]Lawrence uses the same symbolism in the last version of "Two Wives."

[17]Frazer, p. 390.

[18]Frazer describes Cybele, the female partner of Attis, as a Dionysos-like figure whose rituals included the brewing of a liquor resembling wine from nuts gathered from the sacred pine tree. The female of "Ballad of a Wilful Woman" seems to be engaged in brewing such a liquor in the last part of this poem. See Frazer, pp. 409–10 for this reference.

[19]See Roberts, pp. 34–35, for a list of the poems first published in *Look!,* along with titles of earlier published versions when they differ from those in *Look!* Quite a few of the *Look!* poems underwent title changes between extant manuscript drafts and their final versions.

[20]*Letters* 2:1051. In respect to his manuscripts, Lawrence wrote Harry Crosby in this letter, 'I'm afraid I burn most of 'em."

8. *Red-Wolf Meets Star-Road:* Bird, Beasts, and Flowers as *Demonic Revelation*

[1]Lawrence, "The Crown," *Phoenix II,* p. 396.

[2]See Lawrence's comments to Catherine Carswell and Curtis Brown in this connection. *Letters,* 2:737 and 870, respectively.

[3]An example of Lawrence's correction of one such error exists in line 39 of "Sicilian Cyclamens," where he emends a description of greyhound bitches to read "Bending their rosy muzzles pensive down" instead of "Sending their rosy muzzled pensive down."

[4]These descriptions can be found in unsigned reviews in the *Times Literary Supplement* of 13 Dec. 1923, p. 864, and 15 Nov. 1928, p. 852, respectively.

[5]See Roberts, pp. 68–70, for a description of this edition and a brief history of the prefaces that Lawrence wrote for it.

[6]These articles both appear in the same issue of *The D. H. Lawrence Review* 12 (Fall 1979):241–55 and 256–73, respectively.

[7]Gilbert, "Hell on Earth," p. 258.

[8]Trail, "West by East: The Psycho-Geography of *Birds, Beasts and Flowers,*" *The D. H. Lawrence Review* 12 (Fall 1979):247.

[9]*Letters* 2:663.

[10]Ibid., p. 645.

[11]Tedlock, p. 100.

[12]Ibid., p. 96.

[13]*Letters* 2:681.

[14]Ibid., p. 685.

[15]Ibid., p. 702.

[16]Lawrence, "New Mexico," *Phoenix,* p. 142.

[17]Gilbert, *Acts,* p. 166.

[18]This diary reprinted in Tedlock, pp. 87–99.

[19]Keith Sagar, *The Art of D. H. Lawrence* (Cambridge: Cambridge Univ. Pr., 1966). See, in particular, pp. 118, 130, 142.

[20]Trail, "West by East," p. 243.

[21]Lawrence, *The Complete Poems,* p. 995.

[22]See the *Encyclopedia of Philosophy,* vols. 2 (pp. 477–81) and 4 (pp. 496–99), for a summary of the thought of Empedocles and Heraclitus, respectively.

[23]Lawrence, *Fantasia,* p. 214.

[24]Ibid., p. 215.

[25]Gilbert, "Hell on Earth," p. 259.

[26]Davie, Donald, *Thomas Hardy and British Poetry* (New York: Oxford Univ. Pr., 1972). See, in particular, the chap. entitled "A Doggy Demos: Hardy and Lawrence," pp. 130–57.

[27]Abrams, pp. 527–28.

[28]Ibid., p. 552.

[29]Ibid., p. 553.

[30]Ibid., p. 547.

[31]Lawrence, *Fantasia,* pp. 206–7.

[32]This and the following quotation are from Lawrence, *Apocalypse,* pp. 166 and 165, respectively.

[33]Ibid., p. 39.

[34]Ibid., p. 44.

[35]Ibid., p. 43.

[36]Lawrence, *The Plumed Serpent* (New York: Vintage Books, 1959), p. 458.

[37]Ibid., p. 459.

[38]Lawrence develops this theme, including the relation of virginity to true marriage, in *The Plumed Serpent,* p. 431.

[39]Lawrence, *Apocalypse,* pp. 76–77.

9. The Demon at Large: His Presence in The Plumed Serpent Hymns, Pansies, Nettles, *and* Last Poems

[1]Lawrence, *The Plumed Serpent,* p. 183.

[2]Lawrence, *Apocalypse,* p. 163.

[3]Lawrence, *The Plumed Serpent*, p. 347.

[4]Ibid., p. 341.

[5]Ibid., p. 426.

[6]Ibid., p. 430.

[7]Ibid., p. 470.

[8]Tedlock, pp. 172–73.

[9]Lawrence, *Phoenix*, p. 766.

[10]Lawrence tries out a new name for the demon in this essay. He writes: "It is difficult to know what name to give to that most central and vital clue to the human being, which clinches him into integrity. The best is to call it his vital sanity. We thus escape the rather nauseating emotional suggestions of words like soul and spirit and holy ghost." (*Phoenix*, p. 766.)

[11]See "Pan in America" in *Phoenix*, p. 23.

[12]Tedlock, pp. 104–12.

[13]Sagar suggests that Lawrence began MS B in the spring of 1929 ("The Genesis of 'Bavarian Gentians,' " *The D. H. Lawrence Review*, 8 [1975]:47–53). As a comparison of this and other poems in both MS B and MS 79 show clearly, at least the first part of the contents of MS B has to be dated earlier, because Lawrence had completed *Pansies* by then. It also seems that Aldington was mistaken in his assumption that MS B is a continuation of *Pansies*, since at least the first poems in the notebook predate the versions of those poems in MS 79.

[14]Hereafter referred to as "A Propos."

[15]At the end of MS 79, Lawrence lists the poems to be included in *Pansies*. He has listed numerous poems not in MS 79 and extensively rearranged the order of those that are, although he keeps clusters of poems more or less intact. At some later time, Lawrence again reordered the contents of *Pansies*, slightly rearranging previous groupings and inserting still more poems not present in MS 79.

[16]Lawrence, "A Propos," *Phoenix II*, p. 489.

[17]Ibid., p. 490.

[18]Earl and Achsah Brewster reported that Lawrence was correcting proofs of *Nettles* shortly before he died; the book appeared less than two weeks after his death in Mar. 1930.

[19]Lawrence, "A Propos," *Phoenix II*, p. 508.

[20]Lawrence, *Letters* 2:1174.

[21]Earl and Achsah Brewster, *D. H. Lawrence: Reminiscences and Correspondence* (London: Martin Secker, 1934), pp. 308–9.

[22]Tedlock, p. 113.

[23]Lawrence, "A Propos," *Phoenix II*, p. 510.

[24]Ibid., p. 512.

[25]Sandra M. Gilbert, "D. H. Lawrence's Uncommon Prayers" in Robert B. Partlow, Jr., and Harry T. Moore, eds., *D. H. Lawrence: The Man Who Lived* (Carbondale and Edwardsville: Southern Illinois Univ. Pr., 1980), p. 76.

[26]Lawrence, "A Propos," *Phoenix II*, p. 510.

[27]Ibid., p. 511.

[28]Lawrence outlines these rites in chap. 10 of *Apocalypse*.

[29]Lawrence, *Apocalypse,* p. 110.

[30]Ibid., p. 182.

[31]Ibid., p. 77.

[32]Ibid., p. 50.

[33]Aldington printed in the appendix of *Last Poems* a copy of another version of "The Ship of Death" that he says he took from Lawrence's typescript. The typescript itself seems not to have survived. Aldington suggests that this typescript is "part of" "The Ship of Death." Did Lawrence consider ending the MS A version of the poem with it, as pt. 11, perhaps? The enigma is unsolvable; no information about the typescript exists other than what Aldington gives us, and internal evidence does not afford a clear answer to whether the poem is an early or late draft or a complete or partial poem. Consequently, I have had to ignore it in my study of Lawrence's revisions of "The Ship of Death."

[34]Lawrence, *Apocalypse,* p. 110.

[35]See the note to *CP.*

[36]Sagar argues the case for reading the second MS A draft as Lawrence's final one in "The Genesis of 'Bavarian Gentians.' "

[37]Lawrence, "A Propos," in *Phoenix II,* p. 504.

[38]Ibid., p. 506.

Bibliography

I. WORKS BY D. H. LAWRENCE

A. Poems

1. Manuscripts

Diary, 1920–24, including nine poems published in *Birds, Beasts and Flowers.* The Bancroft Library, The University of California at Berkeley.

Notebook containing 165 early versions of poems published as *Pansies.* Humanities Research Center, The University of Texas, Austin, Texas.

Notebook designated as LaL2. University of Nottingham Library, Nottingham, England.

Notebooks (two) containing poems published as *Last Poems,* "More Pansies," and *Nettles.* Humanities Research Center, The University of Texas, Austin, Texas.

Poems designated as LaL4/1–4. University of Nottingham Library, Nottingham, England.

Typescript of *Collected Poems,* vol. 1, including holograph emendations. Humanities Research Center, The University of Texas, Austin, Texas.

2. Books and Pamphlets

Love Poems and Others. London: Duckworth; New York: Mitchell Kennerly, 1913.

Amores. London: Duckworth; New York: B. W. Huebsch, 1916.

Look! We Have Come Through! London: Chatto and Windus; New York: B. W. Huebsch, 1917.

New Poems. London: Martin Secker, 1918; New York: B. W. Huebsch, 1920.

Bay. London: Cyril W. Beaumont, 1919.

Tortoises. New York: Thomas Seltzer, 1921.

Birds, Beasts and Flowers. New York: Thomas Seltzer; London: Martin Secker, 1923.

The Collected Poems of D. H. Lawrence. London: Martin Secker, 1928; New York: Jonathan Cape and Harrison Smith, 1929.

Pansies. London: Martin Secker, 1929; New York: Knopf, 1929; privately printed by P. R. Stephensen, 1929.

Nettles. London: Faber and Faber, 1930.

Last Poems. Florence: G. Orioli, 1932; New York: Viking; London: Martin Secker, 1933.

The Complete Poems of D. H. Lawrence. Collected and ed. with an introduction and notes by Vivian de Sola Pinto and Warren Roberts. London: Heinemann; New York: Viking, 1967.

B. Prose

1. Manuscripts

Holograph of the foreword to *Collected Poems*. Library of the University of California at Los Angeles.

Letter to Edward Marsh, Sept. 1915. Houghton Library, Harvard University.

Letter to Amy Lowell, 18 June 1918. Houghton Library, Harvard University.

Letter to J. B. Pinker, 18 June 1918. Library, Stanford University.

Letter to Amy Lowell, 5 Apr. 1919. Houghton Library, Harvard University.

2. Books

The White Peacock. London: Heinemann; New York: Duffield, 1911. Carbondale and Edwardsville: Southern Illinois Univ. Pr., 1966.

The Trespasser. London: Duckworth; New York: Mitchell Kennerly, 1912. Melbourne, London, Toronto: Heinemann, 1955.

Sons and Lovers. London: Duckworth; New York: Mitchell Kennerly, 1913. Harmondsworth, England: Penguin, 1976.

The Rainbow. London: Methuen; New York: B. W. Huebsch, 1916. Harmondsworth, England: Penguin, 1976.

Twilight in Italy. London: Duckworth; New York: B. W. Huebsch, 1916. London, Heinemann, 1956.

Women in Love. New York: privately printed, 1920. London: Martin Secker, 1921. New York: Viking, 1960.

The Lost Girl. London: Martin Secker, 1920. New York: Thomas Seltzer, 1921. Harmondsworth, England. Penguin, 1950.

Sea and Sardinia. New York: Thomas Seltzer, 1921. London: Martin Secker, 1923. London: Heinemann, 1956.

Aaron's Rod. London: Martin Secker; New York: Thomas Seltzer, 1922.

Psychoanalysis and the Unconscious. New York: Thomas Seltzer, 1921. London: Martin Secker, 1923.

Fantasia of the Unconscious. New York: Thomas Seltzer, 1922. London: Martin Secker, 1923.

Studies in Classic American Literature. New York: Thomas Seltzer, 1923. London: Martin Secker, 1924. London: Martin Secker, 1933.

Kangaroo. London: Martin Secker; New York: Thomas Seltzer, 1923.

The Plumed Serpent. London: Martin Secker; New York: Knopf, 1926. New York: Vintage, 1959.

Lady Chatterley's Lover. Privately printed, 1928. London: Martin Secker; New York: Knopf, 1932. New York: New American Library, 1959.

The Short Novels. The Man Who Died, as *The Escaped Cock*; Paris: Black Sun Pr., 1929. London: Martin Secker; New York: Knopf, 1931. London: Heinemann, 1956.

Apocalypse. Florence: G. Orioli, 1931. London: Martin Secker; New York: Viking, 1932. Viking, 1966.

Etruscan Places. London: Martin Secker; New York: Viking, 1932. Penguin, 1950.

Phoenix: The Posthumous Papers (1936). London: Heinemann; New York: Viking, 1936. New York: Viking, 1968.

The Complete Short Stories. New York: Viking; London: Heinemann, 1955.

Collected Letters. Ed. by Harry T. Moore. London: Heinemann; New York: Viking, 1962.

Phoenix II. Collected and ed. by Warren Roberts and Harry T. Moore. London: Heinemann; New York: Viking, 1968.

Lawrence in Love. Letters to Louie Burrows. Ed. by James T. Boulton. Nottingham: Univ. of Nottingham Pr., 1968.

The Quest for Rananim: D. H. Lawrence's Letters to S. S. Koteliansky, 1914–1930. Ed. by George J. Zytaruk. Montreal and London: McGill-Queen's Univ. Pr., 1970.

Psychoanalysis and the Unconscious and Fantasia of the Unconscious. New York: Viking, 1976.

Letters to Thomas and Adele Seltzer. Ed. by Gerald M. Lacy. Santa Barbara: Black Sparrow Pr., 1976.

The Letters of D. H. Lawrence, Vol. I., September 1901–May 1913. Ed. by James T. Boulton. Cambridge: Cambridge Univ. Pr., 1979.

II. BIOGRAPHIES OF D. H. LAWRENCE

ALDINGTON, RICHARD. *Portrait of a Genius, But . . .* London: Heinemann, 1950.

BREWSTER, EARL, AND ACHSAH BREWSTER. *D. H. Lawrence: Reminiscences and Correspondence.* London: Martin Secker, 1934.

CARSWELL, CATHERINE. *The Savage Pilgrimage.* London: Martin Secker; New York: Harcourt, 1932.

CHAMBERS, JESSIE. *D. H. Lawrence: A Personal Record,* by E. T., 2d ed. New York: Barnes, 1965.

CORKE, HELEN. *D. H. Lawrence: The Croydon Years.* Austin: Univ. of Texas Pr., 1957.

DELANY, PAUL. *D. H. Lawrence's Nightmare: The Writer and His Circle During the Years of the Great War.* New York: Basic Books, 1978.

DELAVENAY, EMILE. *D. H. Lawrence, The Man and His Work: The Formative Years, 1885–1919.* Carbondale and Edwardsville: Southern Illinois Univ. Pr., 1972.

GREEN, MARTIN. *The von Richthofen Sisters: The Triumphant and the Tragic Modes of Love.* New York: Basic Books, 1974.

LAWRENCE, FRIEDA. *"Not I, but the Wind . . ."* Santa Fe: Rydal Pr.; New York: Viking, 1934.

———. *The Memoirs and Correspondence.* London: Heinemann, 1961; New York: Knopf, 1964.

LUHAN, MABEL DODGE. *Lorenzo in Taos.* New York: Knopf, 1932.

MOORE, HARRY T. *The Life and Works of D. H. Lawrence.* London: George Allen and Unwin; New York: Twayne, 1951.

————. *The Intelligent Heart.* New York: Farrar, 1954; London: Heinemann, 1955.

————. *The Priest of Love: A Life of D. H. Lawrence.* Rev. ed. London: Heinemann, 1974.

MURRAY, JOHN MIDDLETON. *Reminiscences of D. H. Lawrence.* Jonathan Cape, 1933.

NEHLS, EDWARD. *D. H. Lawrence: A Composite Biography.* 3 vols. Madison: Univ. of Wisconsin Pr., 1957–59.

III. CRITICAL WORKS ON LAWRENCE'S POEMS

ALVAREZ, ALFRED. "D. H. Lawrence: The Single State of Mind." In *A D. H. Lawrence Miscellany,* ed. by Harry T. Moore. Carbondale: Southern Illinois Univ. Pr.; London: Heinemann, 1961.

AUDEN, W. H. "Some Notes on D. H. Lawrence." *The Nation,* Apr. 26, 1947, pp. 482–84.

————. "D. H. Lawrence." *The Dyer's Hand and Other Essays.* New York: Random; London: Faber and Faber, 1948.

BAIR, HEBE. Free Verse Prosody: The Poetry of D. H. Lawrence. Ph.D. diss., Univ. of Arkansas, 1978.

BAKER, JAMES R. "Lawrence as a Prophetic Poet." *The Journal of Modern Literature.* Mar. 1974, pp. 1219–38.

BARTLETT, PHYLLIS. "Lawrence's *Collected Poems:* The Demon Takes Over." *PMLA* 66 (1951):583–93.

BEAL, ANTHONY. *D. H. Lawrence.* New York: Grove, 1961.

BLACKMUR, R. P. "D. H. Lawrence and Expressive Form." *The Double Agent.* New York: Arrow Editions, 1935.

BLOOM, HAROLD. "Lawrence, Blackmur, Eliot, and the Tortoise." In *A D. H. Lawrence Miscellany,* ed. by Harry T. Moore. Carbondale: Southern Illinois Univ. Pr., 1961.

CLARK, L. D. *Dark Night of the Body.* Austin: Univ. of Texas Pr., 1964.

DAVIE, DONALD. *Thomas Hardy and British Poetry.* New York: Oxford Univ. Pr., 1972.

DRAPER, RONALD P. *D. H. Lawrence: The Critical Heritage.* New York: Twayne, 1964.

ELLMANN, RICHARD. "Barbed Wire and Coming Through." In *The Achievement of D. H. Lawrence,* ed. by Frederick J. Hoffman and Harry T. Moore. Norman: Univ. of Oklahoma Pr., 1953.

FERRIER, CAROLE. "D. H. Lawrence's Pre-1920 Poetry: A Descriptive Bibliography of Manuscripts, Typescripts, and Proofs." *The D. H. Lawrence Review* 6 (1973):333–59.

————. "D. H. Lawrence's Poetry, 1920–1928: A Descriptive Bibliography of Manuscripts, Typescripts, and Proofs." *The D. H. Lawrence Review* 12 (Fall 1979):289–303.

————, "The Earlier Poetry of D. H. Lawrence: A Variorum Text, Comprising All Extant Incunabula and Published Poems up to and Including the Year 1919." 2 vols. Ph.D. diss., Univ. of Auckland, 1971.

————, and Tiedje, Egon. "D. H. Lawrence's Pre-1920 Poetry: The Textual Approach: An Exchange." *The D. H. Lawrence Review* 5 (Summer 1972):149–57.

GILBERT, SANDRA M. *Acts of Attention: The Poems of D. H. Lawrence.* Ithaca and New York: Cornell Univ. Pr., 1972.

GILBERT, SANDRA M. "Hell on Earth: *Birds, Beasts and Flowers* as Subversive Narrative." *The D. H. Lawrence Review* 12 (Fall 1979):256–73.

HASSALL, CHRISTOPHER. "Black Flowers: A New Light on the Poetics of D. H. Lawrence." In *A D. H. Lawrence Miscellany*, ed. by Harry T. Moore. Carbondale: Southern Illinois Univ. Pr., 1959.

HOUGH, GRAHAM. *The Dark Sun.* London: Duckworth, 1956.

JONES, R. T. "D. H. Lawrence's Poetry: Art and the Apprehension of Fact." In *D. H. Lawrence: A Critical Study of the Major Novels and Other Writings*, ed. by A. H. Gomme. New York: Barnes, 1978.

LANGBAUM, ROBERT. *The Modern Spirit: Essays on the Continuity of Nineteenth and Twentieth Century Literature.* New York: Oxford Univ. Pr., 1970.

————. *The Mysteries of Identity: A Theme in Modern Literature.* New York: Oxford Univ. Pr., 1977.

MARSHALL, TOM. *The Psychic Mariner: A Reading of the Poems of D. H. Lawrence.* New York: Viking, 1970.

MONROE, HARRIET. Review of *Collected Poems. Poetry: A Magazine of Verse*, XXXV (Feb. 1930), 273–79.

NAHAL, CHAMAN. "The Colour Ambience in Lawrence's Early and Later Poetry." *The D. H. Lawrence Review* 8 (1975):147–54.

NIN, ANAIS. *D. H. Lawrence: An Unprofessional Study.* Paris: Edward M. Titus, 1932.

OATES, JOYCE CAROL. *The Hostile Sun: The Poetry of D. H. Lawrence.* Los Angeles: Black Sparrow Pr., 1973.

PANICHAS, GEORGE A. *Adventures in Consciousness.* The Hague: Mouton and Co., 1964.

PARTLOW, ROBERT B., JR., AND MOORE, HARRY T., eds. *D. H. Lawrence: The Man Who Lived.* Carbondale and Edwardsville: Southern Illinois Univ. Pr., 1980.

PERKINS, DAVID. *A History of Modern Poetry: From the 1890's to Pound, Eliot, and Yeats.* Cambridge, Mass., and London, England: The Balknap Pr. of Harvard Univ., 1976.

PINTO, VIVIAN DE SOLA. *D. H. Lawrence: Prophet of the Midlands.* Univ. of Nottingham Pr., 1951.

————. "D. H. Lawrence: Letter-Writer and Craftsman in Verse." *Renaissance and Modern Studies* 1 (1957):5–34.

————. "Introduction: D. H. Lawrence: Poet Without a Mask." In *Complete Poems*, pp. 1–21. London: Heinemann; New York: Viking, 1967.

POTTS, ABBIE FINDLAY. *The Elegiac Mode: Poetic Form in Wordsworth and Other Elegists.* Ithaca: Cornell Univ. Pr., 1967.

PRITCHARD, WILLIAM H. *Seeing Through Everything: English Writers, 1918–1940.* New York: Oxford Univ. Pr., 1977.

Review of *Birds, Beasts and Flowers. Times Literary Supplement,* Dec. 13, 1923, p. 864.

Review of *Collected Poems. Times Literary Supplement,* November 15, 1928, p. 852.

REXROTH, KENNETH. Introduction to the *Selected Poems of D. H. Lawrence.* New York: Viking, 1959.

SAGAR, KEITH. *The Art of D. H. Lawrence.* Cambridge: Cambridge Univ. Pr., 1966.

———. "The Genesis of 'Bavarian Gentians.' " *The D. H. Lawrence Review* 8 (1975):47–53.

SANDOVAL, PATRICIA A. D. H. Lawrence: A Study of His Poetic Theories. Ph.D. diss. Univ. of Michigan, 1969.

SHAKIR, EVELYN. " 'Secret Sin': Lawrence's Early Verse." *The D. H. Lawrence Review* 8 (1975):155–75.

SHAPIRO, KARL. "The Unemployed Magician." In *A D. H. Lawrence Miscellany,* ed. by Harry T. Moore, 378–95. Carbondale: Southern Illinois Univ. Pr., 1959.

SPENDER, STEPHEN. *D. H. Lawrence: Novelist, Poet, Prophet.* New York: Harper, 1973.

TEDLOCK, E. W., JR. *D. H. Lawrence: Artist and Rebel.* Albuquerque: Univ. of New Mexico Pr., 1963.

———. *The Frieda Lawrence Collection of D. H. Lawrence Manuscripts: A Descriptive Bibliography.* Albuquerque: Univ. of New Mexico Pr., 1948.

TIEDJE, EGON. "D. H. Lawrence's Early Poetry: The Composition Dates of the Drafts in Ms E 317." *The D. H. Lawrence Review* 4 (Fall 1971), 227–52.

TRAIL, GEORGE Y. "Toward a Lawrencian Poetic," *The D. H. Lawrence Review* 5 (Spring, 1972):67–81.

———. "West by East: The Psycho-Geography of *Birds, Beasts and Flowers.*" *The D. H. Lawrence Review* 12 (Fall 1979):241–55.

VICKERY, JOHN B. "D. H. Lawrence's Poetry: Myth and Matter." *The D. H. Lawrence Review* 7 (1974):1–18.

YOUNGBLOOD, SARAH. "Substance and Shadow: The Self in Lawrence's Poetry." *The D. H. Lawrence Review* 1 (1968):114–28.

IV. RELATED BOOKS AND ARTICLES

ABRAMS, M. H. "Structure and Style in the Greater Romantic Lyric." In *From Sensibility to Romanticism: Essays Presented to Frederick A. Pottle,* edited by Frederick W. Hilles and Harold Bloom, 527–60. New York: Oxford Univ. Pr., 1965.

BEACH, JOSEPH WARREN. *The Making of the Auden Canon.* Minneapolis: Univ. of Minnesota Pr., 1957.

BEDIENT, CALVIN. *Architects of the Self: George Eliot, D. H. Lawrence, and E. M. Forster.* Berkeley: Univ. of California Pr., 1972.

BURNET, JOHN. *Early Greek Philosophy.* Cleveland and New York: World. Reprint of 3d ed., 1963.

CLARKE, COLIN. *River of Dissolution: D. H. Lawrence and English Romanticism.* New York: Barnes, 1969.

CUSHMAN, KEITH. *D. H. Lawrence at Work: The Emergence of the "Prussian Officer" Stories.* Charlottesville: Univ. of Virginia Pr., 1978.

DALESKI, H. M. *The Forked Flame: A Study of D. H. Lawrence.* Evanston: Northwestern Univ. Pr., 1965.

ELIOT, T. S. "Ulysses, Order, and Myth." *The Dial* 75 (1923):480–83.

FRAZER, SIR JAMES GEORGE. *The Golden Bough.* Abridged ed. Toronto: Macmillan, 1922; reprint, 1969.

GROSS, HARVEY. *Sound and Form in Modern Poetry: A Study of Prosody from Thomas Hardy to Robert Lowell.* Ann Arbor: Univ. of Michigan Pr., 1965.

HARDY, BARBARA. *The Appropriate Form: An Essay on the Novel.* London: Athlone Pr., 1964.

HOCHMAN, BARUCH. *Another Ego: The Changing View of the Self and Society in the Work of D. H. Lawrence.* Columbia: Univ. of South Carolina Pr., 1970.

JOOST, NICHOLAS, AND SULLIVAN, ALVIN. *D. H. Lawrence and the Dial.* Carbondale: Univ. of Southern Illinois Pr., 1970.

LANGBAUM, ROBERT. *The Poetry of Experience.* New York: Norton, 1957.

LEAVIS, F. R. *D. H. Lawrence: Novelist.* New York: Knopf, 1956.

———. *Thought, Words and Creativity: Art and Thought in Lawrence.* New York: Oxford Univ. Pr., 1976.

MARINETTI. *Selected Writings.* Ed. by R. W. Flint. New York: Farrar, 1971.

MCDONALD, EDWARD D. *The Writings of D. H. Lawrence.* Philadelphia: Centaur Bookshop, 1931.

MIKO, STEPHEN J. *Toward Women in Love: The Emergence of a Lawrentian Aesthetic.* New Haven and London: Yale Univ. Pr., 1971.

MURRAY, JOHN MIDDLETON. *Son of Woman: The Story of D. H. Lawrence.* London: Jonathan Cape, 1931.

ROBERTS, WARREN. *A Bibliography of D. H. Lawrence.* London: Rupert Hart-Davis, 1963.

VIVAS, ELISEO. *D. H. Lawrence: The Failure and the Triumph of Art.* Evanston: Northwestern Univ. Pr., 1960.

Index